Microsoft®

PhotoDraw™ 2000
by Design

William Tait

PUBLISHED BY
Microsoft Press
A Division of Microsoft Corporation
One Microsoft Way
Redmond, Washington 98052-6399

Library of Congress Cataloging-in-Publication Data
Tait, William, 1942-
    Microsoft PhotoDraw 2000 by Design / William Tait.
       p.   cm.
    ISBN 1-57231-938-0
    1. Computer graphics.   2. Microsoft PhotoDraw.   I. Title.
T385.T338   1999
006.6'869--dc21   99-13773
                                                            CIP

Printed and bound in the United States of America.

1 2 3 4 5 6 7 8 9   WCWC   4 3 2 1 0 9

Distributed in Canada by ITP Nelson, a division of Thomson Canada Limited.

A CIP catalogue record for this book is available from the British Library.

Microsoft Press books are available through booksellers and distributors worldwide. For further information about international editions,
contact your local Microsoft Corporation office, or contact Microsoft Press International directly at fax (425) 936-7329. Visit our Web site at
mspress.microsoft.com.

Acquisitions Editor: Christey Bahn
Project Editor: Sandra Haynes
Manuscript and Technical Editing: LightSpeed Publishing, Inc.

Contents

Acknowledgements

Special thanks to Don Gilbert for great pinch-hitting in the final hour. Don's numerous years of technical writing experience allowed him to step up to the challenge we gave him on this book.

Introduction

Pictures have been used to communicate and record events since humans first painted images on cave walls. The invention of photography brought creative self-expression through pictures to almost everyone; anyone who could afford a camera was given the power to record personal events and "capture the moment" in an image. Now that photography has merged with computer technology, we are witnessing a new revolution in the creation of pictures—digital photography and computer-based editing of photographic images. Now the creative process doesn't stop when you click the shutter; you can continue to evolve and improve the picture using computer software.

Microsoft has added ease-of-use and powerful computer algorithms to the digital image revolution by creating Microsoft PhotoDraw 2000. PhotoDraw is packed with tools that allow you to easily apply a vast range of styles and effects to digital images and to draw, paint, and add text to the mix as well.

PhotoDraw is also one of those products that's just plain fun to use. Starting with a scanner, digital camera, or video frame-grabber attached to your computer—or a stored image file—you can use PhotoDraw to create many types of output. These includes Web graphics, greeting cards, labels, letterheads and more. Many projects can be accomplished almost entirely by using template and wizard steps.

Most of the fun, though, comes when you get out of autopilot mode and begin experimenting with PhotoDraw's effects. After you add text to your photographic images, you'll find yourself quickly engaged in a creative process of trying out effects and styles, keeping or rejecting them, and continuing on to transform a photograph into a unique piece of artwork. PhotoDraw has multiple undo and redo lists so you can always retrace your steps.

Who Uses PhotoDraw?

PhotoDraw 2000 is the graphics complement to Microsoft Office 2000, which tells you that it's an industrial strength product. It's an obvious choice for business users—especially those in small-to-medium sized companies—who need to produce brochures, advertisements, Web pages and so on without spending a lot of time and money in the process. However, versatility doesn't need to mean complexity and PhotoDraw does a lot of things without being complicated.

PhotoDraw is also a great tool for home users; it appeals to a broad range of interests away from the office. Students can spruce up homework and reports; churches and organizations can create fliers, circulars, and posters; photographers and computer hobbyists can get the most out of pictures; and anyone can use e-mail to send pictures to friends and family.

Getting the Most from This Book

The goal of this book is to help you experiment with PhotoDraw's features in an organized and guided manner. This is accomplished by providing projects that make the most of PhotoDraw's tools and effects. Each project is broken into bite-sized steps and illustrated by lots of visual keys to simplify the learning process. You can take your time and learn PhotoDraw at your own pace by following the procedures and examples.

The first part of the book takes you through the basics of using Photodraw. In this section, you'll learn the ropes by putting on the hat of a graphics designer and working through a series of "client" projects. You'll not only learn PhotoDraw techniques, but you'll also gain useful insights into the world of graphic design.

The second part of the book presents fun and easy projects that you can modify for your own use. From designing Web-page graphics, to creating customized calendars, envelopes, and letters, to creating fliers and greeting cards, the chapters in this section get you off to a good start with your own practical projects.

Watch Those Tips

Lots of tips appear in the margins of this book. These tips contain valuable information—shortcuts, hints, cross references, and answers to frequently-asked questions. You'll find them identified by these icons:

 Power Tips give you advanced information that may help you in procedure steps and provide reminders of good practices to follow.

 Keyboard Shortcuts give you the keystrokes to quickly access the most common functions of PhotoDraw.

 Cross Reference Tips point to other areas in the book that contain related information.

 Troubleshooting Tips answer questions that often arise when performing certain activities. They also provide warnings about potential problems.

About the CD

PhotoDraw 2000 by Design includes a CD-ROM containing all the files required for you to complete the projects in the book and a set of completed project files to use as examples. There is also a trial version of Microsoft PhotoDraw 2000 on the CD to let you try out the product before purchasing it. Finally, a set of digital photographic images is provided for you to use in your own PhotoDraw projects or while experimenting with PhotoDraw features.

Having Fun with PhotoDraw

One of the most important aspects of any tool is how much you enjoy using it—especially if it is a tool like PhotoDraw that enhances your natural creativity. By its nature, PhotoDraw is fun to use because it makes it easy to experiment and provides interesting and diverse results. So, while working through the chapters and projects in this book, take a little extra time to explore new features that are introduced here and make them your own by using them in your projects or by playing with them between chapters. But most of all, have a good time getting to know PhotoDraw and creating your own beautiful and original images!

PART 1

PhotoDraw Basics

Getting to Know PhotoDraw

Microsoft PhotoDraw brings powerful imaging technology and smart graphics creation capability to Microsoft Office, enabling you to add professional quality images and graphic elements to your documents. Whatever your graphics needs—custom PowerPoint slides, Web art, illustrations for newsletters and reports, even posters or cool T-shirt illustrations—PhotoDraw makes it fun and easy.

Here, in Part I of *PhotoDraw by Design*, you will learn how the tools work. By its nature, a *by Design* book presents hands-on projects rather than listing tools and their functions. Working with projects allows you to use a variety of tools to create a picture. And that is what PhotoDraw is about: making pictures.

What You Can Do with PhotoDraw

Microsoft PhotoDraw 2000 is a powerful package that combines a large number of tools and effects into a single environment. You can use PhotoDraw to create high-quality pictures anywhere you can imagine using a photograph or designer art. Here are some of the more obvious applications, but these by no means cover all of the possibilities. Pictures created in PhotoDraw can used for:

- Web page banners, backgrounds, button graphics, or feature photographs
- Business letter heads, envelopes, labels, flyers, and advertisements
- Business presentations and slides
- Greeting cards, postcards, tent cards, invitations, and announcements
- Newsletters and book or magazine art
- School projects, homework, and class presentations

With the advent of digital cameras, inexpensive scanners, and quality color printers, photographs are becoming more and more popular as a means to communicate personal and creative ideas. Once you discover how much you can do with this powerful application, you'll probably think of more ways your photographs and PhotoDraw can add professionalism to your desktop-created art.

Using PhotoDraw

There are essentially four main steps to creating projects in PhotoDraw. First, you must open a file or import a picture. You will spend time composing your picture. Most likely, you'll apply effects to at least some parts of the picture. And finally, you either save the file or print it—or both. Let's briefly cover these steps so you get the big picture before we jump into a lot of details.

Bringing Things into PhotoDraw

What does a PhotoDraw project start with? Well, a picture is the obvious answer, but there are many different picture file formats. PhotoDraw reads a large number of these and also takes direct input from scanners, digital cameras, and video capture devices.

Picture File Formats

To work with picture files, you can either open a picture from Photodraw's File menu or insert the picture into an existing PhotoDraw workspace from the Insert menu. If you have pictures, clip art, or drawings in any of the following file formats, you can use them in PhotoDraw:

- JPEG (.jpg, .jpeg)
- Graphics Interchange Format/GIF (.gif, .gfa)
- Portable Network Graphics (.png)
- Tagged Image File Format/TIFF (.tif, .tiff)
- Windows Bitmap format (.bmp, .dib, .rle)
- Windows Metafile format (.wmf, .emf)
- Kodak CD (.pcd)
- Microsoft Image Composer (.mic)
- Adobe Photoshop (.psd)
- PC Paintbrush (.pcx)

- PhotoDraw (.mix)
- WordPerfect graphic (.wpg)
- Targa (.tga)
- AutoCAD 2-D format (.dxf)
- CorelDRAW (.cdr)

- Computer Graphics Metafile (.cgm)
- Encapsulated PostScript (.eps)
- Macintosh PICT (.pct, .pict)
- Micrografx_Designer/Draw import (.drw)
- FlashPix (.fpx)

Open a File

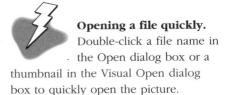

Opening a file quickly.
Double-click a file name in the Open dialog box or a thumbnail in the Visual Open dialog box to quickly open the picture.

1 On the File menu, click Open or Visual Open (shown here).

2 Navigate to the directory containing the file.

3 Select the thumbnail of the picture.

4 Click Open. When you open a file, the picture is automatically sized to fit the screen.

While opening a picture causes the picture space to resize to the image, when you insert an image into an existing picture, the picture space stays the same size.

Insert a File

① On the Insert menu, click From File (shown here) or click Visual Insert.

③ Select the name of the picture.

② Navigate to the directory containing the file.

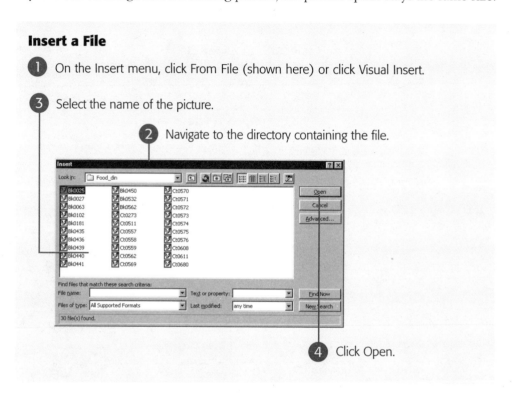

④ Click Open.

Scanners, Digital Cameras, and Video Capture Devices

PhotoDraw recognizes most flatbed scanners and can import pictures directly from them by clicking Scan Picture on the File menu. For other scanner types, you may first need to scan the picture using the software that comes with the scanner and then determine if the file is a compatible file format for PhotoDraw. You can also download directly from digital cameras or video capture devices you have installed.

Import a File from a Digital Camera, a Scanner, or a Video Capture Device

To download from a digital camera, click Digital Camera on the File menu or click the Digital Camera button on the toolbar.

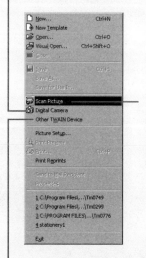

To scan a picture, click Scan Picture on the File menu or click the Scan Picture button on the toolbar.

To download from a video capture device, click Other TWAIN Device.

Linking applications and image acquisition devices. TWAIN specifies an industry protocol standard for linking applications and image acquisition devices. For more information visit *http:www.twain.org.*

See the online Help system for more information about setting up these devices for use with PhotoDraw.

Composing in PhotoDraw

You lay out graphic elements in PhotoDraw the way you might if you were using a drafting table, or several drafting tables. You work with your graphics and text elements on a surface or the computer screen and arrange your composition in a central area: overlapping components, cutting and cropping images, and applying effects. Several pictures are available at one time in PhotoDraw and you can copy picture elements from one to another. You will learn how to use this workspace creatively as you progress through the examples in this book. The image below shows a layout from one of the projects in a later chapter.

The PhotoDraw workspace

Adding Special Effects

A PhotoDraw picture starts with existing photographs, clip art, or line art. To pictures you import, you can add text, draw, paint, or add shapes using PhotoDraw. But the real power of PhotoDraw lies in the way you combine its effects. Here are just some of the effects you can apply to your pictures, elements, and often to text as well:

- Shadows
- Transparency and fade outs
- Blurring and sharpening
- Distortion
- 3-D rendering of text, lines, shapes, and outlines
- Photo touch-ups to fix red eye, remove dust and spots, despeckle, remove scratches, and more
- Artistic and photographic brushes and edge softening
- Gradient color fills, picture fills, and texture fills
- Cutting, cropping, and erasing

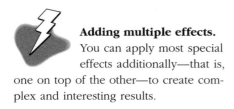

Adding multiple effects. You can apply most special effects additionally—that is, one on top of the other—to create complex and interesting results.

If you're the adventuresome type, you can have a great time playing with the myriad of effects. But PhotoDraw also includes a large set of design templates for entire projects and for individual effects, so that you can usually find something you can use with very little effort.

Saving and Printing PhotoDraw Pictures

PhotoDraw pictures are saved by default in PhotoDraw (.mix) format. Opening a PhotoDraw format picture from the File menu brings in all of the components of that picture so you can edit them. You can, however, save the file in a number of other formats, including those listed on the following page.

- JPEG (.jpg, .jpeg)
- GIF (.gif, .gfa)
- Portable Network Graphics (.png)
- Tagged Image File Format/TIFF (.tif)
- Windows Bitmap (.bmp)
- PC PaintBrush (.pcx)
- Picture It versions 2.0 and 3.0 (.mix)
- Targa (.tga)

If you're not sure in which format to save a particular file, you can click Save For Use In on the File menu and a wizard will walk you through the most common file types.

You can print your composed pictures directly from PhotoDraw and you are provided with many options for laying out and sizing the print, as well as for determining the print quality. There is even an option for printing labels directly from PhotoDraw.

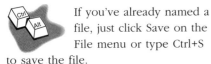 If you've already named a file, just click Save on the File menu or type Ctrl+S to save the file.

Save a File with a New Name or Type

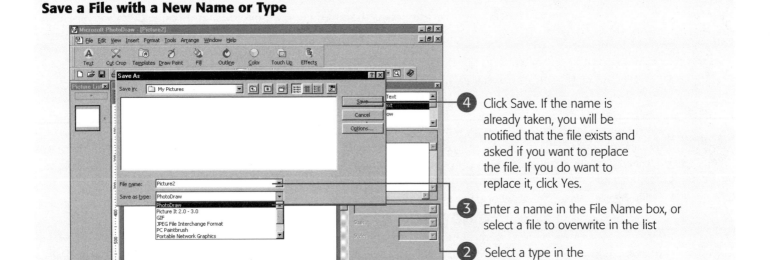

4. Click Save. If the name is already taken, you will be notified that the file exists and asked if you want to replace the file. If you do want to replace it, click Yes.

3. Enter a name in the File Name box, or select a file to overwrite in the list

2. Select a type in the Save As type list.

1. From the File menu, choose Save As.

What You Need to Run PhotoDraw

PhotoDraw is a powerful program and demands a lot from a computer. Every effect that you apply requires graphics algorithms when displaying, saving, or printing the image. You'll find PhotoDraw easiest to work with on later model computers, such as those with Pentium II processors running at 266 MHz or greater, good graphics cards, and at least 32 MB of memory. On computers with less brawn, you might experience some waiting from time to time while PhotoDraw does its thing.

Setting Your Display

Before you start creating art, there are a few things you need to do to make sure your computer performs well.

Display settings determine how many colors your monitor shows (called color depth), and how much information is displayed (number of pixels). It is a good idea to optimize your computer's display settings. Now is a good time to set your display appropriately.

Getting Help

This book is designed to help you learn about PhotoDraw features by taking you on a tour through several projects to gain experience. However, it's not a reference and doesn't try to cover every area of PhotoDraw in detail. The online Help system is usually the place to go first when you have a specific question about PhotoDraw.

PhotoDraw will not run in 16 colors. If your computer is set to 16 colors, an alert will appear the first time you run PhotoDraw. You will be given the opportunity to change your display settings. You can do so by clicking Yes to the prompt; the Display Properties Dialog will appear, the Settings tab will be automatically selected, and PhotoDraw will bring up a help topic with instructions on how to make the necessary changes.

Using Online Help

You can open PhotoDraw Help from the Help Contents And Index button on the toolbar. Or, on the Help menu, click Contents, and then click Index.

The Back button returns the document to the previously selected Help topic.

The Forward button returns to a more recently visited document after clicking the Back button.

The Print button allows you to print the currently selected Help topic or that topic and all subtopics below it.

The Options button opens a menu with various options for navigating Help, printing, hiding the tabs, and setting browser options.

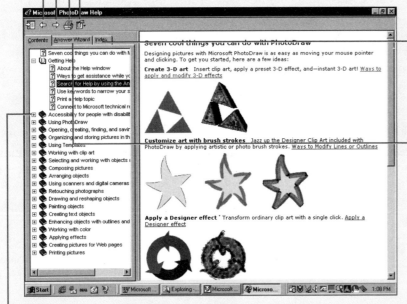

To locate a topic using the Index, click the Index tab and then type a keyword. Double-click an Index topic to view it. Or click the topic then click Display.

To search for any Help topic, click the Answer Wizard tab. Type a keyword, and then press Search. Click any topic to view it.

Click a Contents topic to display it in the document pane. Click the plus button to expand the topics under a heading; click the minus button to collapse them.

Using ScreenTips

ScreenTips provide information about most screen elements. Just pause the cursor over a screen element, such as a button or thumbnail, and the name of that item will appear. When used with a control, such as a slider or edit box, ScreenTips provide suggestions about what you should do or enter. PhotoDraw uses Galleries to display graphical elements and styles to choose from, and ScreenTips are especially helpful for naming these elements. The image below shows a ScreenTip over a gallery item. We'll cover galleries in more detail later in this chapter.

For more information on galleries, see page 23.

ScreenTip in a gallery

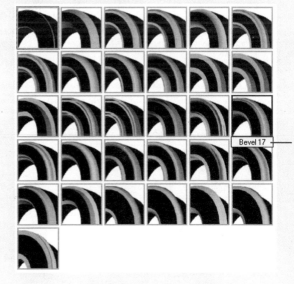

ScreenTip naming a gallery item.

About This Book

All screen captures for the figures used in *Microsoft PhotoDraw 2000 by Design* were made on a computer with display settings configured for 800 x 600 pixels. This determined the layout of the interface elements. If your computer is configured for higher resolution, such as 1024 x 768 pixels, or lower resolution, such as 640 x 480 pixels, your screen will look slightly different than in the book. Higher resolution configurations will have more space between interface elements, lower resolution configurations will have less space. Keep this in mind when the text states that your screen should look like, or similar to, a figure or illustration.

Terms

You may not be familiar with all of the terms used in *PhotoDraw by Design*. Tips will explain those that are either unusual or specific to graphics. Many are similar to, or the same as, those in other Office applications.

Throughout the book, you will be presented with information and tips about what design decisions have been made and the considerations that went into making them. The projects in Part One are generally individual pieces of what would normally be larger projects. In Part Two, you will work through a couple of complete projects, as well as consider the overall design concepts and thought processes that went into them.

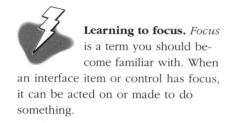

Learning to focus. *Focus* is a term you should become familiar with. When an interface item or control has focus, it can be acted on or made to do something.

Working with the Keyboard and Mouse

In general, Office applications support navigation and control through the user interface. PhotoDraw has a rich set of keyboard shortcuts for navigating, and initiating actions in various controls. While working through the book, you will become familiar with these.

A Tour of PhotoDraw

PhotoDraw uses the familiar Microsoft Office window style, with buttons, a status bar, title bar, and main menu.

The PhotoDraw Window

A PhotoDraw window contains numerous standard Office components and a few components of its own. Some of these elements will probably be familiar to you if you've used other Microsoft products. Some are unique to PhotoDraw, however, so we'll concentrate on those first.

Additional similarities between PhotoDraw and other Office applications include the ability to resize or shrink windows and use standard minimize, maximize, and restore buttons. Standard Windows keyboard shortcuts are used for menu bar items. These are shown throughout the first few chapters of Section One of this book, and any time a new command is used.

Take a few minutes to read about some of the components of PhotoDraw you'll be working with. Then jump in and get to know PhotoDraw firsthand in "Getting Started," later in this chapter.

Where is the Formatting toolbar? The Formatting toolbar is not shown in this illustration because PhotoDraw does not display it by default. To display the Formatting toolbar, click the View menu and, on the Toolbars submenu, check Formatting.

The PhotoDraw Components

The Picture List displays all pictures currently loaded in PhotoDraw.

The standard toolbar contains shortcut buttons for common tasks.

The visual menu provides the most common tasks as visual thumbnail menus.

The menu bar contains all commands for PhotoDraw.

The workpane displays the toolset for the current task.

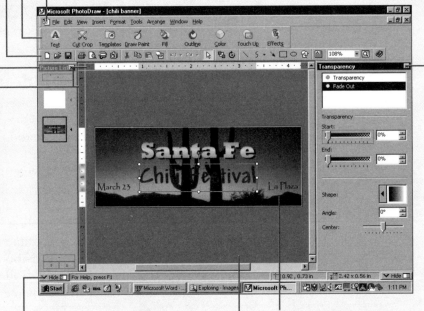

The status bar displays status messages, selection coordinates, and Hide/Show buttons for the Picture List and workpane windows.

Rulers provide visual measurement guides.

The picture space is the area that is rendered when you print or save the picture for a publication.

The scratch space is the work area for holding picture elements that are not rendered.

The Visual Menu

The visual menu provides easy-to-use access to the features you use the most in PhotoDraw. Categories of visual editing are represented by graphical buttons with these labels: Text, Cut Crop, Templates, Draw Paint, Fill, Outline, Color, Touch Up, and Effects. When you click one of these buttons, a list appears with thumbnails and text providing the available options. For example, the image shows the options available from the Text visual menu. All of these options can also be accessed from other parts of the main menu, but they are organized in this menu where you'll more likely to remember where they are.

The Text visual menu

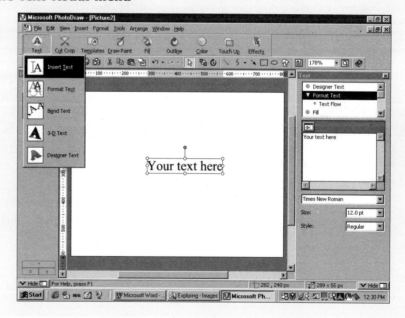

Because there are so many effects and different types of objects available in PhotoDraw, you'll discover there are sometimes different ways of getting to the same place. The visual menu helps to simplify this and presents you with a logical palette of choices.

The Picture Space and Scratch Space

The work area in a PhotoDraw picture is composed of a picture space surrounded by a scratch space, as shown on the facing page. The picture space, initially a white rectangle, provides the canvas for your work. Whatever is inside the picture space is rendered when you print or when you save the file for publication (as a .tiff, .gif, or .png file). The size of the picture space is initially determined by a selection when you open PhotoDraw, but it can be resized, as you'll see later in this chapter.

The scratch space is the gray area surrounding the picture space. This is a handy work area for keeping objects that are not yet ready for the picture space. You can even keep objects in the scratch space for trial, to create and try out different ideas while you compose your picture. Objects are moved on and off the picture space by dragging them to or from the scratch space.

The edges of the white picture space are outlined. The outlines are not part of the image that will be published—nothing outside the picture space is published. Everything inside the picture space is. If a graphic object is both inside and outside the picture space, only the part that is inside will be published. Publishing involves saving a picture in a file format suitable for including in a newsletter, adding to a Web site, printing a poster, or many other uses. Later you will explore the concept of publishing from PhotoDraw.

Saving an image for a later session. The images in the scratch space are only saved between sessions when you save the picture as a PhotoDraw (.mix) file.

The Picture Space and Scratch Space

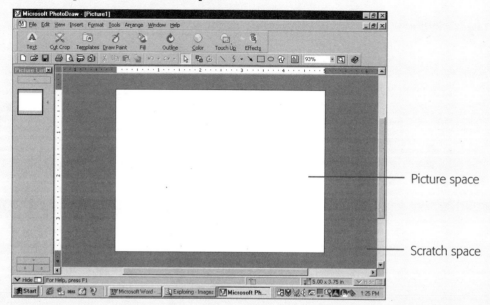

Picture space

Scratch space

The Picture List and Object List

PhotoDraw enables you to keep several pictures open at once. This can be useful when working on parallel ideas (for example, working up different styles on the same project), borrowing components from one picture to use in other pictures, using one picture as a guide or reference for another picture, and so on. Each picture you bring into PhotoDraw appears as a graphical thumbnail in the Picture List in the order in which it was opened. These thumbnails are miniature representations of the picture, so if you change the picture, the thumbnail image changes as well.

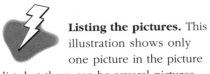

Listing the pictures. This illustration shows only one picture in the picture list, but there can be several pictures listed, each with its own object list. Only one object list can be displayed at any one time.

The Picture List and Object List

Each picture in the Picture List contains a menu button, which can be found on its right. When the menu button is clicked (pressed), the Object List appears showing all of the objects in that picture. The picture above shows an Object List displayed from a picture in the Picture List. You can drag any object from another picture's Object List into your current picture. Also, you can drag any object from your current picture onto the Picture List and a new picture will be created containing only that object.

Compositing Pictures

In graphic design, composing, compositing, or creating a picture is considered assembling an artistically interesting or aesthetically pleasing image from a variety of smaller images. For instance, you might want to communicate the idea of children having fun. You could compose a picture that shows kids involved in several fun activities like riding a Ferris wheel at a fair, playing ball at the beach, bicycling down the street, and so forth. When composed from various appropriate images, the idea of fun is stronger than depicting any one of the activities by itself. Deciding which images are suitable for a composite picture is easier if you have a clear idea of what you want to communicate.

With computer technology, PhotoDraw raises the art of compositing to a new level of ease and creative freedom. Not only can you combine images within a picture, now you are able to drag images from other pictures directly into the one you are creating. After you save the new picture to a separate file, it becomes available as a source of images and ideas for future pictures. Each picture becomes a unique resource, like a good book in your library that you can revisit for inspiration.

The Workpane

Most of the work you do in PhotoDraw will be accomplished through workpanes. Clicking a menu item or toolbar button to perform an action usually opens a workpane. By default, workpanes are docked on the right side of the picture space.

A workpane provides your current toolset. For example, if you are editing a text object, as shown on the following page, the Text Workpane enables you to change the text, set the font, style, alignment, fill color, orientation, and so on. In the case of text, you can even bend it into shapes and add designer font styles.

The Text Workpane

Expand Gallery

The top area of the workpane often contains a list from which you select the toolset that appears in the lower area of the workpane. For instance, selecting Format Text in the Text Workpane displays formatting controls.

The lower area of the workpane contains standard windows controls such as edit boxes, list boxes, slider controls and so on. The one exception is the Gallery, which can be temporarily expanded to provide better access to large numbers of items.

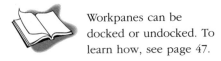

Workpanes can be docked or undocked. To learn how, see page 47.

There are workpanes for most activities and you'll encounter all of them as you work through the examples in this book.

Some of the functions in workpanes open floating toolbars (called floaters in this book) that access additional functions specific to the workpane that launched them.

Galleries

When a workpane has more choices than can be displayed, a gallery, or expanded set of choices is available. Galleries can offer multiple items that have subsets of choices or single items that present all available choices at once. You will work with galleries throughout *PhotoDraw by Design*.

The Designer Effects Gallery

The Designer Effects workpane

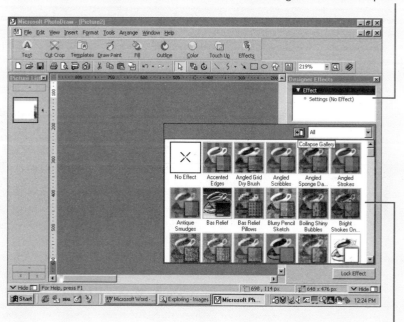

The gallery contains thumbnails.

Getting Started

Now that we've covered some basic terminology, it's time for you to get in and try out PhotoDraw for yourself. In this chapter, we'll cover some basic procedures and get to know a little more about the PhotoDraw program. In the process of these exercises, you'll learn:

- How to open PhotoDraw and select a picture size to work with.
- How to change the picture size once PhotoDraw is open.
- How to insert a picture.
- How to expand and collapse a gallery in a workpane.
- How to add an effect.
- How to move and position objects in your picture.
- How to duplicate objects.
- How to use a floater to paint.
- How to use the Undo and Redo buttons and lists.

About the Exercises

The exercises and procedures in this chapter make the assumption that you have not used PhotoDraw before and that the settings are as they would be if you installed PhotoDraw for the first time. If you encounter screens that do not look like the accompanying illustrations, it might be that you've changed settings somewhere.

Before You Start

You will want to select a location to store the files you make. This destination can be as simple as a single folder for all your files, or a folder for each chapter of this book. Before you start working in PhotoDraw, make a folder or folders on your hard drive in a way that you will remember. Save your files to it as you work. If you are not sure how to do that, look in Windows Help under Folders and then Create. There are work files in each chapter folder, so if you have enough space on your hard disk, you might want to copy the chapter folders from the companion CD. This way, you will have all the work files readily available.

Opening PhotoDraw for the First Time

Now it's time to jump in and get your feet wet. To begin with, you'll simply open a new picture and learn about the available picture sizes.

Open PhotoDraw

 Starting with the Default. If you select the Don't Show This Dialog Box Again check box, PhotoDraw will by-pass this dialog box and open with the Default picture size. To see this dialog box, make sure the Getting Started Dialog Box On Startup check box is selected (point to Options on the Tools menu).

1 Click Microsoft PhotoDraw in the Programs list from the Windows taskbar. The PhotoDraw splash screen appears briefly, PhotoDraw opens, and the Microsoft PhotoDraw dialog box appears on the screen. Several choices are available on the PhotoDraw dialog box:

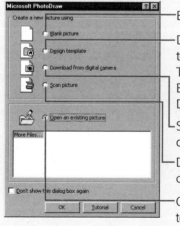

Blank Picture opens a picture with no elements.

Design Template provides a selection of templates to use and steps you through the creation process. Template categories include Web Graphics, Business Graphics, Cards, Designer Edges, and Designer Clip Art.

Scan Picture imports pictures from a connected scanner.

Download From Digital Camera imports pictures directly from a connected digital camera.

Open An Existing Picture allows you to select an image to open.

2 Select Blank Picture and click OK. The New dialog box appears on the screen.

The New dialog box has two tabs at the top—Pictures, and Labels.

You can use the list buttons to control the way the icons display.

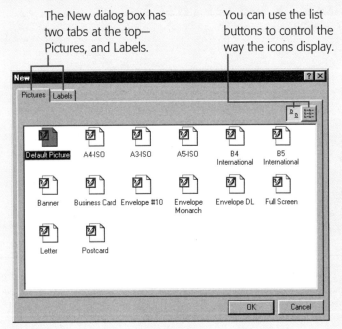

4 Click the Pictures tab. A variety of sizes for standard document styles are represented by the icons. Make sure that Default Picture is selected and click OK.

3 Click the Labels tab. Icons representing a selection of the most common label types appear.

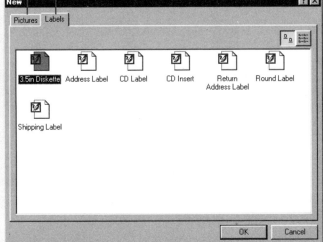

Printing labels. If you choose labels that are to be printed on multiple label forms (such as address labels), you can use PhotoDraw's Print Reprint feature to print the labels.

Open PhotoDraw *(continued)*

5 PhotoDraw creates a new, 5-inch-by-3.75-inch picture.

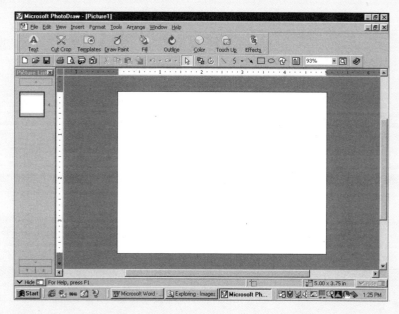

About Picture Size Selections

Before moving on, let's examine the choices PhotoDraw provides for picture sizes. Select the picture size by choosing Blank Pictures when first opening PhotoDraw, or by choosing New from the File menu in PhotoDraw. The following table lists the size of each picture option.

PhotoDraw Picture Sizes	
Item	**Size / Width x Height**
Default Picture	Last setting from Picture Setup dialog box (5 inches x 3.75 inches by default).
Letter	8.5 x 11 inches
A4-ISO	210 x 297 mm
A3-ISO	297 x 420 mm
A5-ISO	148 x 210 mm
B4 International	250 x 354 mm
B5 International	176 x 250 mm
Banner	600 x 64 pixels
Full Screen	Based on current screen display size
Postcard	6 x 4 inches
Business Card	3 x 2.5 inches
CD Insert	4.75 x 4.75 inches
Envelope #10	9.5 x 4.125 inches
Envelope Monarch	7 x 3.875 inches
Envelope DL	220 x 110 mm

 To learn more about ISO standards for paper, and documents, visit the ISO Web site at *http://www.iso.ch/*, where you will find a wealth of information and links to many other standard setting organizations throughout the world. Through this site, you can also find links to documents with information about stationery standards and documents about publishing standards.

There are well over one thousand different classifications of paper. Fortunately, having standard sizes helps smooth the flow of communication. PhotoDraw's preset picture sizes are a mix of common American and International standard sizes. International size standards for paper are determined by the International Organization for Standardization (ISO) and have been adopted by many countries using the metric system of measurement.

Changing Picture Size or Units of Measure

Occasionally you might want to change the size, units of measure, or other properties of the picture you are working on. There are three ways to resize the picture space:

Press the F10 key to activate the main menu. Next press Alt+F to open the File menu list, and then press U to select the Picture Setup item, bringing up the Picture Setup dialog box.

- Click Fit Picture Area To Selection from the View menu to resize the picture space to the selected object.

- Drag the handles attached to the corners of the picture space. These are locked by default and can be unlocked in the Picture Setup dialog box.

- Change height and width values in the Picture Setup dialog box.

Let's try the third method—the Picture Setup dialog box also contains other properties for the picture that are useful to know about.

Change the Picture Size

Picture Size presents a list of standard pictures sizes.

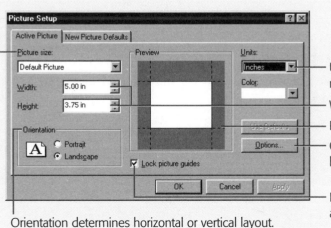

Orientation determines horizontal or vertical layout.

1 Click Picture Setup on the File menu. The Picture Setup dialog box appears with the Active Picture Tab showing. This sets properties for the picture you are working on.

Units provides a list of cms (centimeters), inches, mms (millimeters), or pixels.

Width and Height enable you to set a custom picture size.

Preview area

Options enables you to customize the horizontal and vertical grid spacing.

Lock Picture Guides enables or disables the ability to resize picture visually.

Change the Picture Size *(continued)*

2 In the Units list, click Pixels. The Picture Size width now reads 750 pixels and the height reads 563 pixels.

3 Change the width to 800 and the height to 600.

4 Reselect inches in the Units list. Notice that the picture width and height are displayed in inches.

5 Click the Lock Picture Guides check box to uncheck it. Notice there are now handles at the corners of the white rectangle in the Preview area. When the picture guides are unlocked, these handles enable you to interactively resize your picture by dragging them.

6 For now, click the Lock Picture Guides checkbox again so it is checked.

7 Click the New Picture Defaults tab. New Picture Defaults sets the default choices that are active when you create a new picture. It offers the same options as in the Active Picture dialog box. PhotoDraw remembers changes you make in this dialog box and will apply them when subsequent new pictures are opened.

8 For now, click the Cancel button to return to the current picture. Later, you will work with the Picture Setup dialog box more extensively.

Inserting a Picture

Now that you have a picture space to work in, you need something to work with. Next, you'll insert a picture.

Press F10 to activate the main menu bar. Then press I to open the Insert menu list, and finally press L to select the From File item, bringing up the Insert dialog box.

Insert a Picture

1 On Insert menu, click From File. The Insert dialog box appears.

2 Navigate to the chapters/chap01 folder on the companion CD to locate the file *chapter1a.mix*. Double-click the filename to open the graphic in the PhotoDraw picture space.

Insert a Picture *(continued)*

3 A yellow graphic object with a lavender border appears in the picture space and a thumbnail appears in the Picture List on the left side of the screen.

4 Double-click anywhere inside the graphic object; hold the cursor down and then start dragging. Four arrowheads appear, indicating the cursor is in position to move the object.

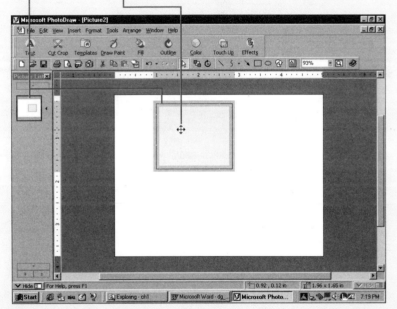

5 To practice moving an object, drag the image object you just inserted a little to the left then release the mouse button. (Notice that the small version in the picture list thumbnail moves too.)

6 Drag the object back to the right and release the mouse button.

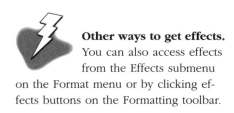

Other ways to get effects.
You can also access effects from the Effects submenu on the Format menu or by clicking effects buttons on the Formatting toolbar.

Adding a Shadow Effect

Next you'll add an effect to the image to get a feel for using the visual menu, workpanes, and the Gallery control. This probably won't be the coolest thing you'll ever do in PhotoDraw, but it'll help introduce you to a few more features.

Add a Shadow Effect

1 Click the Effects icon on the visual menu to open the drop-down list of effects and their thumbnails.

2 Click the Shadow thumbnail to open the Shadow workpane. It will appear docked at the right side of the picture space.

Add a Shadow Effect *(continued)*

3 Position your cursor over the small button at the top of the Shadow workpane for a moment until a ScreenTip appears that says Expand Gallery.

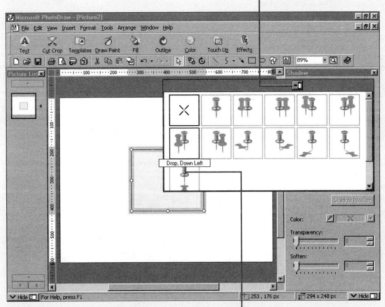

Identifying items.
ScreenTips identify all items in a gallery. Just hold the cursor over any gallery item in any workpane to see its name.

4 Click this button to expand the Shadow gallery. The Shadow gallery changes orientation from vertical to horizontal to display the large number of items. Click the button again to return the gallery to its vertical orientation.

5 Click the Drop, Down Left icon (directly below the No Shadow icon with the X). A narrow shadow appears to the left of the image object.

Now that you've applied the effect, you can move it. You've tried dragging an image already, but there are more accurate ways to move objects in smaller increments, using the keyboard, as you'll see next.

Move the Shadow

1 Click the Shadow Position button in the Shadow workpane. The selection handles disappear from the image object and are now attached to the shadow.

2 Move the cursor anywhere over the object. The cursor displays four arrowheads indicating it is in position to move the shadow. You can now drag the shadow anywhere you want.

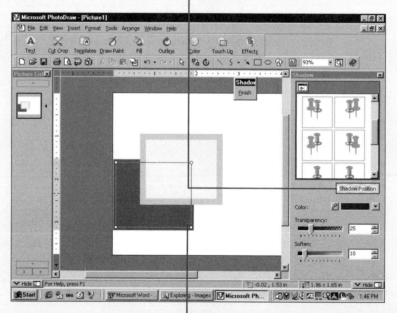

3 Drag the shadow to the left until it is about halfway out from under the image object, and then release the mouse button.

Move the Shadow *(continued)*

4 On your keyboard, press the Left arrow key several times. The shadow moves to the left. Press and hold the Shift key while pressing and releasing the Left arrow key. The shadow moves left 10 pixels. Press the Up arrow key a few times. The shadow moves up. Try the Shift+Up arrow combination.

5 If you decide you don't want the shadow after all, click on the X thumbnail for No Shadow and the shadow disappears.

Duplicating Objects

Often you will want to quickly duplicate an object in PhotoDraw. This is a handy shortcut when you've already done work on one object and you want the same, or similar, effects and properties on another object. Here's how to do that. (This exercise assumes you just finished the previous exercise.)

Duplicate an Object

1 Click the object to select it. The yellow rectangle in the picture space should already be selected since it is the only object so far in your picture space.

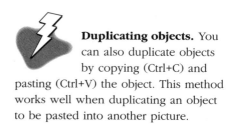

Duplicating objects. You can also duplicate objects by copying (Ctrl+C) and pasting (Ctrl+V) the object. This method works well when duplicating an object to be pasted into another picture.

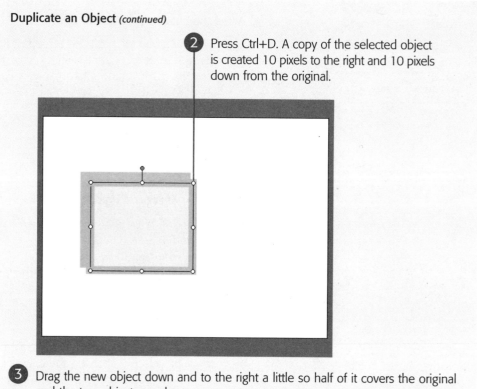

2 Press Ctrl+D. A copy of the selected object is created 10 pixels to the right and 10 pixels down from the original.

3 Drag the new object down and to the right a little so half of it covers the original and the two objects overlap.

Working with the Picture List and Object List

On the left side of the picture space, you will find the Picture List. If you followed the previous exercises, you should see one thumbnail in the Picture List. Because you duplicated the object in the last exercise, the thumbnail should have two graphic objects in it.

In PhotoDraw, only one picture is active at a time. A picture that is open but not selected is called the inactive picture. When multiple pictures are in the Picture List, you can change the active picture by clicking the thumbnail of the picture you want to make active. Let's see how that works now.

Using the Object List to Change the Order of Objects

In this exercise, you'll explore the Object List and how it can be used to arrange the front-to-back order of objects in a picture.

Change the Order of Objects

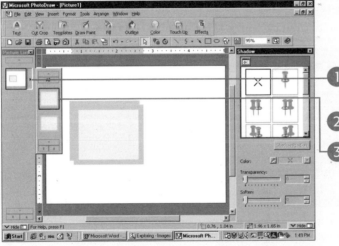

1. Click the small triangle on the right side of the Picture List thumbnail to open the Object List.

2. Click the triangle again to close the Object List.

3. Select the duplicated object in the picture space and then reopen the Object List. Notice a dark blue line surrounds the corresponding object in the Object List. The selected object should be the top object in the list (if not, select the other object in the picture space). This means it is in front of, or on top of, the other object.

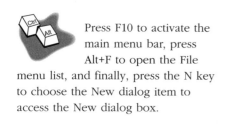

Ordering objects—the Z-order. The Z-order is the front-to-back order of objects. You can change the position of an object in the Z-order by dragging it up or down in the Object List. If one object is on top of another object, it is higher in the Z-order.

Press F10 to activate the main menu bar, press Alt+F to open the File menu list, and finally, press the N key to choose the New dialog item to access the New dialog box.

Change the Order of Objects *(continued)*

④ In the Object List, drag the selected object's thumbnail below the other object's thumbnail. Notice that the objects on the picture space have changed position front to back. This is a quick and easy way to position any object precisely where you want in the Z-order.

⑤ Practice doing this a few times. The Z-order always starts with the top thumbnail in the Object List being the front of the Z-order and the bottom object in the list being farthest back.

⑥ Click the Object List arrow button to close the Object List.

How Much Can PhotoDraw Handle?

With enough memory and hard disk space, PhotoDraw can open as many as 256 pictures. How much memory and hard disk space is enough? That depends on the quantity and size of the graphic objects in each picture. Some people will have pictures with dozens or perhaps hundreds of objects. Others may only have a few. Each person's system will have its own limits. After a while you will learn the limits of your system.

Using the Paint Tools

Now we'll explore the Paint workpane. This introduces another tool we haven't seen yet, called a floater. Floaters are toolbars that are associated with the workpane, but they "float" above the picture space and workpane windows. They contain a few active commands for helping you use the cursor to draw, paint, touch up a photo, and so on.

As we explore the Paint tools, we'll create a second picture and observe the properties in the Picture List.

Use the Creative Paint Tools

1 On the File menu, click New and accept the default picture.

A second picture is created and there are now two picture icons showing in the Picture List.

2 On the Draw Paint menu, click Paint. If you are asked to insert your PhotoDraw Disc 2, do so and then click OK.

The Create Paint floater contains the Paint tools. The Paint button on the Creative Paint floater should be depressed.

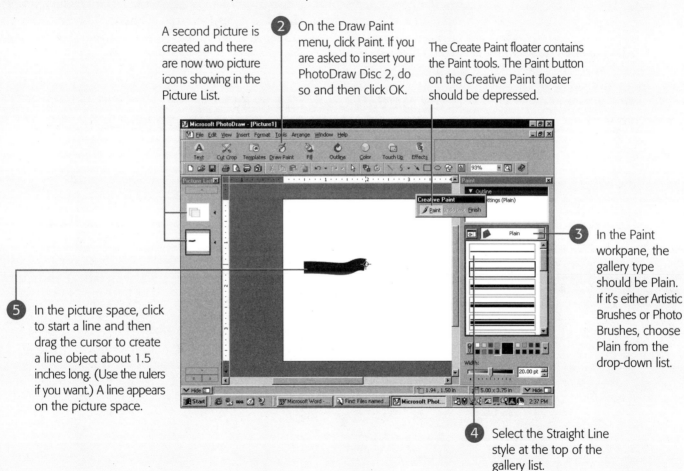

5 In the picture space, click to start a line and then drag the cursor to create a line object about 1.5 inches long. (Use the rulers if you want.) A line appears on the picture space.

3 In the Paint workpane, the gallery type should be Plain. If it's either Artistic Brushes or Photo Brushes, choose Plain from the drop-down list.

4 Select the Straight Line style at the top of the gallery list.

Creative Paint Undo

While working with the Creative Paint tool, you can make as many strokes as you like. At any time if you decide you don't like what you have done, you can use the Undo Last button in the floater to undo the last stroke. When you are satisfied with your work, click the Finish button in the floater to set all the brushstrokes as a single paint object. Now individual brushstrokes are no longer undoable. Clicking Undo on the toolbar will delete all the brushstrokes that make up the single paint object.

Using Multiple Undo and Redo

For each graphic object in each open picture, PhotoDraw keeps a list of up to 20 actions you take. This allows a lot of freedom to try out ideas. If an idea doesn't work, you can undo it and try something else. On the other hand, if you undo an action and then change your mind again, you can reverse the undo with redo.

When you start working on a picture or open a picture for a new session, an undo list is started. Clicking on the small triangle next to the Undo or Redo buttons on the toolbar accesses the lists of actions that can be undone or redone (see the image). Click on the action you want to undo or redo, but remember, if you undo something that is more than one action down from the top of the list, all the actions above it on the list will also be undone. In other words, undo actions are in sequential order.

The undo and redo lists are maintained on your hard disk. Up to two megabytes of hard disk space is used for each picture that is open. So, if you were working between five open pictures, you would use approximately 10 megabytes of space for the undo list. The amount of space actually used will vary with the complexity of your pictures.

Some floating windows have only one level of undo.

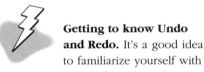

Getting to know Undo and Redo. It's a good idea to familiarize yourself with the Undo and Redo features early on—you'll use them often.

The Undo List

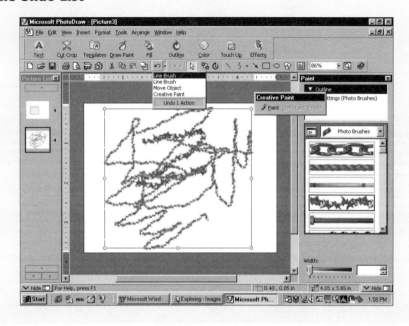

Creating Objects Using the Object List

You can create new objects by dragging objects from the Object List to the picture space. The most recently created picture should be active at this point and should contain a single line. If not, revisit the previous procedure.

Saving for a new project. Sometimes you might do something with a graphic object that stimulates ideas for other possible pictures. You want to explore these possibilities but don't want to stop what you are working on. Drag that graphic object to an empty space on the Picture List to make a new picture and save it with another name. You can come back to it later.

Saving your work. It is a good habit to regularly save your files. All procedures in this book assume that you save the file at the end of each procedure so you normally won't be reminded.

Drag Objects to and from the Object List

1 Open the Object List and drag the object thumbnail from the Object List to the picture space. A new object is created in the picture space and a second object appears in the Object List.

2 Now, without making the first picture active, open its Object List. The Object List displays the two yellow graphic objects.

3 Drag an object thumbnail from this Object List onto the active picture space. You have just added an object from an inactive picture to the active picture. Close the Object List.

4 Here's another trick. From the picture space, drag the currently selected object into the Picture List below the existing two picture thumbnails. A new picture is created with the dimensions of the object you made it from.

5 On the File menu, click Close to close this new picture. When a dialog box asks if you want to save changes to the picture, click No.

6 Save your file. On the File menu click Save As. In the Save As dialog box, navigate to the folder you made for your files. Give this file a name and click OK to save it.

Using the Status Bar

The status bar has several purposes in PhotoDraw. It contains buttons to show and hide the Picture List and workpane, enabling you to create more workspace on your screen if you need it.

The status bar also contains position information and size information. Position information shows the current coordinates of the cursor in the units selected for the picture. Size information shows the size of the current selection. If nothing is selected, the size of the picture space is displayed.

Hiding the Picture List and Workpane

You might want more space to work on your pictures. There are two buttons on the status bar to hide and show the Picture List and current workpane.

Hide the Picture List and Workpane

Closing a window. You can also close the Picture List or workpane by clicking the Close button in the upper right corner or clicking Picture List or workpane on the View menu to uncheck them. To make either of these windows reappear, check the corresponding item in the View menu.

 Click the Hide button at the right end of the Status bar. The workpane disappears and the button now says Show. Click on the button again to show the workpane.

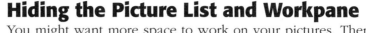

 Click the Hide button at the left side of the Status bar. The Picture List disappears providing you with more working space. The button now says Show. Click on the button again to show the Picture List.

F3 toggles the Picture List on or off and F2 toggles the workpane on or off.

Working with Object and Cursor Coordinates

The key to understanding information presented on the status bar is to know how PhotoDraw locates objects in the picture space. Read the accompanying sidebar if you are unfamiliar with the Cartesian coordinate system (see page 45).

The X and Y Coordinates on the Picture Space.

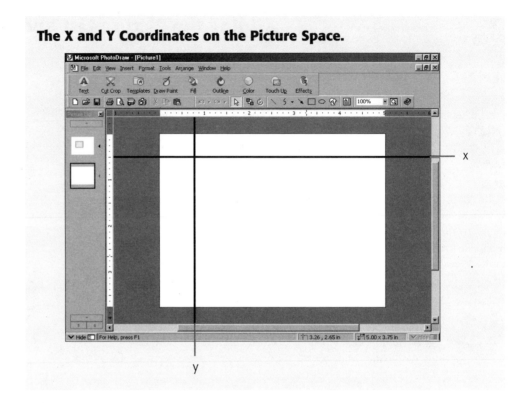

The *X, Y* Grid—Orienting Yourself to the Picture Space

To keep track of locations, PhotoDraw uses the Cartesian coordinate system, which consists of either two or three axes depending on whether two- or three-dimensional space is being described. To locate an object in the PhotoDraw picture space, we need only two axes, labeled *x* and *y*.

The *X*, *Y* Grid—Orienting Yourself to the Picture Space *(continued)*

The *x*-axis represents an imaginary horizontal line (parallel to the top and bottom of your monitor) that can move up and down in the picture space. The *y*-axis represents an imaginary vertical line (parallel to the sides of your monitor) that can move from left to right in the picture space. These two lines always cross somewhere in the picture space at a point called a coordinate point.

Viewing Object Coordinates

The starting coordinate for the picture space is the upper left corner, where both *x* and *y* values are zero. Each object also has its own coordinate grid that starts at 0, 0 in the upper left corner of its bounding box (the area inside the rectangle you see around an object that is selected). This means that if you position an object in the picture space 50 pixels from the left and 60 pixels down from the top, the object's upper left corner is placed at the 49, 59 coordinate in the picture space. (Subtract 1 from 50 and 60 since the counting starts at 0 in each direction.) The status bar position indicator tells you where the 0,0 coordinate of the currently selected object is relative to the 0,0 coordinate of the picture space. The size indicator tells you the size of the selected object in whatever units of measure you are set up to display.

Tracking Cursor Position

There are two ways to track the cursor position. Observe the rulers while moving the cursor around the picture space. A horizontal line on the vertical ruler, and a vertical line on the horizontal ruler, move with the cursor and indicate its location in the picture space. When all objects in the picture space are deselected, the coordinate indicator in the status bar tracks the cursor.

Tracking Cursor Position

Rulers indicate x-y axis
location of the cursor.

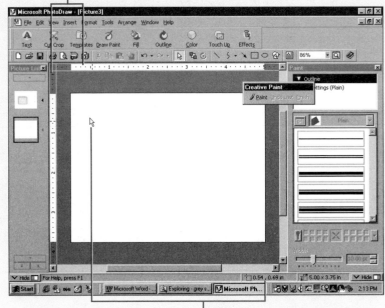

Deselecting an object.
If there are two or more
objects in the picture
space, you can deselect them both by
clicking anywhere away from the objects. If there is a single object, deselect
it by clicking Edit from the main menu
and then clicking Select None. Or press
Alt+E and then press N shortcut.

The coordinate indicator in the
status bar tracks the cursor when
objects are deselected.

Customizing Your Workspace

Sometimes when working in PhotoDraw, you might only have a few objects that require a small workspace. At other times, you might want to make a poster or other large image that contains many small images, thus requiring a larger workspace. You can customize the PhotoDraw workspace.

Repositioning Workpanes, Toolbars, and Menus

Most of the PhotoDraw components can be docked or moved to different areas. They are docked by default. In this exercise, you'll experiment with moving parts of the user interface around.

Move PhotoDraw Windows

Docking a workpane or Picture List. To dock a workpane after it has been undocked, drag it so that the right edge of the workpane is outside the right edge of the PhotoDraw window. To dock a Picture List, drag it so its left edge is just outside the left edge of the PhotoDraw window.

1 On the Draw Paint menu, click Draw. The Outline Workpane appears docked on the right.

2 Position the cursor anywhere in the blue title bar of the Outline Workpane. Drag it into the workspace near the left side of the screen. It is now floating. Drag it back to its original position. It is now docked.

3 Position the cursor over the vertical lines in the main menu bar, the Visual menu bar, and the toolbars, and drag the bars to another location.

4 Now dock them (put them back to their original positions). They can be docked vertically as well as horizontally.

5 Drag the Picture List away from its docked position then put it back.

Move PhotoDraw Windows *(continued)*

6 Click the magnifying glass icon near the right end of the toolbar. The Pan and Zoom floater appears on the screen. This can be moved around the screen but can't be docked. For now, click the Close window button in its upper right corner. You will use this later.

Introducing the Projects

hapter 1 familiarized you with the PhotoDraw interface and some of the tools. This chapter introduces you to the projects used throughout Part 1 of this book. In this chapter, we'll get started on the first project (an easy one to get things rolling), and learn some basics about PhotoDraw.

PhotoDraw by Design is driven by three major design projects. The chapters in the first part of this book step you through the projects to develop your PhotoDraw skills. The projects start out simple and get more complex so you should follow them in order.

By working through the mini-project steps in this chapter, you will learn these important features of PhotoDraw:

If some of the basics slip your mind while working in later chapters, return to Chapter 1.

@ Selecting, grouping, and ungrouping multiple objects

@ Using the Pan and Zoom window

@ Exploring the Object List

@ Drawing straight and curved lines

@ Drawing shapes and changing their fill and outline

@ Creating a text object and changing its color

The Projects in Part 1

The projects we'll cover in Part 1 are based on scenarios you might encounter if you were running a graphic design business or a business that uses graphic design to demonstrate its ideas to customers. You'll wear the hat of a designer (meta-phorically, anyway) and learn PhotoDraw "on the job" as you work on each

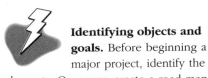 **Identifying objects and goals.** Before beginning a major project, identify the elements. On paper, create a road map of what you need to accomplish and how you can reach that goal. List your objectives and the components. By putting your ideas and goals on paper, you can more readily identify the details necessary to complete the project successfully.

client's piece. As you use PhotoDraw, you'll discover it is a powerful asset in a business setting, as well as for home projects. The techniques you'll learn in Part 1 are useful no matter how you plan to use PhotoDraw.

By contrast, the projects in Part 2 are mostly creative and fun—they are not structured around the concept of a business/client relationship.

Let's look more closely at the projects in this part of *PhotoDraw 2000 By Design* to learn the basics of PhotoDraw:

- ⊚ Our first assignment is to create a map to a rock festival. This lets you get accustomed to some basic techniques you'll use throughout the rest of the book. For this project, the clients are the festival organizers at the Volcanic Rock Festival in Bend, Oregon.

- ⊚ A company called RL&Associates, a value-added reseller of computers, is your second client. As a graphics designer, you'll create several items for this company.

- ⊚ A landscape design company called Curious Coyote is the third business. For this task, you'll take on the role of proprietor of the company and use PhotoDraw to create presentation material.

Map to a Concert

As an introduction to some of PhotoDraw's tools, you will work from a provided picture file, *volcanic map.mix*, to create a map to a concert. This project requires a graphic element, a map element, and a text element. You will make your own version of several of the image objects in an existing map.

RL&Associates

This client has requested several graphics projects, including the following:

- ⊚ **Logo for packing boxes** This is an opportunity to apply the RL&Associates logo to a large, stylized graphic and begin to explore interesting text effects.

- **Poster** Explore concepts of composition, compositing several images, 3-D text, and transparency as you create this piece of art.

- **Announcement card** Customize your own text, using effects and outlines, in this project.

Curious Coyote Landscape Design

The assignment for this company is to assemble a complete set of materials for promotional needs, project design, and documentation use. The typical client is wealthy and wants something unusual, personal, and sophisticated. The graphics and design will project a soft-spoken attention to detail and a sense of intimate relationship with the landscape. You will work with the provided picture files of a landscape design project and develop presentation screens to show the client your landscape designs. The two projects are the following:

- **Pictorial presentation** You'll move and resize existing pictures to present a presentation of landscape elements.

- **Groundmap** You'll use PhotoDraw's drawing tools to make various shapes that represent where the landscape elements will be placed.

Working with the Basics

Your first mini-project is to create a map to a music festival. The Volcanic Rock Festival is held annually near Bend in central Oregon. Although people can find Bend on most maps, the festival site is not so obvious. Festival organizers need to produce a map that helps people get to the concert site from Bend. A PhotoDraw .mix file is included on the *PhotoDraw by Design* CD for you to work with.

You'll practice using the following PhotoDraw tools and functions in this exercise:

- Drawing tools

- Text

- Arrange (placing objects in front of or in back of each other)

Using *mix* files. *Mix* files are PhotoDraw's native file format. All the attributes of the graphic objects in your picture are saved as part of a .mix file. This enables you to open a file, edit the attributes (such as line thickness and color) or a designer effect, and then save the file with another name. You can make as many variations as you need. Note that if you elect to save your file as a different type, such as a bitmap, PhotoDraw will remind you to also save it as a .mix file for future editing. This reminder appears when you close the file.

Opening the Map File

You will need to access the *PhotoDraw by Design* CD for this exercise. If you have been working in Chapter 1 and still have PhotoDraw running, close any open pictures. Then, on the File menu, click Visual Open and skip to Step 3. If PhotoDraw is not open, begin with Step 1.

On the Windows taskbar, click Start, point to Programs, and then click Microsoft PhotoDraw. After a few moments, PhotoDraw opens with the Microsoft PhotoDraw dialog box on the screen.

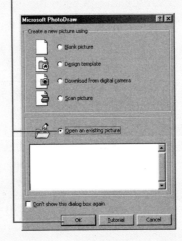

> **Putting PhotoDraw on your desktop.** Create a shortcut of PhotoDraw for your desktop. Then it is always just a click away.

Open the Map File

1. Open PhotoDraw from the Start menu.

2. In the opening dialog box, click Open An Existing Picture and then click OK. The Visual Open dialog box appears.

Open the Map File *(continued)*

3 Locate your CD drive, and then the chapters/chap02 folder.

4 To open the file, double-click the volcanic map.mix thumbnail. A vertical picture space opens with the map picture objects on it. Each line or word is a separate object with its own properties that can be modified.

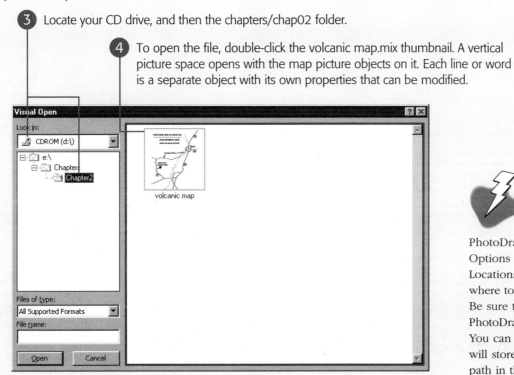

volcanic map

5 Save a copy of the file to your hard drive. Give the file a descriptive name like "chapter 2 number 1" so you will be able to identify it.

Finding the contents. Copy the contents of CD 2 to your hard drive. On PhotoDraw's Tools menu, open the Options dialog and select the File Locations tab. This will tell PhotoDraw where to look for the contents of Disc 2. Be sure that the Prompt To Insert PhotoDraw Disc 2 box is unchecked. You can also specify where PhotoDraw will store your pictures by entering a path in this dialog.

Introducing the Projects

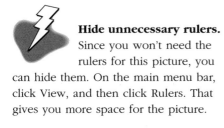

Hide unnecessary rulers. Since you won't need the rulers for this picture, you can hide them. On the main menu bar, click View, and then click Rulers. That gives you more space for the picture.

Selecting Objects

Selecting an object causes that object to receive any actions you perform in PhotoDraw. For instance, if you select one of the text objects in the following example and then open the Effects menu, any of the effects that you use will be applied to this active object.

You can identify which object is active by the highlighted frame that forms around it and by the handle.

Selecting all objects. To select all objects in the entire picture, on the Edit menu, choose Select All. To select all object in just the picture space, on the Edit menu, choose Select All In Picture Area.

Select Multiple Objects

4 With the Shift key still pressed, click the first text object you selected. The object is deselected and only two selected objects remain selected. This illustrates some of the standard Windows behavior you will find throughout PhotoDraw.

1 Click the "Volcanic Rock Festival" text object to select it.

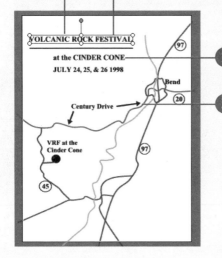

2 While pressing the Shift key, click the Cinder Cone text object. Both objects are now selected.

3 Hold down the Shift key and click to select the light blue line object. Three objects are now selected.

Grouping Objects

By selecting multiple objects, you can group the objects together and subsequently apply similar effects to the objects as a group. For example, if you arrange several objects in a particular way but decide to move them to a different part of the picture, you can move the grouped objects as a single unit, and apply effects to the group. This saves time when a particular effect is to be applied to several objects.

Group and Ungroup Objects

You will see a keyboard shortcut (Ctrl+G) to the right of the Group menu item. Press Ctrl+G to group objects. Press Ctrl+Shift+G to ungroup objects.

1 With the objects selected, open the Arrange menu and then click Group. You could also right-click anywhere within the selected objects and click Grouping and then Group from the list that appears.

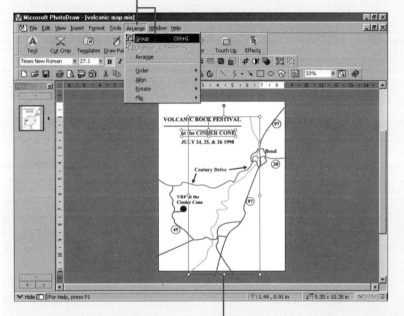

The selected objects are now grouped together and have one common bounding box. They are movable as one object while retaining their positions and proportions relative to each other.

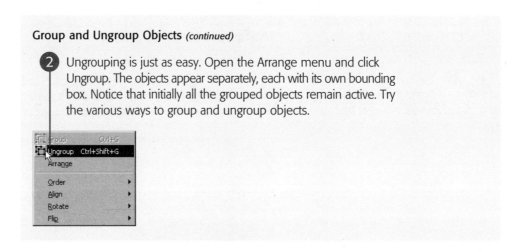

Group and Ungroup Objects *(continued)*

2 Ungrouping is just as easy. Open the Arrange menu and click Ungroup. The objects appear separately, each with its own bounding box. Notice that initially all the grouped objects remain active. Try the various ways to group and ungroup objects.

Zooming with the IntelliMouse. If you are using a Microsoft IntelliMouse, you can zoom using the plus and minus keys.

Zooming to View Objects

There are many times when you need to get a close-up view of an object, or move out to see more objects on the screen. There are several ways to zoom in and out. See the figure on the facing page.

In the exercise on page 60, we'll use the Pan and Zoom window to zoom in and out of the Volcanic Rock Festival map.

Understanding the red rectangle. A red rectangle appears in the Pan and Zoom floating window; this gets smaller as the slider moves up. The rectangle shows the amount of zoom. The picture zooms to the area indicated by the red rectangle.

You can also zoom in the Print Preview window.

The Pan and Zoom window. We'll see how this works in the next exercise.

The Zoom drop-down list. Within the Zoom menu, you'll see the Selection, Fit All, and Fit Picture Area options. The Selection option zooms to the currently selected object. The Fit All option shows all objects in the picture and scratch areas. The Fit Picture Area option zooms to the picture area.

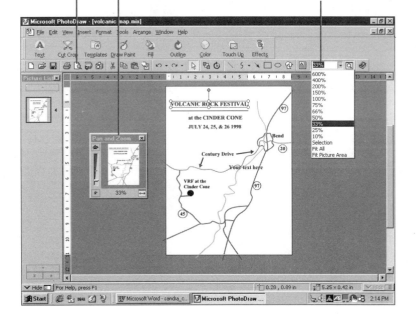

Use the Pan and Zoom Window

2 Position the cursor on the blue Pan and Zoom title bar and drag the floater to a location where it is easy for you to see.

6 Click the Close (floating window) button. The Pan and Zoom window is closed.

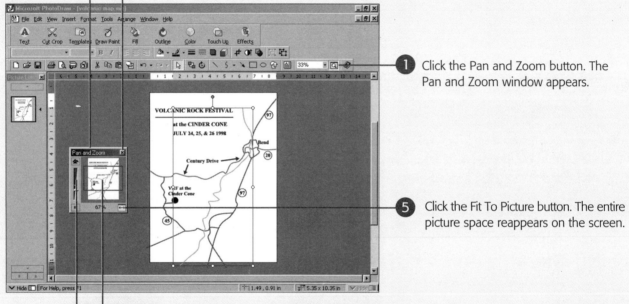

1 Click the Pan and Zoom button. The Pan and Zoom window appears.

5 Click the Fit To Picture button. The entire picture space reappears on the screen.

4 Position the mouse cursor near the center of the red triangle in the Pan and Zoom floating window. Drag the red rectangle a little to the left and release the mouse button. This pans (moves) the visible area in the picture space to match what is under the red rectangle.

3 Slowly move the slider up about one-quarter of the way and release the mouse button.

7 Before continuing, ungroup any grouped objects and save your file.

Working with the Object List

Now is a good time to take another look at the Object List. You can use the Object List to select objects in the picture space (also called the picture area). This exercise lets you explore how objects on the Object List correspond to objects in the picture space.

Explore the Object List

1 In the Picture List, click Object List to open the Object List for the map picture. The first (top) object in the Object List is the text object labeled "Volcanic Rock Festival."

2 Click the All button to select all the objects on the Object List.

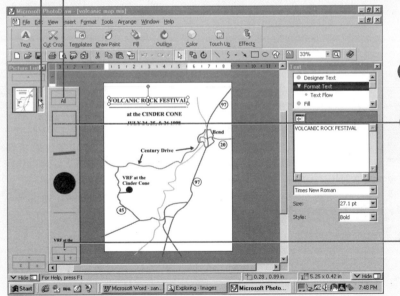

3 Click any white area of the picture space to deselect the objects.

4 Position the cursor over the text object at the top of the Object List. A black line appears around the text object and the corresponding object in the picture space. This identifies which object you have highlighted.

5 Click the down-arrow button to scroll through the list. Move the cursor over other objects in the list, and look at their corresponding objects in the picture area. Scroll to the top of the Object List.

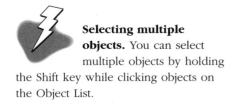

Selecting multiple objects. You can select multiple objects by holding the Shift key while clicking objects on the Object List.

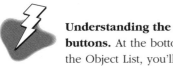

Understanding the buttons. At the bottom of the Object List, you'll find a button with a single triangle, a button with two triangles pointing down, and a button with two triangles pointing up. The single-triangle button scrolls one object at a time, and the dual-triangle buttons scroll up or down one page at a time toward the top or bottom of the list.

Why isn't the Picture List showing? If the Picture List is not showing at the left side of the PhotoDraw screen, click Show at the bottom left corner of the screen.

Explore the Object List *(continued)*

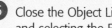 Close the Object List and zoom to fit the picture area by opening the Zoom menu and selecting the Fit Picture Area option.

Working with the Drawing Tools

PhotoDraw makes it easy to draw lines and shapes by providing an AutoShapes floating toolbar that works in conjunction with the Outline Workpane. The AutoShapes toolbar has buttons for drawing:

- Straight lines
- Curved lines in three styles
- Lines with arrow ends
- Rectangles
- Ellipses
- An AutoShapes library provides basic shapes, block arrows, flowchart symbols, stars and banner shapes, and callout shapes resembling cartoon balloons.

The Outline Workpane lets you set properties for these lines and shapes such as line style, width, transparency, and color. The style, which is Plain by default, can also be set to Artistic Brushes for interesting brush effects, or to Photo Brushes for photographic elements.

Drawing a Straight Line

In the next exercise, we'll start out simply by drawing a straight line.

Open AutoShapes in an instant. You can click the Line button on the main toolbar to instantly open the AutoShapes floating toolbar with the straight line tool selected.

Draw a Straight Line

1 Click the Draw and Paint icon on the visual menu to open the drop-down list of Draw and Paint options.

2 Click the Draw icon.

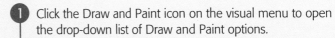
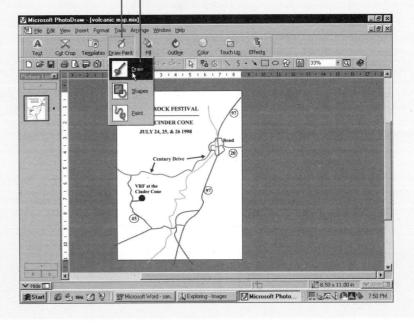

3 If it is not already selected, select the straight line tool in the AutoShapes floating toolbar to activate the workpane controls for the line you are about to draw.

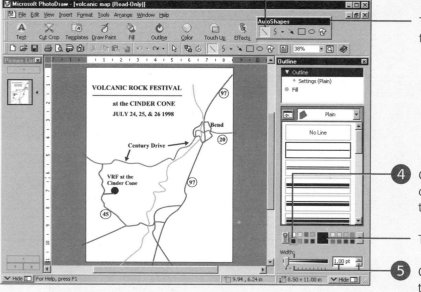

The AutoShapes floating toolbar and the Outline Workpane appear.

4 Change the current line color to black by clicking the small black color square in the Outline Workpane.

The Color Fill square changes to black.

5 Change the line width to 3 by dragging the Width slider until the number to its right is 3. Or click the numbers to select them, and then type 3 and press the Enter key on your keyboard. Or change the numbers by clicking the small arrows to their right.

Using the Shift key while making lines.

Holding down the Shift key while making a line constrains the line to horizontal, vertical or diagonal, 15-degree increments.

Draw a Straight Line *(continued)*

6 Place the cursor below and at the left end of the black horizontal line that is under the Volcanic Rock Festival text object. With the Shift key held down, click, hold down the mouse button, and move the cursor to the right end of the line.

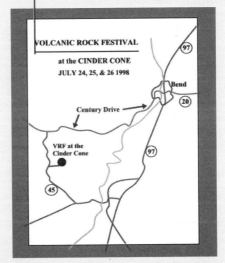

7 Release the mouse button and then release the Shift key.

8 Save your file. Leave the line as part of the picture. This is practice so it's OK to have extra objects.

Drawing a Curved Line

Next we'll try drawing a curved line. However, let's first take a look at the edit points that are available once a curve line is drawn.

PhotoDraw provides an easy solution to editing curved lines. While in Line Editing mode, control points can be moved, deleted from, or added to the line. Each control point is in the middle of a curve. This editing capability takes a lot of the worry out of drawing the line.

Examine Line Edit Mode

1 In the picture area, position the cursor so its point is on the pink line. Click the line to select it, a rectangular box will appear. Right-click in the box.

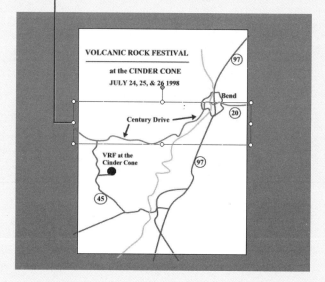

What Line Editing mode looks like.

When PhotoDraw is in Line Editing mode, control points appear on the line and a small Edit Points floater appears near the top of the picture area. You could also have selected Edit Points in the workpane.

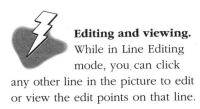

Editing and viewing. While in Line Editing mode, you can click any other line in the picture to edit or view the edit points on that line.

Exiting Line Editing mode. To exit Line Editing mode, you can also click Exit Edit Points in the Edit Points floater or the shortcut menu.

Examine Line Edit Mode *(continued)*

2 On the shortcut menu, select Edit Points to put PhotoDraw into Line Editing mode.

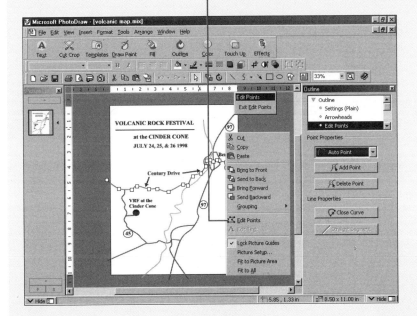

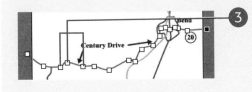

3 Next you draw a line just like this one, so look at the control points and see how they relate to the curves, then press the Esc key on your keyboard to exit Line Editing mode.

Now we'll draw a curved line just above Century Drive by moving from one control point to the next. Remember, control points are always in the middle of curves. After you've tried this procedure, compare the edit points of the original curve to your new curve.

Draw a Curved Line

4 Move the cursor to the next control point, and click and release to set this second control point. Continue this procedure until you have set all except the last control points.

1 To make your own version of the pink line, click the Curve icon on the toolbar. The curve tool is selected in the AutoShapes floating toolbar.

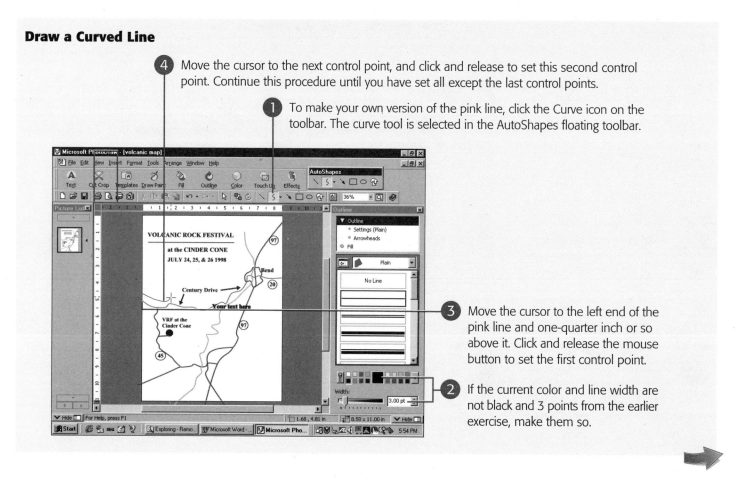

3 Move the cursor to the left end of the pink line and one-quarter inch or so above it. Click and release the mouse button to set the first control point.

2 If the current color and line width are not black and 3 points from the earlier exercise, make them so.

Why aren't the control points visible? The control points are not actually visible until you finish drawing the line and click Edit Points in the Outline Workpane. When you click to set a control point you can only see it by the effect it has on the line to the cursor. (For example, if you move the cursor above the last point, the line will bend up from that point.)

Drawing a curved line. Use the steps outlined on pages 68 and 69 to practice duplicating other curved lines in this map without looking at the original control points.

What's the difference between painting and drawing curves if you can use all the same Outline Workpane tools for both? The answer is painting defaults to Artistic Brushes (although that can be set to other styles) and does not set editable points.

Draw a Curved Line *(continued)*

5 With the cursor positioned at the end of the line, double-click to set the last control point. In a few moments the line appears.

6 Save your file.

Working With Text Objects

While a picture might be worth a thousand words, sometimes you still need words. PhotoDraw provides a variety of text effects and options to work with.

Creating the Text Object

In subsequent chapters, we'll work with quite a few text effects, including 3-D text, bending text, designer text, and more. For now, we'll simply figure out how to create a simple text object, move it, and change its font.

You create a text object by choosing Insert Text on the Text menu; this opens the Text Workpane with a line of default text in the edit window. You then replace that text with your own (by typing new text or pasting text from the clipboard) and optionally change text properties such as font, size, or color. Finally, you can apply any number of effects to the text object if you want.

Create a Text Object

1 On the visual menu, click the Text icon, and then click the Insert Text icon.

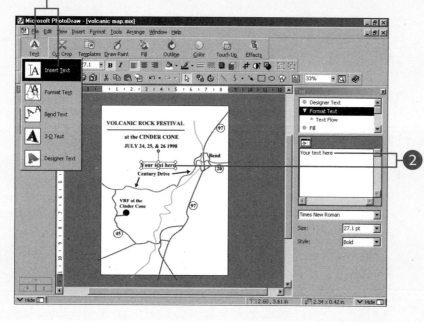

2 In the Text Workpane, replace "Your text here" with your name. The text changes to your name.

Work panes with floating windows. Most workpanes have floating windows containing the basic tools used in that workpane.

Create a Text Object (*continued*)

③ Place the cursor over the edge of the selection rectangle of the text box in the picture area. When the cursor changes to four arrowheads, you can drag the text box.

④ To reposition the text box, drag it onto the white space above the curved lines and then release the mouse button.

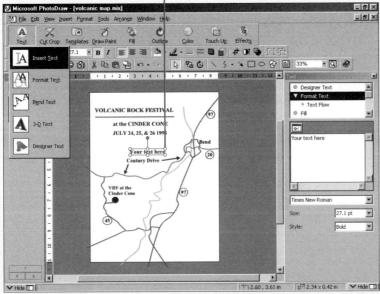

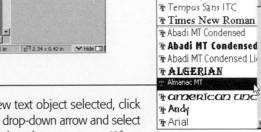

⑤ With the new text object selected, click the Font list drop-down arrow and select a font other than the current one. When the text box is selected, the font of the text object changes.

Changing the Text Color

The color of most PhotoDraw objects is changed by modifying the Fill property. *Fill* can be selected in both the Outline Workpane and the Text Workpane, and it can also stand alone when you click any option on the Fill menu.

Whenever you need to change the color of any object, you can simply select the object and choose a fill type from the Fill menu. (Or, select Fill from the Text Workpane or Outline Workpane if either workpane is visible.)

Change the Text Color

Outline parameters and effects also available to text. In PhotoDraw, outlines can be applied to text objects. Therefore, all the Outline parameters and effects available to lines are also available to text.

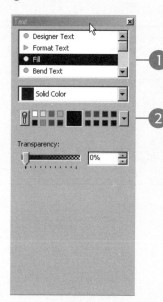

1 In the workpane, click the Fill indicator. Small color boxes appear.

2 Click a color other than the current color. The text object changes color.

AutoShapes, Fill, and Z-Order

Now we'll play with some of the concepts we've covered up to this point: namely AutoShapes, fills, and the ordering of objects. We'll begin by making a shape using the AutoShapes floating toolbar. Then we'll fill that rectangle with a red color and move the object so it covers an existing object. Finally, we'll change the Z-order to put the rectangle under the object.

Making a Shape

Let's make a filled shape using the AutoShapes tool. This is preparation for demonstrating how to work with objects that overlay other objects.

Make a Shape

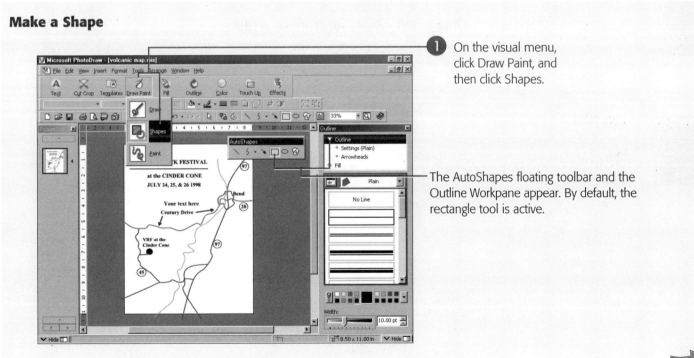

1 On the visual menu, click Draw Paint, and then click Shapes.

The AutoShapes floating toolbar and the Outline Workpane appear. By default, the rectangle tool is active.

The *Z-order* refers to whether one object is in front of (or in back of) another object. This is explained in more detail in Chapter 1.

Make a Shape *(continued)*

 Click and drag a rectangle about 1 inch high and 2 inches wide. Make the line width 3 pixels if it is something else.

Changing Fill Color and Outline Width

On the map, each highway number indicator consists of a text object that (in its Z-order) is on top of a filled shape. We'll give the rectangle a color fill and border, cover one of these highway numbers, and then change the Z-order.

Change Fill Color and Outline Width

3 In the workpane list, click Outline. The Outline tools appear.

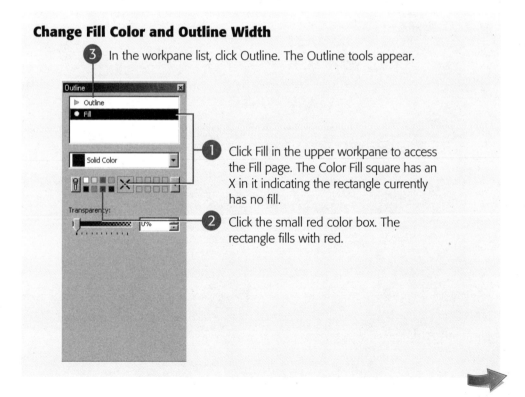

1 Click Fill in the upper workpane to access the Fill page. The Color Fill square has an X in it indicating the rectangle currently has no fill.

2 Click the small red color box. The rectangle fills with red.

First in line. Because the rectangle is the most recent object created, it is first on the Z-order. This means the rectangle is in front of all other objects in the picture.

Refer to the map on page 73.

Change Fill Color and Outline Width *(continued)*

4 Drag the Width slider to 10. The outline of the rectangle becomes 10 pixels wide.

5 Drag the rectangle object on top of one of the highway number indicators. The rectangle hides it.

6 On the main menu bar, click Arrange, and then move the cursor over Order and then click Send To Back. The rectangle changes its position in the Z-order and moves behind the highway indicator.

7 Save the file.

Creating a Proposal Presentation Screen

In this chapter, you will create a colorful cover sheet for a client proposal, which will prepare you to make a landscape layout design in the next chapter. This project provides the opportunity to work with images that you will bring into PhotoDraw. Everything you do in this chapter can be easily applied to many different presentation projects.

By working through the steps in this chapter, you will learn these important features of PhotoDraw:

- Adding objects from an existing picture to another picture
- Setting resolution and background colors for the picture
- Arranging and resizing objects in a picture
- Changing the border styles and colors of images
- Adding text to your picture and setting text properties

An Overview

An on-screen presentation is a walk-through that is presented to a client using a notebook computer. You will create one screen of this presentation in this chapter. The screen contains photographs that you will size and arrange; you will also add borders and text. This provides some basic training for using several PhotoDraw features.

PhotoDraw allows you to open several pictures at the same time. This can be useful for copying images, as well as for reference. For example, we will load one picture that contains the photographic images we want to add to another picture. We will also load the completed presentation, so we can refer to it when necessary.

The Materials You'll Use

Your client, a wealthy industrialist, has recently purchased a large parcel of land in the Southwestern desert region of the United States. He wants his home to be situated in an oasis, with a feeling of privacy, among several rocky outcroppings on the property.

The client wants you to design the oasis landscaping before he designs the house. During your talks with this particular client, you were asked to present several possibilities for the name of the property. Out of your proposals, the client chose the name "SunDog." A colloquialism for the term parhelion, a sun dog is a bright spot on the halo of the sun. A fitting name for the property—an oasis that will be a bright spot in a desert environment ruled by the sun.

While visiting the property, you photographed the rocks and adjacent area. Working from the photographic images, you will first create a presentation screen and, later in the next chapter, develop the ground plan laying out the rocks, water area, and plants.

Taking your photographs. When shooting photographs for projects, take more than you think you will need. Seemingly unrelated subject matter can sometimes be useful. PhotoDraw accepts a variety of digital input formats, including direct input from scanners, digital cameras, video capture devices, and all common picture file formats, so you have many choices. If your images are on film, you can either scan them or have a service bureau put them on Photo CD. By taking your own photographs, you will have unique subject matter selected specifically for your project.

Working from Photographs

When designing something like a landscape that exists in three-dimensional space, familiarity with the space and what it contains will help you visualize its possibilities. Photographs are an excellent way to demonstrate the design principles. You'll use PhotoDraw to arrange the photographs in a presentation.

From the many photographs you took, you selected those that represented the shape of the rock masses—the largest objects. These will form the perimeter of the oasis and give you a clear sense of what the shape of the open interior space will look like.

Before beginning, you will open three files to work with. You will need your own workspace file; the file containing the photographs taken onsite (to add to your workspace); and the finished presentation screen, so you have an example to work from.

This procedure assumes that you still have the CD that accompanies *Photo-Draw by Design* in your CD-ROM drive. If not, insert that CD.

In the next procedure, you'll open a blank picture for composing your work, and then you'll load the file containing scanned photographs for your project. Finally you'll load a sample file showing the finished results.

After you've loaded the finished sample picture, you'll notice that the scanned images are labeled.

The images are of the main rock formations that bound the oasis. You will use these images to create a project presentation screen.

Open Three Pictures

1 Open PhotoDraw and create a default picture. If PhotoDraw is already open, then close all pictures first and create a new default picture by clicking New on the File menu.

2 Open a second picture in PhotoDraw by navigating to the chapters/chap03 folder on the CD that accompanies *PhotoDraw by Design* and loading *desert 1.mix*.

3 Use the Zoom drop-down list box on the toolbar to set the zoom to 50 percent.

4 Open a third picture in PhotoDraw by loading *SunDog presentation screen1.mix*, also in the chapters/chap03 folder. Notice that the zoom changes.

Composing the Presentation Screen

Before continuing, let's look at the elements of the presentation screen and the order in which you will create them. If necessary, zoom out so you can see the whole presentation screen. Remember that you can hide the Picture List to obtain more screen space, if you need it.

In the remainder of this chapter, you will perform these activities in the following order:

Organizing your work. When working on your own projects, try to first determine the order in which actions will be taken and make a list of these actions. This will save you time and help you develop a sense of the logical order of working with PhotoDraw's graphic elements and tools.

- **Create the background.** First you will create a new picture using the default PhotoDraw settings, then you'll change the size and background color. You will save this picture on your hard drive.

- **Add and resize the images.** If you don't already have *desert 1.mix* open, you will open that file. Then after creating a new picture, you will drag the images from the *desert 1.mix* Object List into the new picture and loosely arrange them.

- **Align the images.** Using the Arrange Workpane, you'll arrange the images in precise locations.

- **Add image borders** Using the Outline Workpane, you'll use the Artistic Brushes setting to add interesting borders to each image.

- **Add text.** You'll finish the presentation screen by adding title text and labeling the images.

Creating the Presentation Background

Computer display measurement units. Computer monitors are built to display pixels, so whenever you are creating a picture for onscreen use, set up the picture space using pixels as the unit of measure.

The background size and shape of a picture is determined by how the picture space is set up. First you will open the picture and then change the properties for the background.

Changing the Background Resolution and Color

On the File menu, click Picture Setup to open this dialog box without using the shortcut menu.

Remember, you are making a presentation to a client using a notebook computer. In this case, we've chosen 800 by 600 pixels as a background resolution because most current notebook computers support this resolution. Also, we want to set the background color to black. Both the resolution and the background color are changed using the Picture Setup dialog box.

Change the Background Resolution and Color

1 Right-click anywhere in picture area or picture space and select Picture Setup from the shortcut menu. The Picture Setup dialog box appears.

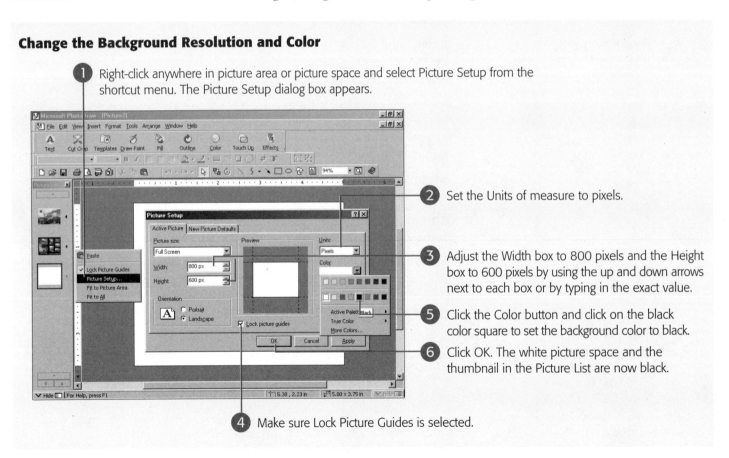

2 Set the Units of measure to pixels.

3 Adjust the Width box to 800 pixels and the Height box to 600 pixels by using the up and down arrows next to each box or by typing in the exact value.

5 Click the Color button and click on the black color square to set the background color to black.

6 Click OK. The white picture space and the thumbnail in the Picture List are now black.

4 Make sure Lock Picture Guides is selected.

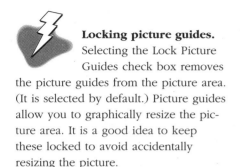

Locking picture guides.
Selecting the Lock Picture Guides check box removes the picture guides from the picture area. (It is selected by default.) Picture guides allow you to graphically resize the picture area. It is a good idea to keep these locked to avoid accidentally resizing the picture.

Adding and Resizing the Images

We're composing the presentation screen with the large image on the left, two smaller vertical images to the right, and three smaller horizontal images at the far right. This creates a visual feeling of movement from left to right, the way western cultures read and write.

All the objects in our design are aligned to provide the viewer with more details as he or she looks from left to right, which leads to the next screen in the presentation. Also, by showing the photographs first, the client gets a sense of the actual landscape before moving on to a much more abstract ground plan.

To compose the picture, we will need to place the images on the background and size them to fit in the overall picture. First we will add the horizontal pictures, then the two vertical pictures, and finally we will insert one large picture on the left. All will be resized to fit the picture.

Dragging Objects from the Object List

Occasionally you will want to use image objects from one picture as part of another picture. PhotoDraw makes that easy, enabling you to drag objects from one picture's Object List directly into an active picture.

In this case, the images for our presentation are stored in an existing *desert 1.mix* Picture file, so we will open that picture and drag the pictures we need from it to our presentation screen.

Drag Objects from the Object List

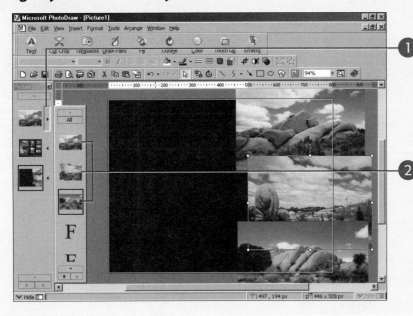

1 Click the arrow next to the *desert 1.mix* thumbnail. If you opened this picture after the others, the thumbnail will be lower in the Picture List. The Object List opens and your new picture is still the active picture.

2 From the *desert 1.mix* Object List, drag the three small horizontal image thumbnails to the right side of the black picture space, keeping them in the same vertical order as in the Object List. The images can overlap. We'll resize and place them next.

Saving often. Before dragging images, make sure the new picture is active (black picture space on the screen) and save the file to your hard drive (Ctrl+S). Saving often prevents problems later on.

Arranging Images

Now we'll resize and arrange the three pictures to fit on the presentation screen. The PhotoDraw Arrange Workpane enables you to resize, position, rotate, or flip objects. In this case, you'll resize the images using this workpane. You can tell PhotoDraw to maintain proportions and then simply set either the width or height to resize the entire picture proportionally.

The positioning is a rough estimate, so dragging the pictures works well at this stage. Looking at the example presentation screen, you'll see that the three

Remember to save your file after you complete each procedure.

horizontal pictures need to be aligned vertically on the upper right side of the presentation screen.

Arrange the Horizontal Images

1 Select the bottom image.

2 From the Arrange menu, click Arrange to open the Arrange Workpane. When it appears on the right, the Size and Position view is visible.

4 In the workpane, change the Width setting to 180 pixels. (Leave the Maintain Proportions check box selected so you don't have to change the Height setting.) and press the Enter key on your keyboard. The image is resized to 180 pixels wide while maintaining its original proportions.

3 Drag the horizontal slider to bring the three image objects into view. You will resize them.

5 Resize the two remaining images proportionally using the same method and the same Width setting of 180 pixels.

6 Position all three pictures by dragging them near the right side in a vertical column and toward the top of the picture space. (Use the finished presentation screen as a guide.)

Creating a Proposal Presentation Screen

Arranging the Vertical Images

To finish, let's add two more pictures from the *desert 1.mix* Object List and then resize them in a similar manner to the previous steps.

Arrange the Vertical Images

1. Look at the middle pictures in the example presentation picture.

2. From the Object List, drag the two small vertical images that correspond to the horizontal images in the example presentation screen into your picture. (Don't add the picture of the large rock yet; we'll insert a larger version of that picture next.)

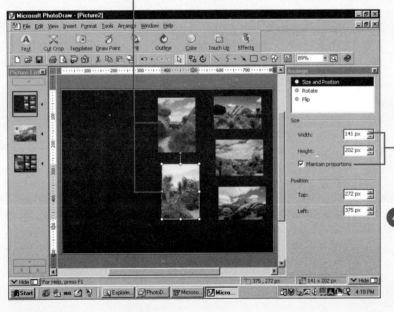

3. Resize the images at 141 pixels wide, leaving the Maintain Proportions check box selected.

4. Drag these two resized images next to the three resized horizontal images, as in the finished example picture.

Image Scaling

PhotoDraw uses algorithms to scale images. Mathematical formulas calculate what the image currently looks like and, based on the algorithm, calculate the number of pixels and colors that will best represent the resized image. This is drawn to the screen in a new size. When scaling an image to a smaller size, the algorithm has more than enough data and chooses the best from what already exists, discarding the surplus pixels. This produces an image that is quite good. Scaling an image to a larger size is different. In this case, the algorithm must calculate new data to add to the image to re-create a larger, similar-looking image. *Similar* is the key term, since added data is only an estimation of what the larger image should look like. Considering this, whenever possible keep your original images large and scale down when necessary.

Adding the Final Image

The biggest picture in this presentation screen must be added from a separate bitmap file on the accompanying CD.

In the next procedure, you'll resize and roughly position the largest image on the left of the picture space. Remember to check out the *SunDog presentation screen1.mix* picture if you need to get an idea of where you are headed with this project.

Add the Final Image

1 From the Insert menu, click Visual Insert, navigate to the chapters/chap03 folder on the *PhotoDraw by Design CD*, and load *vertical rock*.

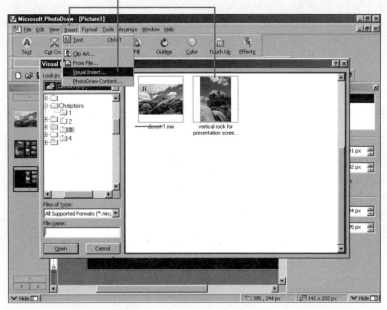

2 Using the Arrange Workpane as before, resize this image to 313 pixels wide, leaving the Maintain Proportions check box checked.

3 Place all your image objects as in the finished picture. You will position them precisely in the next procedure.

Aligning the Images

Let's line up the images first, and then add outlines around each image to make the images appear to float slightly against the background.

Position the Images

① Select the large image on the left side of your picture.

③ For the uppermost of the two smaller vertical images, enter the Position coordinates of 25, 394.

④ For the lower vertical image, enter the Position coordinates of 274, 394.

⑤ Select the top horizontal image and enter the Position coordinates of 25, 590.

⑥ Select the middle horizontal image and enter the Position coordinates of 184, 590.

② Type in Position coordinates of Top 25, Left 24, and press the Enter key.

⑦ Select the bottom horizontal image and enter the Position coordinates of 355, 590.

Arranging and aligning objects. The arrangement of objects in a picture has a lot to do with how the user sees the overall image. In the presentation screen, you want the viewer to visually settle on any one of the several images. Arranging the images so their outside edges are aligned gives an overall continuity that invites the viewer to stop anywhere, rather than imparting the feeling that the visuals are demanding continual movement. Objects with offset edges tend to bounce the viewer around.

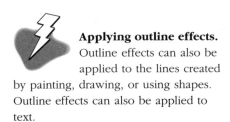

Applying outline effects. Outline effects can also be applied to the lines created by painting, drawing, or using shapes. Outline effects can also be applied to text.

Adding Image Outlines

PhotoDraw automatically defines outline borders around all objects except for shapes, lines, or painted objects. You can use the outline around pictures for framing them or for adding effects. An outline is essentially the same as a plain line surrounding the object, so any attribute that can be set for a line can also be set for an outline. Borders can be set with widths of up to 150 points. They can be composed of any of the Plain line styles in any color, or with styles from any of the Artistic Brushes or Photo Brushes.

Colors in the desert are mostly semi-neutral and, except for cactus flowers in the spring, not very brilliant. To make the desert images stand out, I chose black as the background color. As such, the images lack a certain individuality. In this case, we'll use the PhotoDraw Outlines feature to help them stand out.

Selecting Artistic Brushes

Lines and outlines in PhotoDraw can be used quite effectively by adding effects such as brushes and edge softening. From the Outline visual menu button, you can choose from the following options:

- Plain, which provides a palette of various line types based on straight edge lines.

- Soft Edges, which blurs the edge of the line or outline. This can be used with any other line style and enables you to select the softness of the edge as a parameter.

- Artistic Brush styles, which apply various brush strokes to the line or outline.

- Photo Brush style, which replaces the line with a linear photograph. This tends to give it a framed look.

In this example, we'll use an Artistic Brush since we want a subtle effect.

Select Artistic Brushes

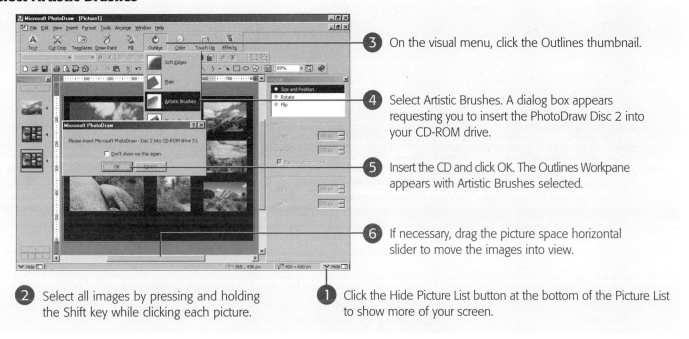

3 On the visual menu, click the Outlines thumbnail.

4 Select Artistic Brushes. A dialog box appears requesting you to insert the PhotoDraw Disc 2 into your CD-ROM drive.

5 Insert the CD and click OK. The Outlines Workpane appears with Artistic Brushes selected.

6 If necessary, drag the picture space horizontal slider to move the images into view.

2 Select all images by pressing and holding the Shift key while clicking each picture.

1 Click the Hide Picture List button at the bottom of the Picture List to show more of your screen.

Applying Outlines

The next couple of procedures walk you through the process of selecting and adding a specific Artistic Brush as an outline for your images. If you can't find the specific brush suggested right away, don't worry—any brush will work to give you the idea.

Creating a Proposal Presentation Screen

Apply Outlines

1. Scroll down through the brushes and hold the mouse over each graphic to display the name.

2. Locate the Pen - Technical Point brush and click it. The outline appears around the image in the default blue color.

Changing Outline Attributes

This procedure should be performed immediately after completing the preceding procedure. Note that all images should be currently selected.

Change Outline Attributes

1 Select Settings. A different set of tools appears in the workpane.

3 Click the Color button. A color selector list box appears.

An outline design tip. The blue in the image is mixed with some black and de-emphasizes the outline, allowing the image to float slightly away from the background while the subdued outline maintains a distinct boundary.

2 Change the Placement setting from On Top to Beneath. You should see the progress indicator start. When it stops, the inside edge of the outlines will be underneath the images.

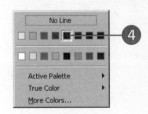

4 Change the outline color by clicking the Variation 5 square in the color selector. (Hold the mouse over each color square to see the variation number.)

Creating a Proposal Presentation Screen

Adding Text

Microsoft PhotoDraw provides a broad assortment of text types, fonts, and colors. PhotoDraw uses text mostly for labeling and titles, as opposed to a word processor which generally manipulates large amounts of text. In the presentation, screen text is used as a design element as well as to convey information, so we'll make good use of PhotoDraw's text capabilities.

Adding Title Text

The space underneath the images is for title text that identifies the name of the future oasis home. It also acts as a visual foundation on which the images rest.

Add Title Text

1 On the visual menu, click the Text thumbnail, and then click Insert Text. The Text Workpane appears and a selected text box appears in the middle of the picture space.

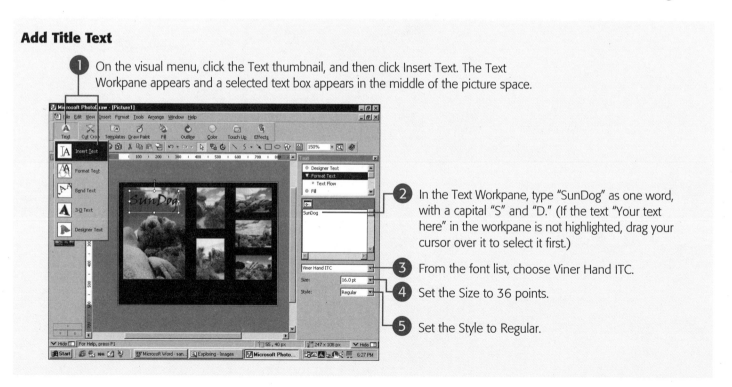

2 In the Text Workpane, type "SunDog" as one word, with a capital "S" and "D." (If the text "Your text here" in the workpane is not highlighted, drag your cursor over it to select it first.)

3 From the font list, choose Viner Hand ITC.

4 Set the Size to 36 points.

5 Set the Style to Regular.

Changing Text Color

The following procedure for changing the fill text color assumes that the Text Workpane is open. You can get more creative by using options from the Fill button on the visual menu.

Change the Text Color

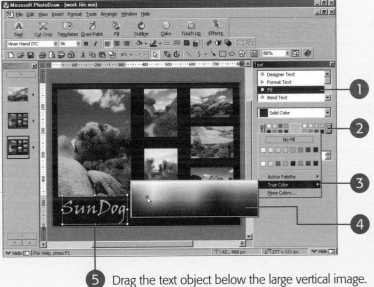

1. In the Text Workpane, click Fill. Color selection tools appear in the workpane.

2. Click the Color button on the far right side of the color selection squares.

3. On the color selector list box that appears, select the True Color item. A gradient color panel appears.

4. Move your cursor over the colors and find a shade of orange that you like and then click it. The panel disappears and the text becomes orange.

5. Drag the text object below the large vertical image.

By clicking on any text object to give it focus, you can move it 1 pixel at a time using the keyboard arrow keys. You can also press and hold the Shift key, and then use the arrow keys to move objects 10 pixels at a time.

Duplicating Text Objects

Now we'll use a shortcut to create the second part of the title. This needs to be a separate text object because the size and color will be different. But to get started, we'll simply make a copy of the text object we just created and change the text and size.

Duplicate a Text Object

1 With the "SunDog" object selected, press Ctrl+D to make a duplicate object.

2 Drag the duplicate to the right, below the small images.

3 Double-click the duplicate text object. This puts you back into text editing mode and you can now change the duplicate text.

4 In the workpane, change the word "SunDog" to "an Oasis homesite".

5 Change the font size to 24 points and leave everything else as is.

Changing the Color

The next step changes the color of the second label. The method is similar to the way you changed text color earlier.

Change the Color

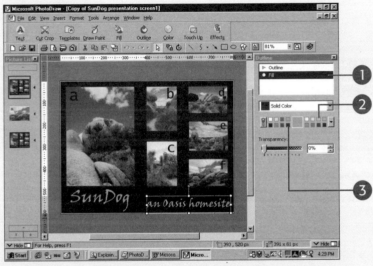

1 Click Fill in the workpane.

2 Click the blue color square at the bottom left of the Color Fill square. The Color Fill square turns blue, and eight variations of blue now appear to the right of the Color Fill square.

3 Choose the third from the left on the top row. This provides a color close to the example presentation.

4 Position the text object so it fits below the small images.

Try using true color. You can experiment with the True Color selector if you want to get a more precise match for the sample presentation.

Adding Labels—The Finishing Touch

To complete the presentation screen, you only need to add labels to the images. We've already gone through the steps for creating text, so you know how to create and position the a, b, c, d, and e labels on the pictures.

Add Picture Labels

1. From the Text visual menu, click Insert Text and type the letter a in place of "Your text here."

2. Set the Font to Lucida Sans Typewriter, the Size to 36 points, and the Style to Regular.

4. Position this letter in the left corner of the large image.

6. Choose Format Text in the workpane.

3. Click Fill and set the color to black.

5. Make a copy of the letter a (by pressing Ctrl+D) and position it in the corner of every other image.

7. Select each letter and replace the letter a with the letter that corresponds to that picture, as in the example presentation.

Things to Explore on Your Own

Here are a few exercises to expand on what you've just learned:

- Practice matching the colors of text for a while to get a feel for it. Try other color combinations for the text to get a feel for how different text colors change the overall picture. To change the variations of a current color, access the True Color panel and select a color either lighter or darker than the current color.

- Try other outlines around the image objects. Try using a different outline for the large image object. Try different colors for the outlines. Explore changing the settings for outlines.

- Try laying out (composing) the image objects in different ways. What would the picture look like if the large image were on the right instead of the left? What if the three small horizontal images were in the middle?

- Try setting the background color to something other than black.

Working with AutoShapes and Align Tools

See Chapter 3, "Creating a Proposal Presentaion Screen," for a description of the project.

In this chapter, we will create a ground plan for the SunDog oasis site. The landscape layout graphic will include shapes labeled with letters that correspond to the presentation screen you made in Chapter 3. It will also have a compass.

To build on some of the skills you've learned, you'll apply techniques to make freeform shapes, align objects, and rotate objects. By working through the steps in this chapter, you'll learn these important features of PhotoDraw:

- Rotating a line
- Aligning objects
- Using the AutoShapes Curve, Freeform, and Ellipse tools
- Shaping lines by editing control points

Creating a Complete Ground Plan

For the ground plan, we'll use the images from the *SunDog presentation screen1.mix* file to see what the objects look like. We'll also refer to a copy of the finished project (the *sundog ground plan1.mix* file) for reference. These files are located in the chapters/chap04 folder on the companion CD.

You will create some shapes that represent rock formations, using the finished drawings as a guide. The rocks only define the perimeter of the space in which the landscape and house are located, so the shapes will serve as outlines. After creating the rock shapes, you will make other shapes that represent a stream, a pool, palm trees, and other landscape plants.

Getting Started

Let's begin with the basic shapes needed in the ground plan. Start PhotoDraw, if it's not already running.

As you did in previous chapters, make a new picture using pixels as the units of measure. Set the size to 800 by 600 pixels and leave the background white. Leave the picture guides locked. You will make new pictures throughout *PhotoDraw by Design*—the procedure will no longer be spelled out unless something unusual is required.

In the next procedure, you'll open the sample files *sundog groundplan1.mix* (the finished project), and *SunDog presentation screen1.mix*, the project we did in Chapter 3. Then you'll drag a compass object from the finished project into your project so you can reference it while you make your own compass.

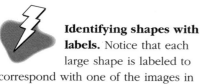

Identifying shapes with labels. Notice that each large shape is labeled to correspond with one of the images in the presentation screen picture you made in the previous chapter.

Ordering and the Object List. When creating your picture, the objects are placed in the Object List relative to their Z-order (front to back). The most recently created object is placed at the top of the list (in front of all other objects). Logically, the compass should be at the bottom of the list since you are creating it first. For fast access, it has been moved to the top.

Open the Sample Files

1 Open the file *sundog ground plan 1.mix* in the chapters/chap04 folder on the *PhotoDraw by Design CD*.

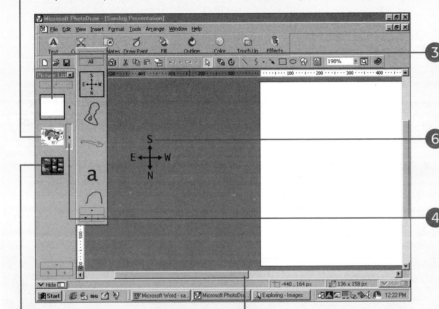

3 In the Picture List, click the thumbnail of your new, empty picture to make it the active picture.

6 Drag a copy of the small compass into your picture and place it in the scratch space. This allows you to refer to it as you make your own compass.

4 Click the Object List arrow to open the *sundog ground plan 1.mix* Object List. As you make your picture, the order that the objects appear in your Object List will differ from that in *sundog ground plan 1.mix*.

2 Open the file *SunDog presentation screen 1.mix* in the chapters/chap04 folder on the *PhotoDraw by Design CD*.

5 Scroll to the right in the picture area to make room for the compass on the scratch space.

Using visual directions and symbols. Sometimes you'll present objects that relate to other pictures with different points of view. The directions of a compass will not always work. Other directions might be: inside and outside; back, front, and sides; up and down; and so on. Visual symbols such as colored shapes or numbers orient the viewer. In this picture, a green dot means a palm tree and a gold oval is a flannel bush. Remember to define the symbols for your viewer.

See Chapter 2, "Introducing the Projects," for more information on grouping objects.

Making a Compass

The next part of this project provides you with PhotoDraw drawing experience. To create a compass, you'll need to draw a straight line; apply arrows to each end; duplicate the arrow line and rotate it 90 degrees; center the cross axis; and label north, south, east, and west points. This compass should end up looking like the one you dragged from the finished file.

The reason for creating the compass in this manner is to give you some practice with lines, arrow points, rotation, and grouping. If you want a quicker way to create a compass object, click AutoShapes on the toolbar, click Block Arrows, and then click the Quad Arrow shape. PhotoDraw usually has a shortcut for most tasks, including this one, but we'll take the scenic route in this case to get a bit of exercise.

Working with Groups

Occasionally you will want to keep several objects together, especially if you are working with many objects in a picture. As explained in Chapter 2, PhotoDraw allows you to group objects together, move the group as a single object, and apply effects to all the objects in a group.

In the finished picture, the compass elements have been grouped together. In our project, we'll ungroup them so you can see the elements. Then we'll get set to draw a line.

Ungroup the Objects

1 Click the compass group to select it if it is not already selected.

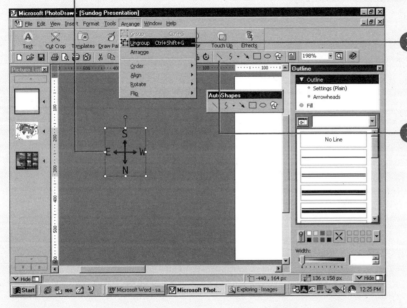

2 On the Arrange menu, click Ungroup. The compass is ungrouped into its component objects.

3 On the toolbar, click the Line tool to bring up the AutoShapes floater and Outline Workpane.

Right-click anywhere in the picture space. Point to Grouping on the shortcut menu that appears and choose Ungroup or Group.

Getting more workspace. To obtain more screen space, you might want to move the AutoShapes floater to the right end of the visual menu, where it is out of the way but readily available.

Using ruler when drawing. You can use the cursor location indicator in the rulers to tell where to start and stop drawing a line when referencing another object for measurement.

Ungroup the Objects *(continued)*

5 Click the small black Color Fill square to set the color of the new line to black.

4 Change the line Width to 2 points.

Working with Lines

The Line tool should still be active from the previous procedure. If it is not, click it to make it active. For this exercise, use the compass you dragged as a reference for size and placement.

Create the Compass Spokes

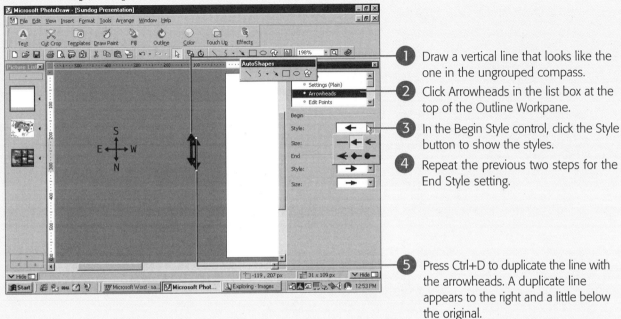

1. Draw a vertical line that looks like the one in the ungrouped compass.

2. Click Arrowheads in the list box at the top of the Outline Workpane.

3. In the Begin Style control, click the Style button to show the styles.

4. Repeat the previous two steps for the End Style setting.

5. Press Ctrl+D to duplicate the line with the arrowheads. A duplicate line appears to the right and a little below the original.

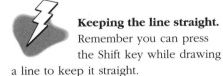

Keeping the line straight. Remember you can press the Shift key while drawing a line to keep it straight.

Judging line length. To see the length of the original line, select the line and look at the object size in the status bar.

Next, let's rotate the duplicated line 90 degrees. For this example, you'll open the Custom Rotate tool to do this. The duplicated line should be selected before continuing.

Rotate One Spoke Line

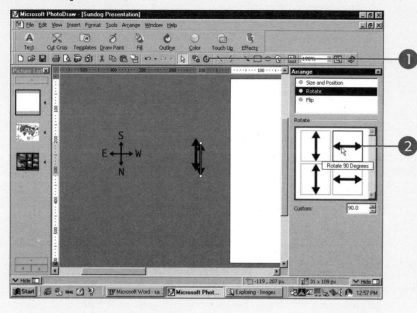

1. On the toolbar, click the Custom Rotate button. Or click Custom Rotate on the Rotate submenu of the Arrange menu. The Arrange Workpane appears with the Rotate settings tools active.

2. Select the Rotate 90 Degrees thumbnail. The duplicate line rotates 90 degrees.

You can also click Rotate Right on the Rotate submenu of the Arrange menu instead of opening the Custom Rotate tool.

Positioning the Objects

Next we'll align the two objects so they cross each other in the middle. The object you just rotated remains selected.

Align the Objects

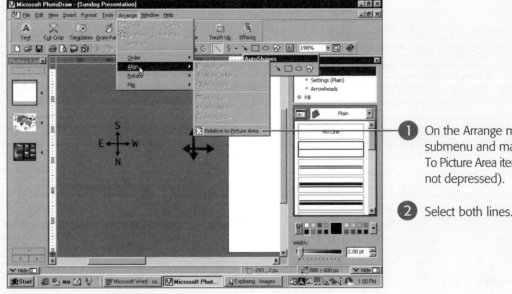

① On the Arrange menu, open the Align submenu and make sure the Relative To Picture Area item is turned off (button not depressed).

② Select both lines.

Items to check before aligning objects. Always select the Relative To Picture Area item before aligning objects. It should be off when aligning objects relative to each other and on when aligning objects relative to the picture area.

Align the Objects *(continued)*

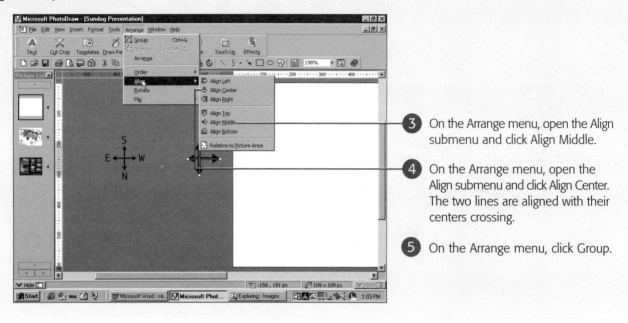

③ On the Arrange menu, open the Align submenu and click Align Middle.

④ On the Arrange menu, open the Align submenu and click Align Center. The two lines are aligned with their centers crossing.

⑤ On the Arrange menu, click Group.

To select both lines, press the Shift key and click the first line you made.

Group the Objects

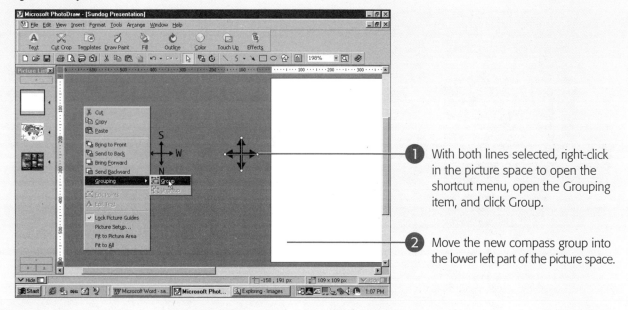

1 With both lines selected, right-click in the picture space to open the shortcut menu, open the Grouping item, and click Group.

2 Move the new compass group into the lower left part of the picture space.

Making the Direction Points

Now that we have the compass lines, we'll create the letters that designate north, east, south, and west.

Create the Text Objects

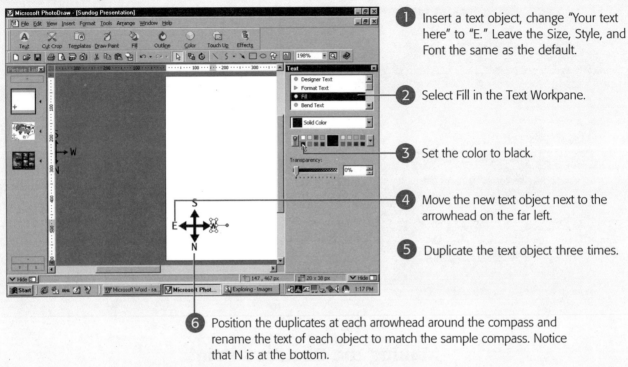

1. Insert a text object, change "Your text here" to "E." Leave the Size, Style, and Font the same as the default.

2. Select Fill in the Text Workpane.

3. Set the color to black.

4. Move the new text object next to the arrowhead on the far left.

5. Duplicate the text object three times.

6. Position the duplicates at each arrowhead around the compass and rename the text of each object to match the sample compass. Notice that N is at the bottom.

Using arrow keys for nudging. Use the arrow keys to nudge the text objects one pixel at a time as you line them up with the arrows.

Selecting and Grouping Objects

It's time to group all the objects that make up the compass. As you've seen, you must select all the items to group them. So far, we've used the Shift key while selecting the objects to do this. Then we've grouped the items using either the Group command on the Arrange menu or the shortcut menu equivalent. This time

Press Ctrl+Shift+G to Ungroup objects.

we'll try a new technique for selecting and grouping. The lines are grouped at this point, so we'll ungroup them first and then group everything together.

Group the Line and Text Objects

1 Click the central group of lines with arrowheads to select it and ungroup the objects using one of the techniques you've learned.

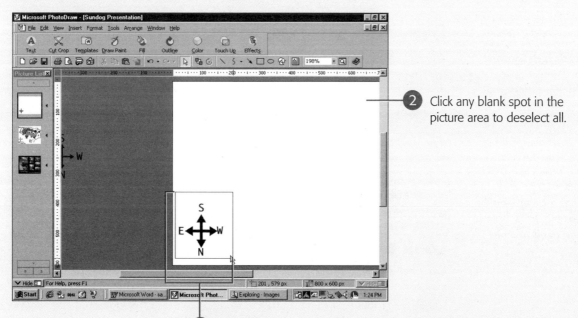

2 Click any blank spot in the picture area to deselect all.

3 Place the cursor above and to the left of all the compass objects, and then drag the cursor down and to the right of all the objects. (Drag with the left mouse button pressed and release it when you are done.) All objects in the compass should be selected.

Drawing Shapes in the Ground Plan

PhotoDraw shapes can be drawn using any of the tools on the AutoShapes toolbar. In Chapter 2, you worked with drawing curved lines and using edit points. In this section, you'll get more exercise using the drawing tools in a detailed project setting.

Using the right tool for the job. The landscape project demonstrates the types of shapes best drawn with these three types of tools: the Curve tool works best for smooth objects (such as the natural shapes of rocks); the Freeform tool is good for angular objects (in this case the outline of a house); and the Ellipse tool is good for oval and circular shapes (used liberally in landscape designs to show bushes and trees).

The drawing tools we'll use in this project are the Curve tool, the Freeform tool, and the Ellipse tool. Both the Curve and Freeform tools create control points. The Curve tool creates a curve at every control point (unless it's directly in line between two other control points). The Freeform tool creates an angle at every control point. You can think of the Freeform tool as a straight line drawing tool with control points. The Ellipse tool is great for drawing oval shapes.

Look at the Target Picture

Once again make *SunDog presentation screen1.mix* the active picture and briefly look at the images, taking mental note of what each one looks like, along with the letter labels that identify them. Image a will be the object at the west end of the ground plan; b and c are the rock formations and pathway near the southeast corner; d is the rock formation along the east end; f is the long rock formation along the south side. Together these images form a rough, elongated "U" shape, inside of which the house, pool, and gardens will be located. These procedures give you practice making freeform shapes that can be closed and filled with color, or open and unfilled.

As in the previous exercise, you'll begin by moving a copy of a sample object into your workspace so you have a model to work from.

Get a Copy of the Target Shape

1 Click the picture thumbnail in the Picture List to make it active and scroll the picture area to the right to make room on the scratch space.

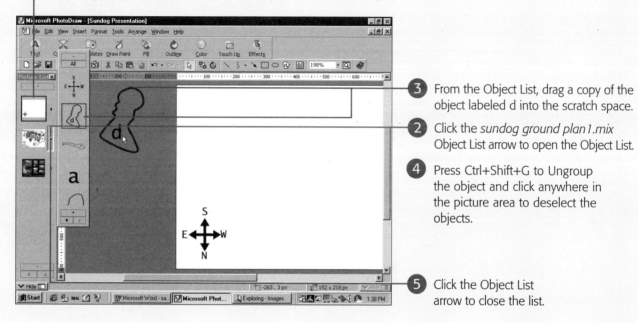

3 From the Object List, drag a copy of the object labeled d into the scratch space.

2 Click the *sundog ground plan1.mix* Object List arrow to open the Object List.

4 Press Ctrl+Shift+G to Ungroup the object and click anywhere in the picture area to deselect the objects.

5 Click the Object List arrow to close the list.

Using the Curve Tool for Complex Shapes

Learning to use the curve tool takes some patience until you get a feel for it. Next, you'll create a very rough approximation of the target shape and then use the point editor to refine it.

It is often easiest to begin by counting the number of bends in the object you are drawing. (In this case, it's easier because that object has control points.) Then try to create the same number of control points when you draw your rough approximation. You can fix most objects in the edit stage, even adding or deleting control points. Don't worry about connecting the end with the beginning at first pass—you can do that in the point editor too.

Before beginning this next step, take a good look at the control points in the target object. To see the control points of object d, select the object, and choose Edit Points in the Outline Workpane. When you enter the point editor, you'll see 20 points on the shape that you dragged in from the sample. When you create your own version of this object, you'll want to set 20 points in order to get every curve. Don't worry about any of the settings under Point Properties in the workpane for now. After looking at the control points, click Exit Edit Points in the floater to go back to Selection mode.

Positioning your screen. If needed, scroll the picture area so you can see the shape on the scratch space and provide room to work.

Zooming in. You can use Zoom tools to allow more precise placement of control points.

Draw a Curve Shape

① Click the Curve button on the Toolbar. The AutoShapes floating toolbar and the Outline Workpane appear.

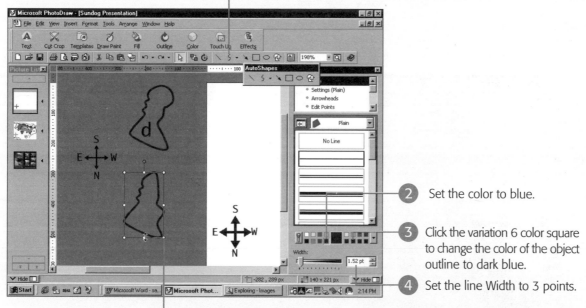

② Set the color to blue.

③ Click the variation 6 color square to change the color of the object outline to dark blue.

④ Set the line Width to 3 points.

⑤ Referring to the copy of object d that you dragged onto the scratch space, click and release once to set a control point for the lower left corner. While setting control points work your way around to the right (counterclockwise).

⑥ Duplicate the shape on the scratch space as closely as you can by continuing to click and release to make control points. Don't worry about accuracy—just generally attempt to place control points in the right areas.

⑦ Place the final control point on top of, or as near as possible to, the first. Double-click to finish drawing.

Shaping the Drawing

Now that you've finished drawing the control points, you can shape them into the final form. Then to finish the rest of the rock objects (a and f), just copy them from the finished *sundog ground plan1.mix* file.

Edit the Points

① Right-click and select Edit Points menu from the shortcut menu.

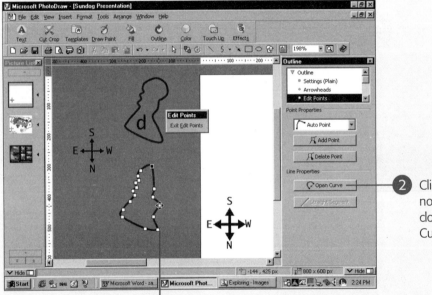

② Click Close Curve if the curve is not closed. (If the curve is closed, this button will say Open Curve.)

To move an existing point, place the cursor on the point you want to move. The cursor becomes a diamond shape. Drag the point to where you want it.

Edit the Points *(continued)*

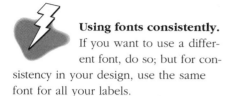

Using fonts consistently.
If you want to use a different font, do so; but for consistency in your design, use the same font for all your labels.

3 When done, click Exit Edit Points in the floater.

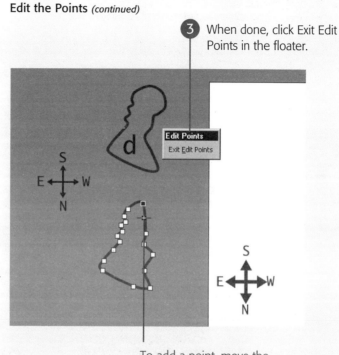

To add a point, move the cursor near a section of the line not on a control point. The cursor becomes a black square with crosshairs. Click to add a point.

Press Ctrl+D to duplicate a selected object.

4 Duplicate the d label from the scratch space and put it in your new shape.

5 Group the d label and the outline and move them into place.

6 Delete the target objects from the scratch space.

Copy Additional Rock Objects

1 Click the Object List arrow to open the *sundog ground plan1.mix* Object List.

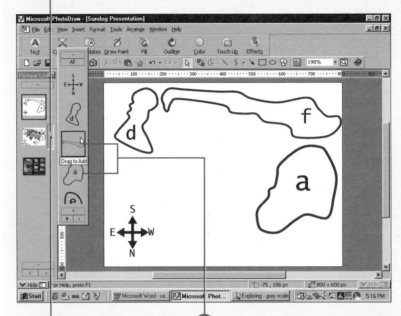

3 Click the Object List arrow to close the Object List.

2 Drag copies of shapes a and f from the *sundog ground plan1.mix* Object List into the picture area, referring to *sundog ground plan1.mix* for placement of the objects.

Fixing points. If necessary, use Edit Points to change the shape of your house object. When finished, click Exit Edit Points in the floater.

Using the Freeform Tool for the House Object

From conversations with the architect, you know the basic shape of the house. To make an object that will represent the house, you will use another tool from the AutoShapes floater—the Freeform tool. You will also fill this object.

Create a Freeform Shape

1 Click the Object List triangle to open the *sundog ground plan1.mix* Object List.

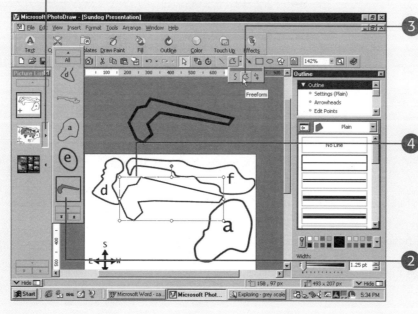

3 On the toolbar, click the arrow and click the Freeform button from the list of Line tools. Or click the AutoShapes button, select Lines, and click the Freeform button.

4 Click to set your first control point where the upper left corner of the house object will be. Work your way around clockwise, setting control points every place the outline changes direction (at corners). Set the last point on top of the first.

2 Drag a copy of the brown house object to the scratch space above the picture area.

Set the Color of the House

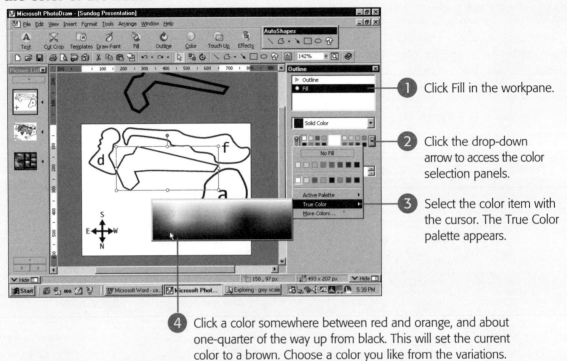

1. Click Fill in the workpane.

2. Click the drop-down arrow to access the color selection panels.

3. Select the color item with the cursor. The True Color palette appears.

4. Click a color somewhere between red and orange, and about one-quarter of the way up from black. This will set the current color to a brown. Choose a color you like from the variations.

5. Set the outline color to black and, if you have not already done so, move your house object into position inside the rock objects (as shown in the sample layout).

6. Delete the object on the scratch space and save your file.

Creating a Pool and a Stream

Between objects a and f, there is a natural spring that provides enough water for the house and a pool. You will use Edit Points to change the shape of the pool.

Change the Shape of the Pool

1 Open the *sundog ground plan1.mix* Object List and drag a copy of the light blue pool shape onto your picture area, inside the house and rock shapes.

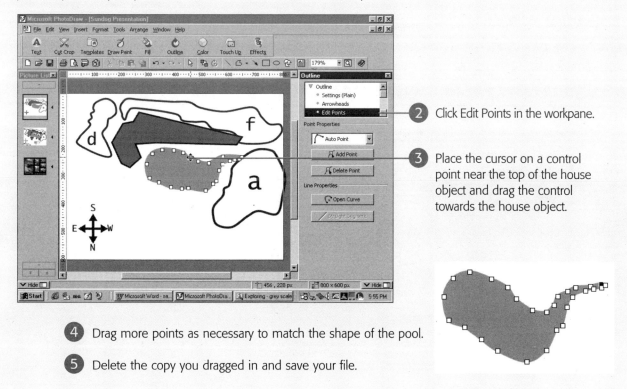

2 Click Edit Points in the workpane.

3 Place the cursor on a control point near the top of the house object and drag the control towards the house object.

4 Drag more points as necessary to match the shape of the pool.

5 Delete the copy you dragged in and save your file.

Making the Palm Trees

The leaves of palm trees make a large dome-shaped canopy. You will make an oval shape and duplicate it for the palms. Use the Ellipse tool from either the toolbar or the AutoShapes floater. The largest palms are about 75 pixels in diameter and perfectly round. To represent all the palm trees, you only need three sizes. After you've drawn the first tree, you will duplicate the green circle twice and resize the duplicates. From these you can make copies for all the trees.

Use the Ellipse Tool

1 Close the *sundog ground plan1.mix* Object List.

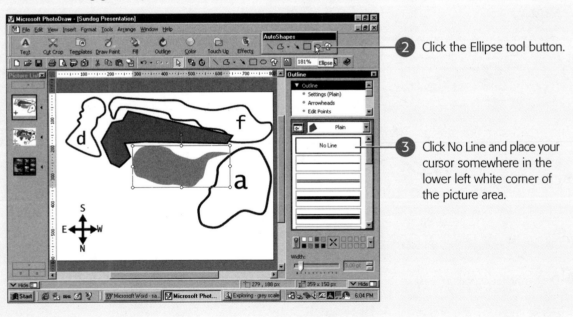

2 Click the Ellipse tool button.

3 Click No Line and place your cursor somewhere in the lower left white corner of the picture area.

Use the Ellipse Tool (continued)

④ To make a perfect circle, press and hold the Shift key, and then drag out a circle.

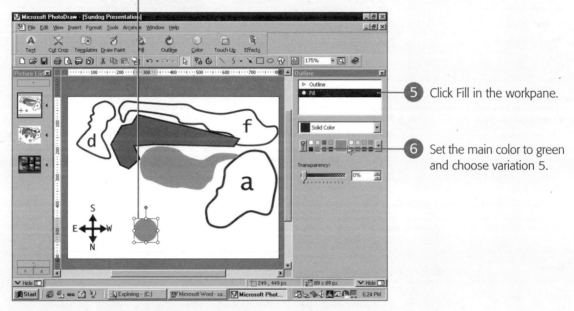

⑤ Click Fill in the workpane.

⑥ Set the main color to green and choose variation 5.

Judging size with rulers. On the top ruler, the size of the selected circle is indicated with a light blue band of color. This will change size as you interactively change the size of the object.

Why can't I accurately resize? To resize more accurately, uncheck Snap To Grid in the View menu. Otherwise, you can only resize to increments set in the Customize Grid settings under Options in the Picture Setup dialog box.

Judging the size with the status bar. Use the selection size information at the right end of the status bar to gauge the size of an object.

Resize and Duplicate the Palm Trees

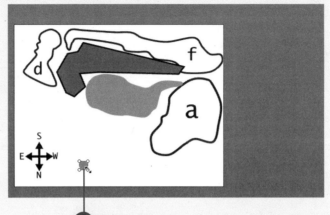

1. Resize the green circle to about 91 pixels by dragging the top right corner of the selection box. This is the size of the largest circle.

2. Make two duplicates of this circle.

3. Select a duplicate circle and resize it to about 61 pixels.

4. Select the second large duplicate circle and resize it to about 48 pixels.

5. Make *sundog ground plan1.mix* the active picture and look at how the green circles are distributed.

6. Return to your picture and make copies of the green circles. Distribute them in a manner somewhat similar to *sundog ground plan1.mix*.

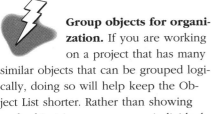

Group objects for organization. If you are working on a project that has many similar objects that can be grouped logically, doing so will help keep the Object List shorter. Rather than showing each object in a group as an individual object, groups appear in the Object List as single objects. This will keep you from having to scroll so far to find individual objects.

Completing the Ground Plan Diagram

To complete this landscape plan, you just need to add the gold-colored ellipses that represent the flannel bushes and the legend in the lower left corner that defines the shapes of the palm trees and flannel bushes.

By creating and duplicating the palm trees, you've already worked with the Ellipse tool. The only difference between the palm tree and flannel bushes in this diagram is that the flannel bushes are elongated ovals, rotated at different angles. You can continue to practice the techniques you've learned and create the remainder of this diagram, or move on to the next chapter.

Flannel Bushes

The last landscape object in this picture will be the gold-colored ovals. In keeping with the theme of the oasis, there will be massed plantings of flannel bush—a large shrub that grows in hot desert regions with little water. In early springtime these are covered with thousands of 2- to 3-inch flowers of a pure golden yellow, just like sunlight.

Make Shrubbery

1 Use the Ellipse tool to make an oval object 80 by 20 pixels.

2 Set its color to a clear gold.

3 Make six duplicates.

4 Move one of the duplicates between object a and the stream that runs out to fill the pool.

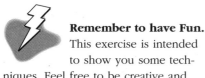 **Remember to have Fun.** This exercise is intended to show you some techniques. Feel free to be creative and experiment with object placement, color, and so forth.

Make Shrubbery *(continued)*

⑤ Place your cursor over the green control point. The cursor becomes a Rotate cursor.

⑥ Drag the Rotate control point to rotate the object so it aligns with the stream and object a.

⑦ Drag object e from the *sundog ground plan1.mix* and place it in about the middle towards the bottom of the picture space.

⑧ Referring to *sundog ground plan1.mix,* place and rotate the remaining ovals in the picture area.

⑨ Save your file

Legend

Complete the ground plan by adding a legend at the lower left corner of your picture below the compass. The legend shows a circle object next to a text object with the words "Palm Trees" and an oval object next to a text object with the words "Flannel Bush." Make copies of the circle and oval objects from the existing objects in the picture. Create the text objects in a blue Lucida Sans Typewriter font with a size of 12.0 points. When positioning these objects, you may need to move the compass a little to accommodate the legend. Refer to the final layout of this project for details.

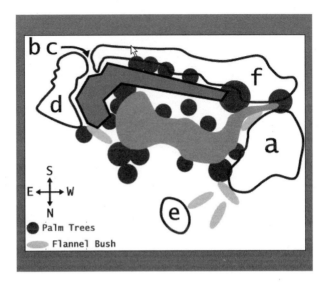

Refining Images and Text

In Chapters 3 and 4, you made a presentation screen and ground plan for the SunDog oasis site. As part of the overall presentation to the client, you want to illustrate the main types of flowering plants that will be part of the landscape. This will give the client a clear picture of how the oasis will look.

You already photographed flowers at the site in the spring and scanned them. Now you need to make them into compositions and add interesting text to identify the plants.

By working through the steps in this chapter, you will learn these important features of PhotoDraw:

- ❧ Cutting out an image
- ❧ Resizing an image to the picture
- ❧ Cropping an image using different techniques
- ❧ Sharpening an image
- ❧ Applying a designer effect to an image
- ❧ Saving a picture in TIFF format

Cutting Out and Cropping Images

Microsoft PhotoDraw provides tools that allow you to select portions of an existing picture and precisely cut them out of the picture or crop them down to size.

In this chapter, we'll work through examples of both cutting and cropping pictures. After you get the idea, feel free to come back and experiment with some of the unique features you've learned.

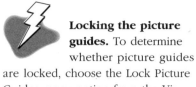

Locking the picture guides. To determine whether picture guides are locked, choose the Lock Picture Guides menu option from the View menu. Select the check box if it's not already selected.

Getting Started

You need to bring an image into PhotoDraw before you can cut or crop it. In this example, we'll work with a scanned photograph that is in file format, so we will use the Insert menu. However, you can also bring scanned art directly into PhotoDraw by using the Scan Picture command on the File menu or on the standard toolbar.

Insert the Picture and Zoom Out

1 Start PhotoDraw and make a blank picture 800 x 600 pixels. Make sure picture guides are locked.

2 Insert the file *flannel bush wide closeup.bmp* from the chapters/chap05 folder on the *PhotoDraw by Design* CD.

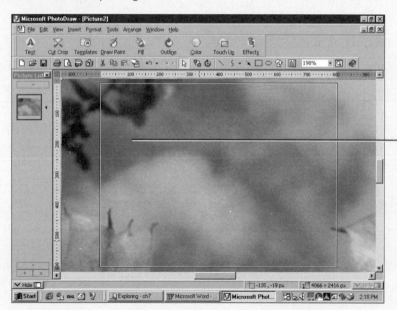

The image that appears in PhotoDraw is much too large for the picture space and the outline of the picture space shows through.

Zooming in and out. The minus key on the keyboard zooms out and the plus key zooms in, one level at a time. For example, if your display resolution is 800 x 600 pixels, try pressing the minus key on the keyboard number pad three times. You can now use the sliders to move the flannel bush image so you can see all of it.

 Getting a different design effect. Another design possibility is to use the main element for most of the composition. If part of the image is in bright sunlight and another part in shade, the text can be placed in front of the darker, shaded area.

Insert the Picture and Zoom Out *(continued)*

 Position your cursor near the center of the picture space outline and use the keyboard to zoom out until the picture fits within the picture area. Alternatively, select Fit All on the Zoom drop-down menu.

Composing and Positioning

The next step of cutting or cropping is to compose your picture. For example, the part of the flannel bush image displayed in the picture space is not a particularly useful, interesting, or balanced composition. Therefore, we will cut out the part of the picture we need using PhotoDraw's Cut Out tools.

The finished presentation screen will include the words "flowers of SunDog." It would be best to use a part of the image that gives you a large section of flowers and provides a separate area for the text. In this case, an image with a flower element and a sky element would work well.

Cutting Out Images

Let's cut out a couple of images. One will be used for the project in the rest of this chapter. The other will give you more practice and allow you to experiment with other design possibilities. (See "Things To Explore on Your Own" at the end of the chapter.)

Creating the First Composition

Before you cut out a piece of the flannel bush image for your first composition, consider whether or not resizing might make it look better.

Looking at the image on your screen, you see two bright yellow flowers in the picture space. Currently the top and bottom of the flower on the left barely fit inside the picture space. It would make a better composition if that flower had some room around it and if there were a bit more sky in which to put the text elements. Reducing the size of the image would benefit the overall look of the composition. However, you don't want to scale down the whole flannel bush image—just the part that you will use. To do that, you will cut out a piece of the image that is larger than the picture space. The first thing you will do is cut out the piece of the flannel bush image you want to use for your first composition.

This is a fairly straightforward procedure using the rectangular cut out shape. By default, PhotoDraw puts the cut out image into a separate picture. You can disable this by clearing Put In New Picture in the Cut Out Workpane check box. But for this procedure, we'll use the default action.

Using the handles to resize. You may need to reduce the size of the flannel bush picture by dragging the corner handles inward.

Cut Out and Crop an Image

① Drag the large flannel bush image to the left until the picture space encloses the part of the image, as shown.

Cut Out and Crop an Image *(continued)*

2 Click the Cut Out item on the Cut Crop menu. The Cut Out Workpane appears with the By Shape item selected. The Cut Out floating window also appears above the picture.

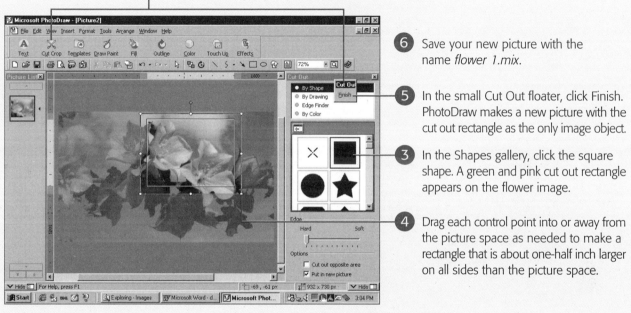

6 Save your new picture with the name *flower 1.mix.*

5 In the small Cut Out floater, click Finish. PhotoDraw makes a new picture with the cut out rectangle as the only image object.

3 In the Shapes gallery, click the square shape. A green and pink cut out rectangle appears on the flower image.

4 Drag each control point into or away from the picture space as needed to make a rectangle that is about one-half inch larger on all sides than the picture space.

Making the Second Composition

You will now make the second composition—the entire image will be composed of flowers. We won't use this composition subsequently in this chapter, so you can skip this procedure if you want.

If necessary, zoom out so you can see the entire flannel bush image. A little bit to the left of where you cut out the previous image object you'll see a cluster of three flowers—one flower points to the upper right, one to the upper left, and the third (which is in the shade) points straight down. This demonstrates all the elements of a good composition—a strong, sunlit element with a shaded area that is large enough to place a readable text element.

Once again, it will be beneficial to cut out an image object larger than the picture space and resize it so all three flowers fit into the space.

Cut Out a New Image

1 Move the large flannel bush image to the right and up a little to position the picture space around this group of flowers.

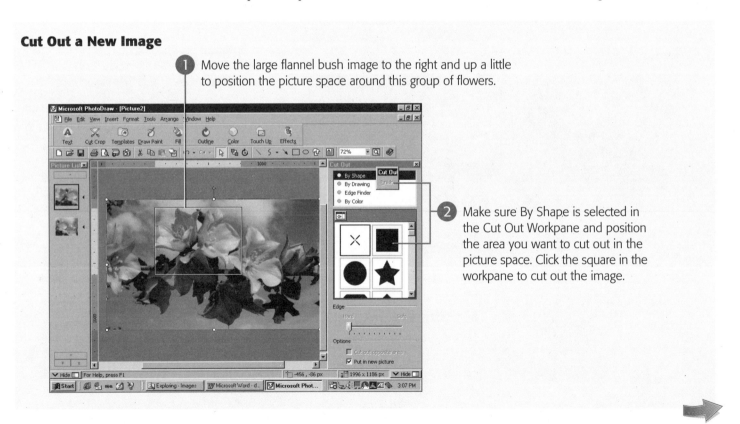

2 Make sure By Shape is selected in the Cut Out Workpane and position the area you want to cut out in the picture space. Click the square in the workpane to cut out the image.

Using the put in new picture option. At the bottom of the Cut Out Workpane you'll see a check box labeled Put In New Picture. If you clear that box, the cut out image object will be placed in the picture where the cut out was made. For this project, however, you want individual, separate pictures to work with, so leave it selected.

Cut Out a New Image *(continued)*

3 Adjust the cut out rectangle with about the same amount of extra room around the sides of the picture space as in the last procedure.

4 Click Finish in the Cut Out floater. PhotoDraw makes another picture and places a thumbnail in the Picture List.

5 Save this picture as *flower2.mix*.

6 Close the *flannel bush wide closeup* picture and click No if PhotoDraw asks whether you want to save changes.

Resizing Images

When you made your new pictures from the cut out image, PhotoDraw used its default units settings—inches—and created a new picture area the same size as the image object that was cut out. The client's presentation will be shown on a monitor with a resolution of 800 by 600 pixels. Let's change the size of the picture space before we resize and sharpen the images.

Each reader will probably have a slightly different cut out image size. My *flower 1.mix* image turned out to be 960 by 724 pixels. If your numbers are vastly different, don't worry. The finished height needs to be 640 pixels, which leaves a little overlap of the 800-by-600-px picture space. We'll use the Crop tool to crop out the overlapped image.

Sharpening Images

When working with photographs in PhotoDraw, you'll often want to sharpen the original image, especially if it was taken with a poor lens or will be displayed at a larger size. Sharpening an image in PhotoDraw tends to add contrast, which usually reduces the number of available colors. If you are reducing the image, you want as many colors as possible to produce the scaled image. You will get better results if you resize before sharpening so that the greatest number of colors is available in the reduced image.

Resize the Image to the Picture

1 Make *flower 1.mix* the active picture.

2 Set the picture space dimensions to 800 by 600 pixels.

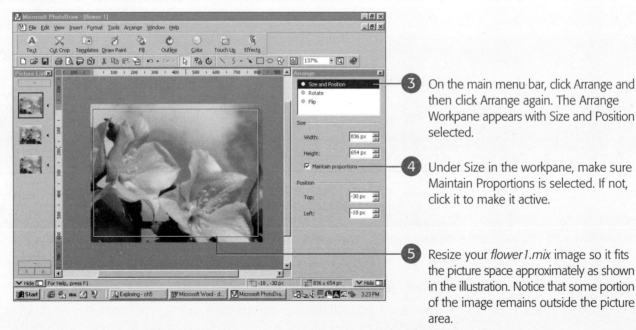

3 On the main menu bar, click Arrange and then click Arrange again. The Arrange Workpane appears with Size and Position selected.

4 Under Size in the workpane, make sure Maintain Proportions is selected. If not, click it to make it active.

5 Resize your *flower1.mix* image so it fits the picture space approximately as shown in the illustration. Notice that some portion of the image remains outside the picture area.

Resizing and the undo button. Resizing images is often a trial-and-error procedure. You may need several attempts to get it right. Remember that you can take advantage of PhotoDraw's Undo button and the Undo list to back out of most operations in PhotoDraw, including resizing.

 Save the file.

 Make a duplicate of this image and drag the duplicate onto the Picture List for a later procedure. You will try two different crop techniques, so you need a second copy.

Cropping the Picture

Now that you have resized the image, it is still larger than the picture space and needs to be cropped to fit. Let's consider the best way to do that. The most common way to size the image to the picture space is to use PhotoDraw's Crop tool. However, you can use a shortcut method by publishing your picture as an image for screen presentation using Save For Use In from the File menu. The second method helps improve performance if you have a slower computer.

We'll go through both ways so you can choose which will work best for you. Let's start with the Crop tool.

Using the Crop Tool

You can use Cut Crop on the visual menu to access the Crop tool. However, to take you through the various ways of accessing tools, several alternatives will be presented. Make sure that the image on the picture space is selected before beginning this procedure.

Refining Images and Text

Crop the Image

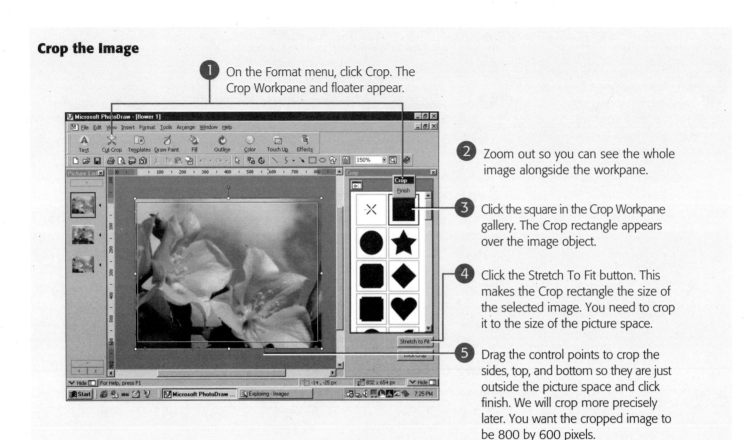

1 On the Format menu, click Crop. The Crop Workpane and floater appear.

2 Zoom out so you can see the whole image alongside the workpane.

3 Click the square in the Crop Workpane gallery. The Crop rectangle appears over the image object.

4 Click the Stretch To Fit button. This makes the Crop rectangle the size of the selected image. You need to crop it to the size of the picture space.

5 Drag the control points to crop the sides, top, and bottom so they are just outside the picture space and click finish. We will crop more precisely later. You want the cropped image to be 800 by 600 pixels.

Cropping to Precision

This time you will drag the control points to fine-tune the image to the right size.

Crop to Precision

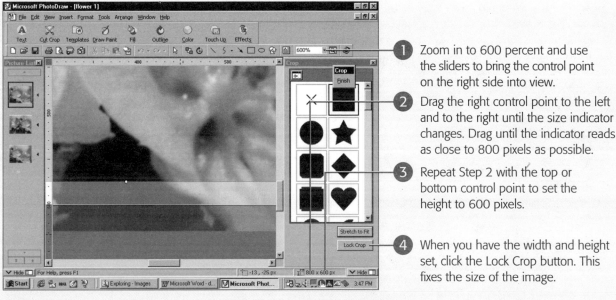

① Zoom in to 600 percent and use the sliders to bring the control point on the right side into view.

② Drag the right control point to the left and to the right until the size indicator changes. Drag until the indicator reads as close to 800 pixels as possible.

③ Repeat Step 2 with the top or bottom control point to set the height to 600 pixels.

④ When you have the width and height set, click the Lock Crop button. This fixes the size of the image.

⑤ Open the Align submenu on the Arrange menu and verify that the Relative To Picture Space button is selected. If it isn't, click to select it. Then align the middle and the center.

 When I resize my image—why don't I see the new image size right away? It might take a few moments for the resize to update. On slower machines, you may have to release the mouse button with the size indicator not exactly at the number you want. For instance, if dragging from inside the picture space toward the edge to get 800 pixels, you might have to release the mouse button when the size indicator reads 799 pixels. Then when the indicator updates, it will give you a true reading.

 Re-cropping an image. If you want to come back later and change the size, click the Finish command on the Crop floater instead of the Lock Crop button. To make the cropped image larger again, select the image; access the Crop Workpane; click the square crop shape; click the Stretch To Fit button, and the image will return to its original size. You can then re-crop it to whatever size you want.

Using an Alternate Cropping Method

What if my image appears to have changed sizes? If you access an image and believe it to be smaller than you remember it, you may have inadvertently cropped it. To fix this, select the object, open the Crop Workpane, click the square shape, and then click the Stretch To Fit button. The object will revert to its original size.

Now let's look at the second method of cropping a larger object to the size of the picture space. The key to this technique is that whatever is inside the picture space is saved as a .png file at the same pixel resolution as your original image. When you insert the .png file back into your file, it is cropped.

For this procedure, you will need another duplicate of the larger image object. When you resized the image for the *flower 1.mix* picture, you saved a duplicate in a temporary picture. Then you tried the first crop method. Now let's use that duplicate for the second crop method.

Insert the Duplicate

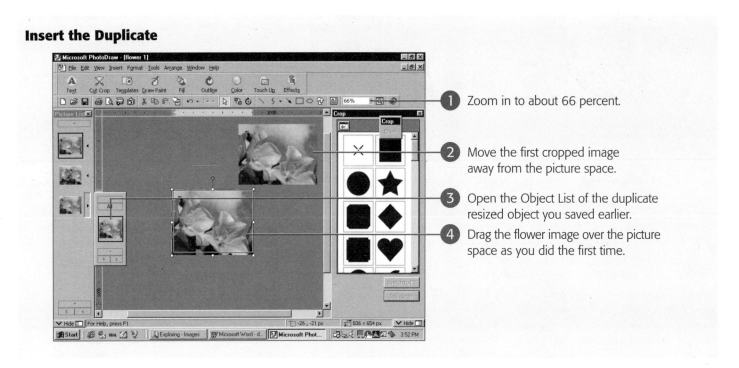

1. Zoom in to about 66 percent.

2. Move the first cropped image away from the picture space.

3. Open the Object List of the duplicate resized object you saved earlier.

4. Drag the flower image over the picture space as you did the first time.

Checking the file format. The Save For Use In Wizard provides information about how the file will be saved. The .png (or ping) file format was developed more recently than .gif, .tif, or .bmp and has many benefits. Files saved in .png format will work in other Microsoft Office products.

Crop an Image with *Save For Use In*

① On the File menu, click Save For Use In. The Save For Use In Wizard appears.

② Click the In An On-Screen Presentation option to make it the selected choice.

③ Click Next.

Crop an Image with *Save For Use In* *(continued)*

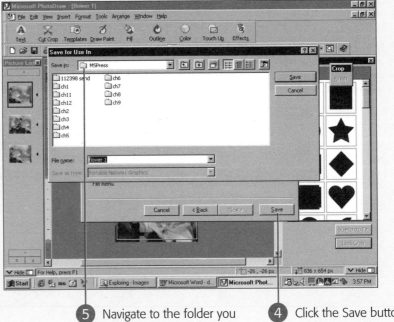

⑤ Navigate to the folder you want, name the file, and click Save.

④ Click the Save button and the Save For Use In dialog box appears.

⑥ Insert the .png file you just saved using Visual Insert from the Insert menu. The image is inserted into your picture at 800 by 600 pixels, the exact size of the picture space.

Using the Align Center and the Align Middle tools. Use the Align Center and Align Middle tools from the Align menu (accessed from the Arrange menu) to align the image object with the picture space. Remember to click Relative To Picture Area at the bottom of the Align menu if it is not already selected.

Crop an Image with *Save For Use In* (continued)

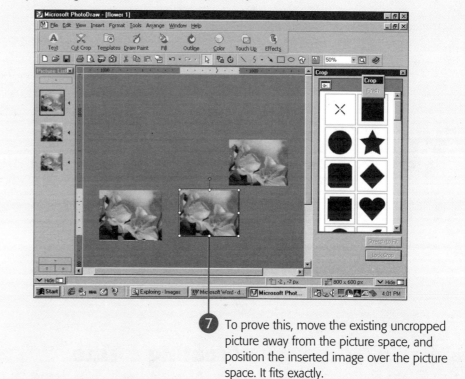

⑦ To prove this, move the existing uncropped picture away from the picture space, and position the inserted image over the picture space. It fits exactly.

Sharpening The Image

Next you will sharpen the image object. The cropped image in the picture space should be 800 x 600 pixels. Close the Crop Workpane if it is open, and make sure the image on the picture space is selected.

Sharpen the Image

1 Click Blur and Sharpen from the Effects menu on the visual menu bar. The Blur and Sharpen Workpane appears.

2 Zoom in and adjust the screen so you can see the whole image.

3 Drag the slider or type in numbers to change the blurriness or sharpness of the object. Set the sharpness to 20 and press the Enter key.

Getting the desired sharpness. Dragging left results in more blur, dragging right makes the image sharper. Now more individual flower parts stand out. You could sharpen the image more, but you don't want the sky to stand out too much; otherwise the text will be difficult to see.

Creating a Title

As in most of the projects in this book, the text elements are an important part of the overall design. Now that the image is complete, let's move on and create an interesting title for the first screen.

A Look at the Finished Sample

The flower screens provide the client with pleasing pictures. There aren't many flowers that stand out in the desert so anything you can do to enhance the feeling of floral beauty improves the presentation.

You can use text elements to make the flowers stand out. With PhotoDraw, you can also make text elements that are visually interesting in themselves.

Open the Sample Picture

Open the *flower1.tif* picture from the chapters/chap05 folder so you can see what it looks like. Notice that there are two different text objects:

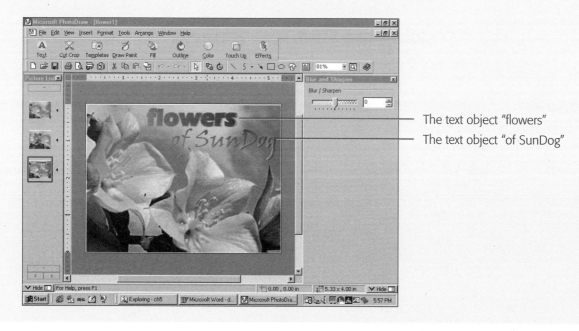

The text object "flowers"

The text object "of SunDog"

The Target Effect

The "flowers" text object is purple and blue. These colors are complementary to the golden yellows of the flannel bush flowers and make the flowers stand out. The text also uses a transparent gradient so it seems to come out of the sky to provide a feeling of three-dimensional space. Behind the colored text is a second copy of the object, formatted one point larger and with the Bas Relief effect applied to it. Making this text larger allows the colored text to be positioned on top of the Bas Relief text, aligned on the left side. This makes the colored text appear to lift away, further enhancing the 3-D effect. The text object "of SunDog" uses the same strategy in reverse. Placing the grayscale Bas Relief text in front visually pushes the text object back in space, so the flowers appear to rise toward the viewer.

Creating the First Text Element

First you will create the text element "flowers" using several PhotoDraw features.

Insert and Size the Text

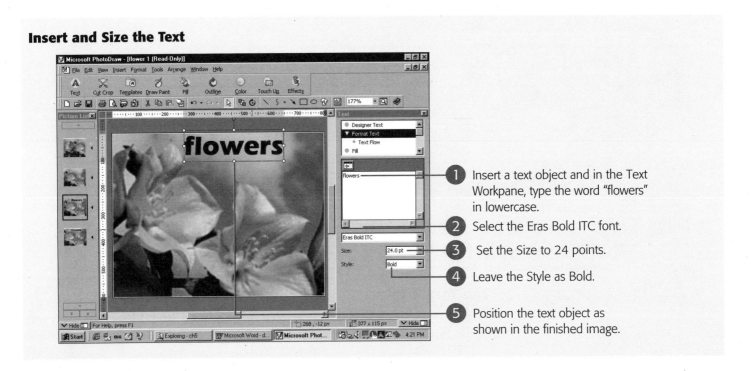

1. Insert a text object and in the Text Workpane, type the word "flowers" in lowercase.

2. Select the Eras Bold ITC font.

3. Set the Size to 24 points.

4. Leave the Style as Bold.

5. Position the text object as shown in the finished image.

Making the Color Fill

Now we'll use a two-color gradient text fill for the "flowers" text object. The Fill Workpane has two gradient fill options: Two-Color Gradient and Designer Gradient. A two-color gradient fill changes from one color to another color. In the workpane, you choose the two colors to use and their Transparency settings—as well as other options including the center (balance) of the fill, a shape to apply to the fill, and the angle to apply to the gradient. The Designer Gradient option is a collection of some interesting presets for different combinations of the Two-Color Gradient.

Make a Two-Color Gradient Text Fill

1. In the Text Workpane, click Fill.

2. In the drop-down list, choose Two-Color Gradient. The Two-Color Gradient tools appear in the workpane.

3. For the Start color, access the Active Palette and select a purple you like.

4. For the End color, again access the Active Palette and select a fairly bright blue.

5. Click Transparency on the Effects menu on the visual menu bar. The Transparency Workpane appears.

Make a Two-Color Gradient Text Fill *(continued)*

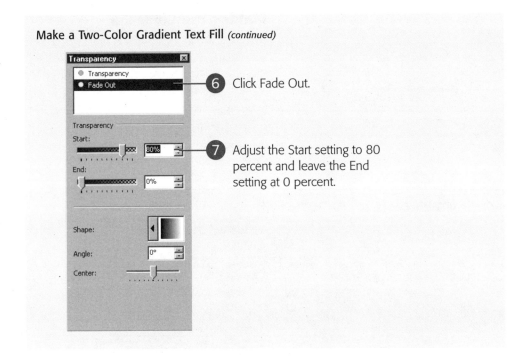

6 Click Fade Out.

7 Adjust the Start setting to 80 percent and leave the End setting at 0 percent.

Creating the Bas Relief Effect

This procedure adds a subtle shadow effect to the "flowers" text object. The Shadow option on the Effects menu is a quick way to add a shadow, which gets applied evenly to all letters. The following technique adds a shadow that increases from left to right, to accentuate the fade-in effect.

Make the Bas Relief Effect

① Make a duplicate of the text element and move it aside for now. Note that the duplicate is placed in front of the original on the Z-order, so it will be the main letter object.

② Select the original text element to create the shadow effect.

③ From Effects on the visual menu, click Designer Effects. The Designer Effects menu opens.

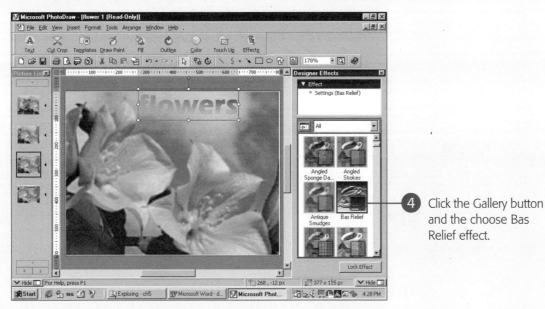

④ Click the Gallery button and the choose Bas Relief effect.

⑤ Select both text objects.

⑥ Open the Align submenu from the Arrange menu and deselect Relative To Picture Space if it is selected.

Make the Bas Relief Effect *(continued)*

8 Access the Align Middle and Align Left tools to align the two text objects.

9 Move the two selected text objects into position as in the finished image.

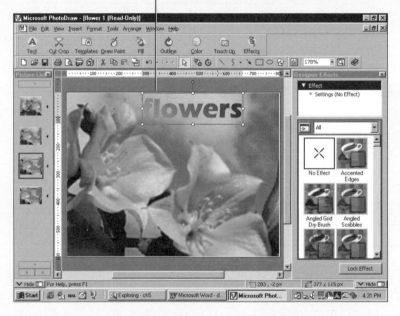

Creating the Second Text Element

Now that you know the steps for creating the first text element, you can create the second text element. This text object is similar to the first but uses a different font and size, a reverse color gradient, and different words. In this procedure, we'll simply outline the steps and let you do the rest by referring back to the original steps, if necessary.

Create the Text

1 Insert the text and create a text object that says "of SunDog." Use Viner Hand ITC Font sized to 20 points. (See the "Insert and Size the Text" procedure earlier.)

2 Make a two-color gradient fill using the same colors as the first text element but in reverse. Use the same Transparency settings: the Start setting at 80 percent and the End setting at 0 percent. (See "Make a Two-Color Gradient Text Fill.")

3 Apply Bas Relief to the front object. Use a 20-point font size for the background text. (See "Make the Bas Relief Effect.")

4 Align these objects the same way you aligned the first text element.

5 Position these objects as in the finished image.

Publishing Pictures

You will want to publish the composite image for use in your presentation. You have already tried the Save For Use In Wizard earlier in this chapter; now let's try another way to save your picture. Follow these steps to save your picture as a TIFF file:

Save a File in TIFF format.

1 On the File menu, click Save As.

2 In the Save As dialog box, navigate to the folder in which you want to save the file.

3 In the Save As Type drop-down list, choose Tagged Image File Format.

4 Name your file

5 Click Save.

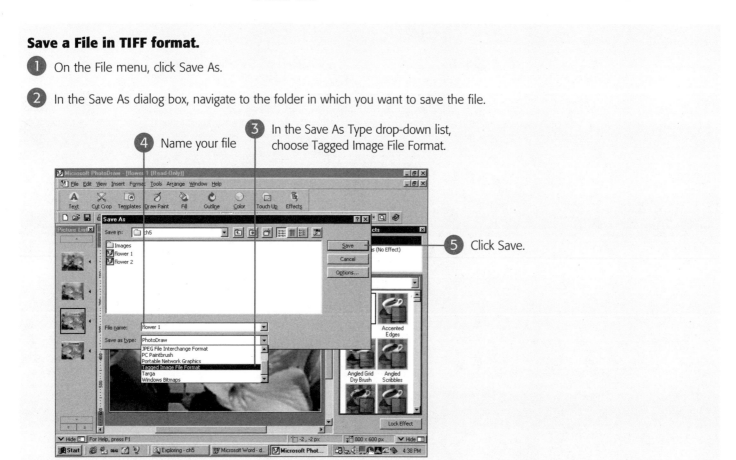

Things To Explore on Your Own

Here are some variations you might like to try on your own:

- Make the *flower2.mix* file you cut out of the flannel bush image similar to *flower2 with text.mix* on the CD. To do this, sharpen the image to 20, insert a text object with the word "Flowers" and set the font to Baskerville Old Face Bold, 48 points. (Use any light blue Fill that you like.) Then set Bend Text to Quarter Circle Down, set the Outline to 3 points. and the Outline Color to a medium to dark blue. Next, position the text and image as in the finished file. Repeat for the "of SunDog" text using the Bend Text Quarter Circle Up selection and set the Outline to 2 points. Save it as a bitmap file—the saved picture consists of only those parts of the objects that are inside the picture space.

- On the CD, look at the picture file *flower4.mix* and see if you can make *flower3.mix* similar by adding text. Set the text to "ground cover." Set the text size to 64 points. On the workpane, select Designer Text and choose the red outlined text in the upper left corner of the gallery. Choose a light blue-violet fill color. In the Shadow Workpane, select the Drop-Down Right shadow effect, choose a dark purple color, and soften it to 90. Click the Shadow Position button and use the arrow keys on your keyboard to move the shadow up 4 pixels and left 4 pixels. Click Finish in the floater.

Creating a Package Design

In this chapter, we'll turn our attention to RL&Associates, the computer VAR in San Francisco.

First we'll design graphics for RL&A's computer shipping boxes. RL&A uses the name "Wave Systems" to designate their custom-built computers. Their logo graphic is a simple outline of a breaking wave enclosed in a vertical oval with the words "Wave Systems." Our graphics will be placed on the sides and ends of their shipping boxes. The wave shape will be the common element carried through to a new design for the side graphic. This will give you a chance to learn more about PhotoDraw's Curve tool.

The graphic design used for the box ends will be a collection of RL&A employee portraits. To compose this collection, you will work with PhotoDraw's tools for resizing and cropping pictures, erasing areas by color, and applying colorizing techniques to a picture.

The text included in this design provides more opportunities to explore creative PhotoDraw text effects, including 3-D text.

The Box Sides—Drawing a Wave Shape

The box sides are the largest graphical element of the box and we'll do this design first. There are three parts to creating this graphic: setting up the picture, drawing the wave, and adding text. All of these involve interesting PhotoDraw techniques.

Setting Up the Picture Size

Creating a graphic to be used on a box 22 by 20 inches creates some interesting problems. PhotoDraw has a size limit for any one object of 4000 by 4000 pixels. If you tried to cover a 22-by-20-inch area at 300 pixels per inch, you might need an image that is 6600 by 6000 pixels (considering that one or more of the graphic objects in the picture might be as large as the box). Fortunately, box graphics can be printed at a much lower resolution, so 150 pixels per inch will be fine in this case and will work for our example.

How do you use PhotoDraw to create a picture that will printed at 150 pixels per inch? PhotoDraw's Options dialog box lets you choose from three picture quality settings: Web, Typical (Photographic), and Professional (Best For Printing). The Professional setting will achieve 300 pixels per inch (ppi) resolution. So if we use this setting to create a picture half the size that we want (11 by 10 inches in this case), the resulting picture will be 150 ppi when saved as a TIFF (.tif) or Windows bitmap (.bmp) file and then scaled by the printer to 22 by 20 inches.

Printing at the lower pixel-per-inch resolution will make the image look coarser, but cardboard boxes have a very absorbent surface that benefits from printing at lower resolutions—since each pixel is larger, it won't get lost by being absorbed into the cardboard.

With that said, let's create a picture that can be printed 22 by 20 inches at 150 pixels per inch for the side of the box.

Create a New Picture for the Box Side

1 Create a new picture in PhotoDraw with inches as the Units of Measure, a Width of 11 inches and a Height of 10 inches.

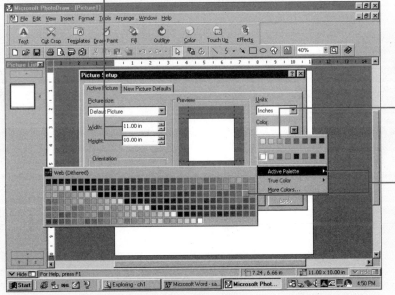

4 Click OK.

3 Click the Color button again to access the color variations. On the top row, choose variation 3, the third from the left.

2 Click the Color button in the Picture Setup dialog box, access the Active Palette, and choose the color that is second from the right on the third row.

Working with a background color. Whenever you create graphics that will be printed on a colored background, it is a good idea to set up the picture space color as close as possible to the final background color so you can see how the final product will look. Before saving your file for printing, you'll want to change the picture space color back to white. When you save to a file format such as .tif, .tga, or .png, PhotoDraw uses white as the alpha channel—that is the transparent area, so only the graphic will be printed, not the background.

Choosing the best Picture Quality setting. At the end of this project, we will change the Picture Quality setting back to Typical (Photographic), which is best for most purposes.

You can also access this from the View menu or by pressing F11.

Set the Picture Quality

1 On the main menu, click Tools and then click Options. The Tools Options dialog box opens.

3 Under Picture Quality, click Professional (Best For Printing) to set the defaults for saving files to 300 pixels per inch

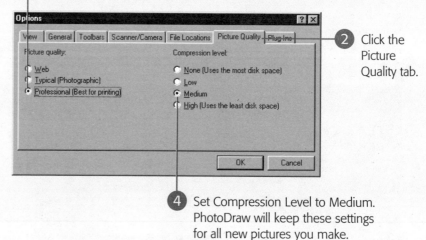

2 Click the Picture Quality tab.

4 Set Compression Level to Medium. PhotoDraw will keep these settings for all new pictures you make.

5 Click OK and then click Fit To Picture Area in the Zoom list.

6 Save the file with the name *chapter4 wave.mix*.

Working with Control Points

The wave object in the *wave outline 1.mix* file is the first object you'll create for your new project. Before continuing, here's a short overview of PhotoDraw point properties. In Chapter 4, you worked with control points when drawing a freeform object and you saw how to move the points to control the shape. Now we'll look at the properties that can be set on each point to further control the shape. There are four settings for point properties in PhotoDraw's Edit Points tool:

@ **Symmetric Point** Provides controls to change the curve shape symmetrically on either side of the control point.

@ **Smooth Point** Provides controls to change the gradual shape of the curve at the control point.

@ **Corner Point** Provides controls to change the curve to an angle at the control point.

@ **Auto Point** Determines automatically how the curve will be shaped and doesn't provide any controls.

In addition to the control points, every line has a Segment property, which is either Straight Segment or Curved Segment. You can click on the line to select it and then change the Segment button in the Line Properties area to change it.

In previous chapters, we've used the PhotoDraw default Auto Point for control points. Now, however, we have three sections of the object that need to be perfectly straight. This means different settings must be used.

Examining the Wave File

Before continuing, you might want to examine each of the control points in this graphic to visualize the effect of changing point properties. A little exploration can go a long way. After you play with the control points, be sure to undo all changes before continuing.

Examine the Wave File

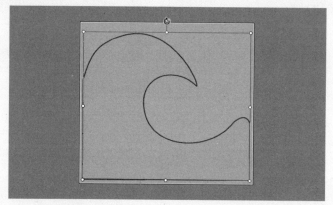

1 Open the *wave outline 1.mix* file in the chapters/chap06 images folder of the *PhotoDraw by Design* CD.

2 Position the picture so you can see all of it. Notice there are only nine control points on the wave object.

Examining the Edit Points and Line Properties

Notice when you click once on the control point that is closest to the top of the wave shape, the Smooth Point type is selected in the Outline Workpane and two control handles extend from the control point. The placement and length of each control handle determines the exact curve of the top of the wave shape.

Try opening the list and choosing Auto Point to see what happens, then click Undo to return the curve to its proper shape, and choose Edit Points again to go to the next point.

As you examine each of the control points on the curves, notice how each set of handles controls its section of a curve. Sometimes two control points become selected at once. Click again on the point you want to select, the other point will be deselected. Notice that when you select the control points on the straight sections, they are all Auto Points.

On the right side of the shape, click the straight vertical segment (not a control point). The Bottom button under Line Properties on the workpane becomes active.

Click the Curve Segment button. The segment changes shape and the button now says Straight Segment. Click the button once again to change the segment back to a straight line.

Creating the Wave

When you create the wave, you'll want the line segments on the left, bottom, and right to be straight segments. All straight segments in this graphic have Auto Point settings for the end points. All other points are set to Smooth Point. The first step is to bring in the model wave and sketch the control points.

Drag in the Model Wave Object

1 Make the empty picture you created (*chapter6 wave.mix*) the active picture and zoom out.

Drag in the Model Wave Object *(continued)*

2 Open the Object List of *wave outline 1.mix.*

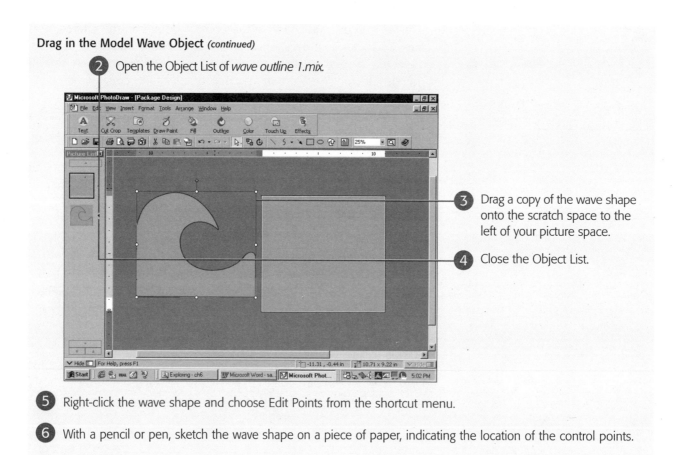

3 Drag a copy of the wave shape onto the scratch space to the left of your picture space.

4 Close the Object List.

5 Right-click the wave shape and choose Edit Points from the shortcut menu.

6 With a pencil or pen, sketch the wave shape on a piece of paper, indicating the location of the control points.

Move your picture space back into full view before continuing. Next we'll use the sketch to draw the nine control points.

Draw the Control Points for the Wave Object

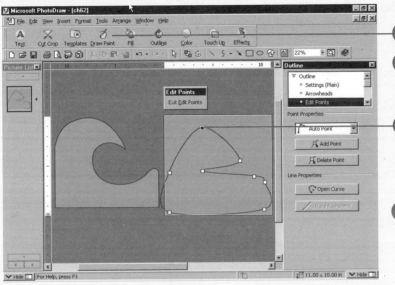

1. On the Draw Paint menu, click Draw.

2. Change the line Width setting to 4 points. You can leave the default blue as the current color.

3. Using your sketch as a guide, set the nine control points to make the wave shape. The shape will look quite different than you want. The object is to set the control points.

4. Right-click and choose Edit Points from the shortcut menu.

Comparing shapes. For comparison, you might find it helpful to drag the model wave on top of your wave. To edit your wave object while the two objects are overlaid, open the Object List and click your object. To view the control points of the model wave, select it in the Object List and click Edit Points in the Outline Workpane. Try changing the color of your wave to red, for instance, to see the differences.

Creating a Package Design

Draw the Control Points for the Wave Object *(continued)*

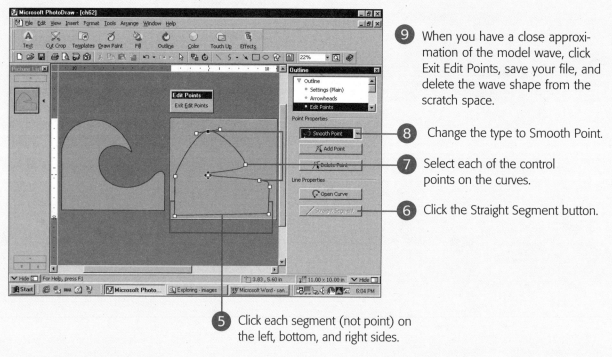

9 When you have a close approximation of the model wave, click Exit Edit Points, save your file, and delete the wave shape from the scratch space.

8 Change the type to Smooth Point.

7 Select each of the control points on the curves.

6 Click the Straight Segment button.

5 Click each segment (not point) on the left, bottom, and right sides.

As you change the point style, make an initial adjustment to the control handles to make the shape roughly what it should be. When you have changed and adjusted each point, go back and refine the entire shape, moving points and adjusting control handles as needed.

 Changing the shape. When you adjust the Smooth Point controls, remember that you can change the length of the control handles, as well as the angle, to affect the shape.

 Why doesn't my figure match the sample? It's OK if the shape is not identical to the copy from *wave outline 1.mix*. Becoming familiar with the tools is our goal at this time. You can practice more on your own.

Making a bold statement. When designing something that is seen only briefly, and is as large as a computer shipping box, you want the graphics to be big and bold. That way people get the message at a glance. Remember that what looks wide or thick on a computer screen can become lost when printed on a large surface.

Adjusting the Line Width

There is another file on the CD called *wave1.mix* in the chapters/chap06 folder. Open it to see what your final graphic will look like. It is a large file and may take a few minutes to open. You'll notice the outline on the wave shape is much wider than the one you just made. You used a narrow line width to create the shape more easily. Now you will change the width of your shape's outline and adjust it to fit the picture space.

Adjust Line Width and Fill for the Wave

1 Make your picture the active picture.

2 On the View menu, click Fit To Picture Area.

3 Change the line Width to 32 points. Part of the line will probably extend outside of the picture space.

4 Access Edit Points and move the four control points of the straight line segments so that the outside edges of the lines are inside the picture space.

5 Click Exit Edit Points in the floater.

Creating a Package Design

Adjust Line Width and Fill for the Wave *(continued)*

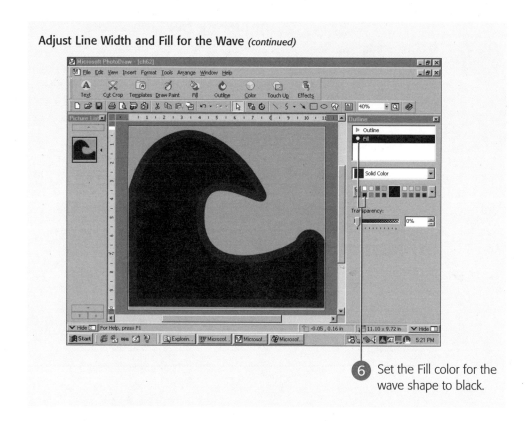

6 Set the Fill color for the wave shape to black.

Adding Special Effects to Text

Now it's time to create interesting text. Look at the finished picture again. We'll add text that says "Wave Systems" to the bottom of the picture. In this case, we'll use a nice texture fill for the letters.

Create the Wave Systems Text

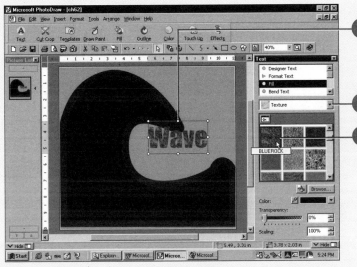

1. Insert a text object with the word "Wave." Set the Font to Impact and the Size to 120 points.

2. In the Text Workpane, select Fill and choose Texture.

3. Click on the Blue Rock thumbnail. The text fills with the selected texture.

4. Make a duplicate of the text object.

5. Double-click the duplicate to enter text editing mode and change the duplicate text item to "Systems."

6. Select both text objects and move them into place at the bottom of the wave shape, comparing them with the finished file.

Create the Wave Systems Text *(continued)*

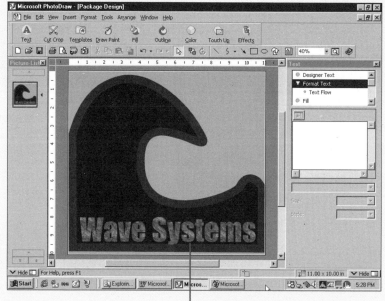

 Turn off Relative To Picture Area. Remember to turn off Relative To Picture Area if it is active.

7 Use the Align tools (found on the Arrange menu) to align the bottoms of the two text objects.

8 Group both text objects.

Choose Outline and Fill

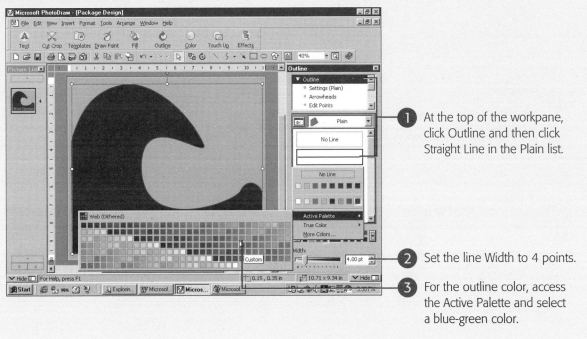

1. At the top of the workpane, click Outline and then click Straight Line in the Plain list.

2. Set the line Width to 4 points.

3. For the outline color, access the Active Palette and select a blue-green color.

Adding Designer Text

Next you will make the 3-D text objects using Designer Text. Most effects that can be applied to pictures can also be applied to text. There are lots of different effect combinations in PhotoDraw's Designer Text gallery. Like most Designer galleries in PhotoDraw, you can tweak any of the parameters once you apply the text.

Create the 3-D Text Objects

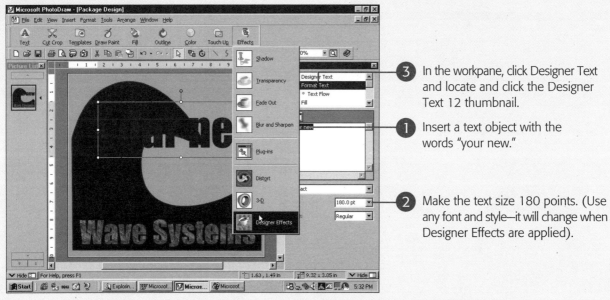

3 In the workpane, click Designer Text and locate and click the Designer Text 12 thumbnail.

1 Insert a text object with the words "your new."

2 Make the text size 180 points. (Use any font and style—it will change when Designer Effects are applied).

4 Repeat the first two steps, but change the text to "computer" and change the Size to 210 points.

5 Position the text objects as in the finished picture.

Duplicating an object. Duplicate and edit the text before applying special effects.

Creating a Color-Filled Text Object

Now we just need to create the final text object, which is the plain color-filled word "from." This text object is interesting because PhotoDraw makes it easy to match the color fill from an existing text object—in this case, it takes the color from the 3-D Designer Text object added earlier.

Create a Color-Filled Text Object

1 Insert another text object with the word "from."

2 Set the Font to Arial Rounded MT Bold, 70 points.

3 Place the text object above the "Wave" object.

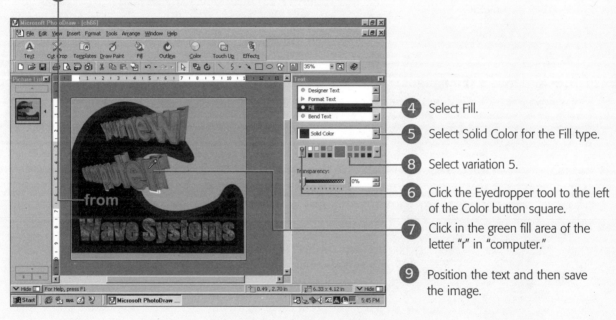

4 Select Fill.

5 Select Solid Color for the Fill type.

8 Select variation 5.

6 Click the Eyedropper tool to the left of the Color button square.

7 Click in the green fill area of the letter "r" in "computer."

9 Position the text and then save the image.

Making the Box End Graphic

The graphic you just completed will work for both sides of the shipping box. Now you will make a graphic for the ends of the box. In this project, you will learn more about PhotoDraw's Cut Out and Color tools.

Creating a Package Design

Working with vertical space. The end of a computer shipping box is tall and narrow—a "strong vertical," which presents a challenging design problem. We'll use a scanned 35-millimeter filmstrip to frame several employee portraits to fit the vertical space. We communicate RL&A's personality at the same time.

Using PhotoDraw, you can cut out and erase by shape, by drawing, or by color. You'll use the PhotoDraw Erase tool to quickly erase sections of an object by color, a job that would take hours if using a drawing tool. The Crop tool removes the area around an object and just allows cropping by shape as an option. Note that you can crop by drawing or color using the Cut Out tool and checking Cut Out Opposite Area.

You'll also learn some cropping and resizing techniques that are useful when working with a variety of portrait sizes. Finally, you'll see how to fix a lighting problem in a photograph using tools from PhotoDraw's Color menu.

Create the Picture and Insert the Images

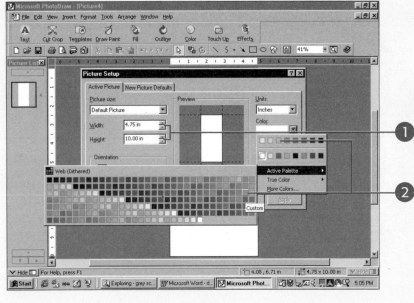

1 Make a new picture 4.75 by 10 inches (using inches as Units of Measure).

2 Make the color the same as the side graphic. (On the Active Palette in the Picture Setup dialog box, choose the color second from the right on the third row, then choose variation 3.)

Create the Picture and Insert the Images *(continued)*

3 From the *PhotoDraw by Design* CD chapters/chap06 folder, insert the following images into your picture: *filmstrip.bmp*, *mary.bmp*, *amyl.bmp*, and *richard1.bmp*.

4 Zoom out as needed.

5 Move the filmstrip image to the right of the picture space.

6 Move the images of people to the left of the picture space.

Erasing By Color

First let's work with the filmstrip. You want the cardboard background to show through the sprocket holes in the filmstrip so you somehow need to remove the white. You could do that by cutting out each sprocket hole one at a time; however, there is an easier way.

Position the Filmstrip and Erase the Sprocket Holes

2️⃣ With the filmstrip selected, on the Cut Crop menu, click Erase to access the Erase Workpane.

1️⃣ Use the Align tools to align the filmstrip object with the middle and center of the picture space.

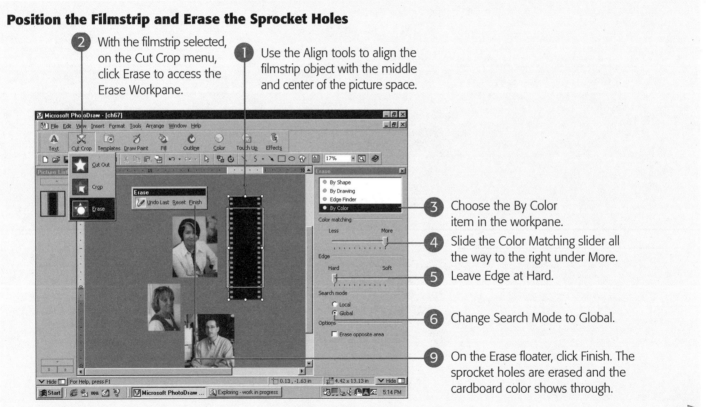

3️⃣ Choose the By Color item in the workpane.

4️⃣ Slide the Color Matching slider all the way to the right under More.

5️⃣ Leave Edge at Hard.

6️⃣ Change Search Mode to Global.

9️⃣ On the Erase floater, click Finish. The sprocket holes are erased and the cardboard color shows through.

Aligning with the Relative To Picture Area option.
Since PhotoDraw only saves what is on the picture space, you can align the top of this graphic with the top of the picture space and let the bottom extend beyond the bottom edge. Remember to activate Relative To Picture Area.

Position the Filmstrip and Erase the Sprocket Holes *(continued)*

7 Move the cursor over the filmstrip image. It is now a crosshair and will select whatever color is directly under the intersection of the lines. Position it over the center of the white sprocket hole at the top left side of the filmstrip image.

8 Click once. In a few moments all the sprocket holes fill with the cerise color that occurs at this stage of the erase operation.

10 From the Effects menu, click Blur And Sharpen and select a setting of 10 to sharpen the filmstrip image.

Working with Photographs

Before you start working with the images of people, open *box end demo.mix* from the chapters/chap06 images folder. There will be several stages of change to the image objects. Each stage has been saved into that picture. As you work, you can compare what you are doing with what has been provided for you. Open the file, zoom out to 25 percent, and scroll right and left to see the various image objects.

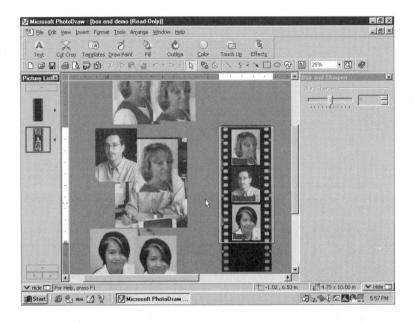

In the *box end demo.mix* picture there are three scanned photographs of people: Mary is at the top, below her picture is Richard, and Amy is below them. Start with the image of Mary, which will go at the top of the filmstrip.

The images in this file will be referred to as you progress through this part of the project. The cropped image of Mary on top of the original Richard image is there for a reason. Don't move it. You'll see why shortly.

Crop and Size an Image

1 Make your picture active.

2 Duplicate the image of Mary that you put on your scratch space.

3 Crop the duplicate to be similar in size to the middle-sized image of Mary in the demo picture.

4 Duplicate the cropped image object.

5 On the Arrange menu, click Arrange. The Arrange Workpane opens.

7 Move the resized image object near the top of the filmstrip image.

6 With the duplicate image of Mary selected, change the Width to 2.5 inches with Maintain Proportions checked (active). Press Enter.

Creating a Package Design

Cropping to an Overlay

After resizing, you want all three images to be the same size so they look like they belong together on the filmstrip. Unfortunately, each original image is a different size. Here's a way to solve the problem. It involves some judgement calls on your part, so what you end up with may not be precisely the same as what I did. That's OK. What matters is that you learn the procedure and how to apply it so you can be consistent within your own projects.

Deciding where to position images. How did I know where to position Mary's picture? I made some aesthetic judgements. The first was to leave some space above Richard's hair so the top of his head wouldn't look like it was crammed against the top of the cropped image. Then I tried to center Mary's image over Richard's face so it would be close to the center when I cropped his image. Make your best guess.

Add Richard's Photograph—Part 1

1. Select and duplicate the picture of Richard.

2. Make the demo picture active and look at how the cropped picture of Mary is positioned on top of the original picture of Richard. You want to do the same in your picture.

3. Make your picture active again and select the duplicate cropped picture of Mary.

4. Right-click and choose Bring To Front from the shortcut menu.

Add Richard's Photograph—Part 1 *(continued)*

5 Move the picture of Mary onto the picture of Richard and position it as it is in the demo picture.

Add Richard's Photograph—Part 2

1 Select the picture of Richard, leaving Mary's picture where it is.

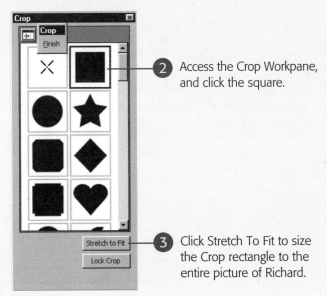

2 Access the Crop Workpane, and click the square.

3 Click Stretch To Fit to size the Crop rectangle to the entire picture of Richard.

4 Drag the Crop control handles in to line up the edges with Mary's picture.

5 Click Finish in the Crop floater.

6 Select Mary's picture, right-click, and choose Send To Back from the shortcut menu.

7 Access the Arrange Workpane again and, with Maintain Proportions checked, change the Width to 2.5 inches and press the Enter key.

8 Move the resized image onto the filmstrip under Mary's picture.

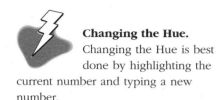

Changing the Hue.
Changing the Hue is best done by highlighting the current number and typing a new number.

Correcting the Color of an Image

Before cropping and resizing the image of Amy, you need to fix the green cast caused by fluorescent lights when this photograph was taken. As with resizing, you will obtain more satisfying results doing color correction on a complete image rather than on a piece that has been cut out from that image. This is because the color correcting algorithms have more data to work from. So let's roll up our sleeves and get to work.

Fix the Tint, Hue, and Saturation

1 Duplicate the Amy image so you will see how much change occurs and scroll so you can see the entire Amy image on your screen.

3 Make sure Correct Selection is highlighted at the top of the workpane.

2 On the Color menu, click Tint. The Color Workpane appears.

6 Under Settings, change the Hue slider to 70. This makes it more green.

7 Change the Amount to -20 to reduce the amount of green a little.

4 In the Color Workpane, click the Automatic button to let PhotoDraw perform the color correction from an area you select.

5 Click Amy's shoulder where the seam runs left to right.

Creating a Package Design

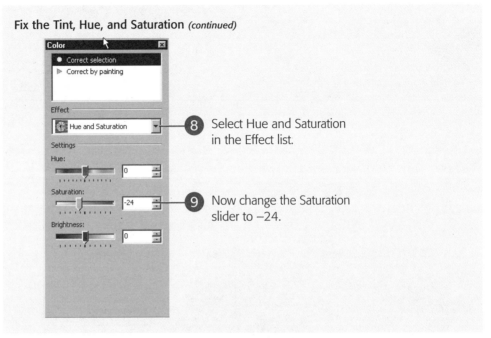

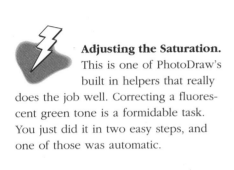

Adjusting the Saturation. This is one of PhotoDraw's built in helpers that really does the job well. Correcting a fluorescent green tone is a formidable task. You just did it in two easy steps, and one of those was automatic.

8 Select Hue and Saturation in the Effect list.

9 Now change the Saturation slider to −24.

Cropping and Resizing Amy's Image

You can now crop and resize Amy's image to the same size as the images of Richard and Mary. Follow the procedure for Richard to accomplish this and place Amy's cropped and resized image below the other two on the filmstrip.

A design issue

Now that we've completed the major mechanics of preparing your image objects, you might want to stop a minute to see if there is anything that could be done to refine the overall look.

The filmstrip sprocket holes at the bottom are cut off by the edge of the picture space. If you move the filmstrip up eight pixels, both the top and bottom sprocket holes are inside the picture space. This is a small change, but one that feels more compositionally complete. Remember that anything outside the picture space will not save to a printable file.

Adding Text Labels

To finish this side of the box, you can add text objects for the names of the employees, using the same font you used for the Wave Systems text objects on the side of the box. Check the font and edge size on the finished file and work out the colors by yourself. Try several combinations of fill and edge colors to see how they look. Try to imagine how this will look if printed 9.5 by 20 inches.

Remember to change your Picture Quality setting in the Options dialog box back to Typical before continuing to the next chapter.

Things To Explore on Your Own

For more in-depth exploration of the skills learned in this chapter, try some or all of the following:

- Use the Curve tool to create a variety of shapes with all the different styles of control points.

- Try out a variety of AutoShapes in the Outline Workpane, AutoShapes floater.

- Try applying pictures to shapes or text. In addition to the pictures in the PhotoDraw gallery, you can click the Browse button and apply any picture from your hard drive if its file format is supported by PhotoDraw.

- In the additional images folder on the companion CD, there are a variety of scanned photographs. Open some of them and try applying various color correction tools to see what happens. Try a lot of settings with each tool so you get an idea of how these tools can be used to create unusual effects.

7

Creating a Poster with PhotoDraw

 Stochastic printing. Until recently, a standard four-color offset method would be used to print this type of piece (a poster). The color would be separated on the film and a half tone screen would be applied to produce the small dots that the press prints. These small dots of cyan, magenta, yellow, and black (CMYK) are arranged in a *rosette pattern,* because the half-tone screen for each color is made at a different angle than the others. Today a method called *stochastic printing* has become very popular. This method breaks up the colors and scatters them somewhat like an airbrush. This allows lower-resolution images to be printed while achieving results that are quite acceptable for all but the highest quality glossy magazines.

In Chapter 6, we used employee photos to create a parking-carton graphic for RL&Associates. In this chapter, we will create a poster for that client. The resolution of the poster will be 9 by 12 inches at 300 pixels per inch. This will result in a printable size of 18 by 24 inches at 150 pixels per inch. Although this may not seem like high resolution for commercial graphics printing, it will look quite good with stochastic printing.

To build a dynamic composition, you will use several scanned photographs of RL&A employees, and a scanned image of a printed circuit board. Then you will use Erase and the alpha channel fade out function for compositing. Next, you will add dynamic 3-D text to enhance the illusion of space. Normal text will finish off the piece.

In the process, you'll encounter two different Cut Out techniques and learn how the Erase function works. You will also learn about how to use transparency in PhotoDraw to blend images together. Finally, you'll get an advance preview of the 3-D features that are covered in depth in the next chapter.

A Look at the Poster Image

Let's take a quick look at the project you will create in this chapter. Open it to get an idea of what you will do to make this image.

Building on the personal touch, the people that form the company have been grouped together from individual photographs. Visually, this imparts a more personal feeling of people who work together and interact with each other. Let's identify the people in the poster.

Open the File

1 Open the *rl&a poster.mix* file in the chapters/chap07 folder on the CD. This is a large picture and may take a short while to open.

Rowan is in back.

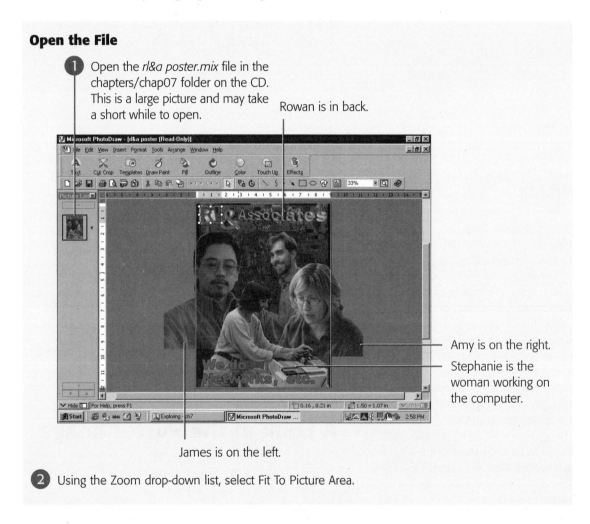

Amy is on the right.

Stephanie is the woman working on the computer.

James is on the left.

2 Using the Zoom drop-down list, select Fit To Picture Area.

Working with Reflected Light

In the poster, the light will come from behind and a little above Stephanie, as you can tell by the highlights on Stephanie's shoulder. Logically, the light hits Amy and Rowan's faces since they are facing somewhat toward the light. What is not so obvious is how the reflected light hits James. Reflected light bounces in the opposite direction from the main light source, but, since it is indirect light, it is weaker and does not produce bright highlights. Since James is on the side away from the light and facing away from the light source, it is the reflected light that illuminates the side of his face that is toward the others. When shooting photographs, try to get several shots of everyone with light coming from different directions so that when you start putting together compositions, you will be able to use the light source as part of your design. This allows you more control of how your pictures look and, in many cases, will make the difference between good and really good-looking pictures.

Manipulating Image Size

To produce the illusion of 3-D space, a common trick artists use is to make similar objects different sizes. This produces an illusion of some objects being closer than others. In this composition, I have employed this by making Amy, Rowan, and James larger than Stephanie, who is really the focus of attention. This produces a visually dynamic tension and a feeling that the others are surrounding her. The dynamic tension is further enhanced by the fact that Stephanie is leaning slightly forward and Amy is leaning slightly toward her, while James and Rowan are vertical.

Working with the PC Board Image

The poster's backdrop is an image of a printed circuit board. This was scanned by simply laying the board on the scanner. If you have a scanner, you have access to an unlimited supply of photograph quality images to bring into PhotoDraw. This can range from photographic prints to magazine pictures to real objects, such as this PC board.

The scanner light left a white border around the image, which will need to be erased. Because of the solid white color of this border, we can use PhotoDraw's Erase By Color feature to erase the background.

Open a New Project

1 Leave *rl&a poster.mix* open and open a new picture, setting the Picture Settings as follows:

2 Set Units to Inches.

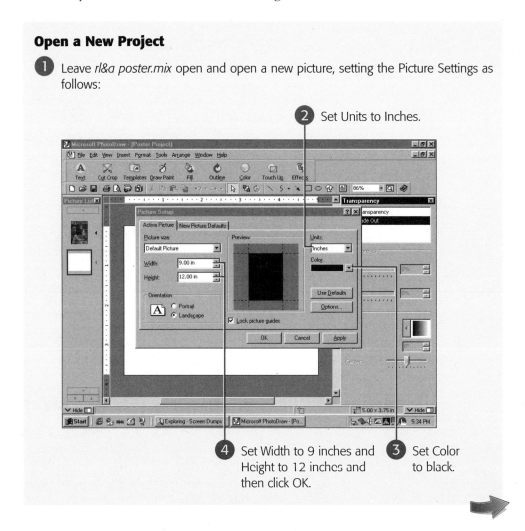

4 Set Width to 9 inches and Height to 12 inches and then click OK.

3 Set Color to black.

Why is my machine slowing down? In this picture, you will be working with several fairly large image objects that may slow down some computers if all are opened at once. If you experience performance problems, bring each image into your picture separately, modify the picture, save the file, and then go on to the next image.

Open a New Project *(continued)*

⑤ Click Options on the Tools menu to open this dialog box, and then click the Picture Quality Tab.

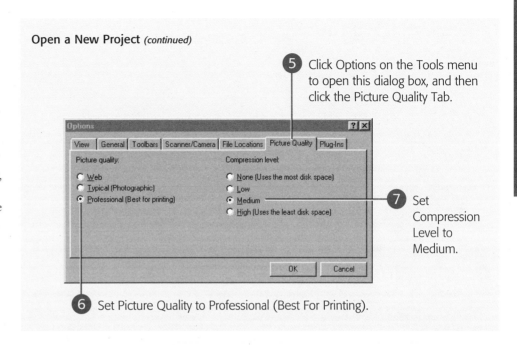

⑦ Set Compression Level to Medium.

⑥ Set Picture Quality to Professional (Best For Printing).

 Erasing before resizing. It's easier to use the Erase feature to make any corrections to an image before resizing. If you resized the image first, there would be artifacts around the edges between the white background and the image. That would make cleaning it up much more time consuming and probably result in a lower-quality image.

Erasing and Resizing

The printed circuit board image needs to be resized and, as mentioned, the white background around the board removed. When you use the Erase feature in PhotoDraw, the erased area becomes transparent, so that objects behind it show through.

Erase the White BackGround

1 Open the picture *pc board.bmp* in the chapters/chap07 folder on the CD.

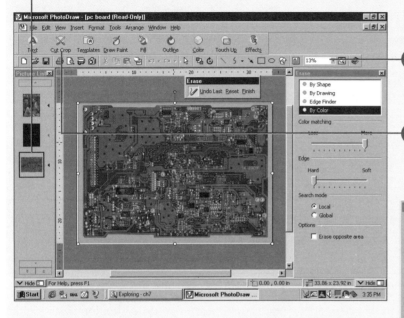

2 In the Zoom drop-down list box, choose Fit All.

3 Click Options on the tools menu and set Picture Quality to Professional (Best For Printing).

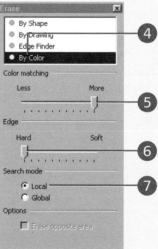

4 Choose Erase from the Cut Crop menu and in the Erase workpane, select By Color.

5 Move the Color Matching slider all the way to the right under More.

6 Set the Edge slider all the way to the left under Hard.

7 Set Search Mode to Local.

8 Click anywhere in the white area around the printed circuit board between the board and the edge. In a few moments, the white area is filled with the cerise default Erase selection color.

9 Click Finish in the Erase floater.

Resizing the PC Board Image

Now that the white background is gone, you can resize the image. Notice that the object's selection box remains where the outside edge of the background was. This is OK. When you resize the whole image to fit the width of the picture space, the narrow transparent boundary will allow the black background to show through and provide a border that frames the image object.

Resize the PC Board Image

1 Open the Arrange Workpane.

2 Make sure Maintain Proportions is checked, set the Width to 9 inches, and press the Enter key.

3 Making sure that Relative To Picture Area is active on the Align menu, click Align Center and Align Top to place the PC board graphic at the top and center of the picture space.

Cropping the PC Board

Erasing the white background has left space around the board image. To make the file a little smaller, you want to crop the image to the edges of the board.

Crop the PC Board Image

1 Click Crop on the Cut Crop menu.

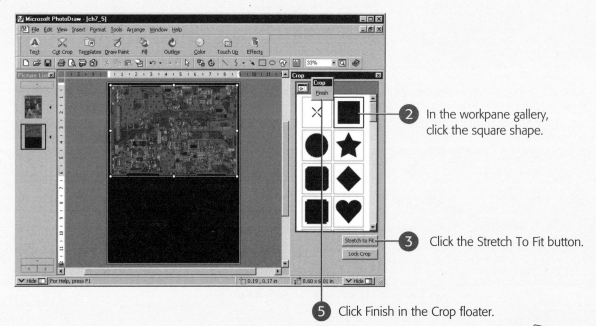

2 In the workpane gallery, click the square shape.

3 Click the Stretch To Fit button.

5 Click Finish in the Crop floater.

4 Zoom in so you can clearly see the edges of the printed circuit board, then crop to within one or two pixels outside of each edge. (If you have trouble with this step, just move on to Step 5—the point is to get the idea.)

6 On the Align menu, make sure Relative To Picture Area is active and then use the Align Center and Align Top tools.

7 Move the image down 6 pixels by pressing the Down arrow key on your keyboard six times.

Using the arrow keys. Remember you can use the arrow keys to nudge the crop line. Settings for this are in the Options dialog box on the Tools menu.

Giving your object focus. If at any time you try moving an object with the arrow keys and it won't move, it probably doesn't have focus. Click it to give it focus, and then use the arrow keys.

Fading Out the PC Board

To help make the people's images stand out, we will now make the printed circuit board fade out toward the bottom. This will make it visually recede into the picture.

Fade the PC Board Image

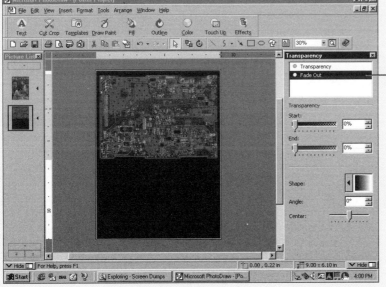

From the Effects menu, click Fade Out. The Transparency Workpane appears with Fade Out selected.

Fade the PC Board Image *(continued)*

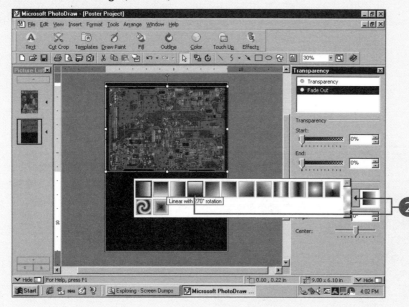

 Click the left arrow in Shape and choose the icon that says Linear With 270 Rotation in the ScreenTip (fourth from the left). The expanded Shapes gallery displays 14 thumbnails representing how transparency will be distributed throughout an image. Black is 100 percent transparent and white is 100 percent opaque.

Fade the PC Board Image *(continued)*

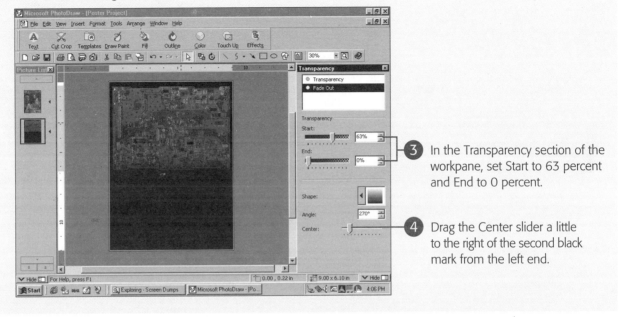

3 In the Transparency section of the workpane, set Start to 63 percent and End to 0 percent.

4 Drag the Center slider a little to the right of the second black mark from the left end.

Working with the Employee Images

The images of the RL&A employees have been scanned to maintain as much quality as possible. As you bring each person's image into the composition, you will need to erase the areas around them, position that person in the poster, and then apply a fade out effect to the image.

Here's a small overview on cutting, cropping, and erasing in PhotoDraw before you continue on. The PhotoDraw Cut Crop menu provides the following items:

- **Cut Out**   Removes an area of an object and optionally puts that object in another window.
- **Crop**   Removes an area around an object.
- **Erase**   Makes the area around an object transparent.

Cropping is generally done by applying a shape to an object and removing the area outside the shape. Erase and Cut Out functions are more flexible. If you examine the workpanes for Cut Out and Erase, you'll notice they are very similar because the task is the same in both cases: to delineate an irregular object so it can either be cut out or the area around it erased. Both Cut Out and Erase Workpanes contain the following options:

- **By Shape**   Uses a shape to delineate an object, similar to the Crop tool.
- **By Drawing**   Enables you to draw around the object to delineate it.
- **Edge Finder**   Uses PhotoDraw algorithms to determine the edge.
- **By Color**   Uses color to delineate the object.

We've used the By Color option already with the PC board. In this section, we'll erase using By Drawing and Edge Finder.

Rowan's Image

We'll work on Rowan's image first. We need to insert this image, delineate the person from the background, erase the background, and position the image.

Erasing By Drawing

Erase By Drawing gives you the most control over the delineation process. However, this also means that it can be the slowest, since the more points you choose around the outline the higher the resolution of the edge will be. For this project, you can make the drawing as accurate or inaccurate as you like. Just remember, this should be fun and it's only an example to learn about PhotoDraw.

Erase the Background

1 Insert *rowan.bmp* from the chapters/chap07 images folder on the CD.

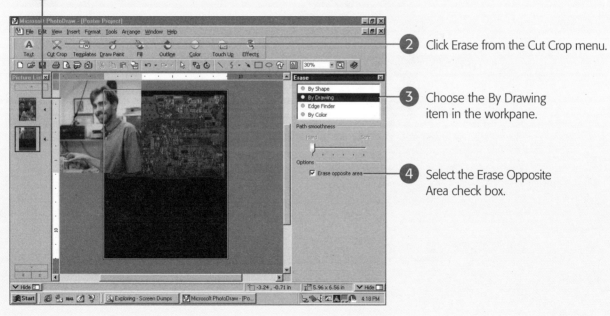

2 Click Erase from the Cut Crop menu.

3 Choose the By Drawing item in the workpane.

4 Select the Erase Opposite Area check box.

5 Zoom in to 50 percent.

6 Start anywhere you like and click the edge of Rowan's image; then work your way around the figure, setting control points wherever you need them. You want to end up with Rowan's entire image inside your Erase selection. It is usually better to have a few too many control points than not enough, but we're just practicing.

Fixing a mistake.
Use the Undo Last or Reset buttons in the Erase floater if you make a mistake.

7 Click Finish on the Erase floater. The area outside your selected area is erased, leaving an image of Rowan with a transparent background.

8 Click Blur and Sharpen on the Effects menu and move the slider to the right to 10. This sharpens the image slightly.

Alpha Channel Transparency

When you erased the area around the figure of Rowan, the selection rectangle remained around the new image. The area between the figure and the selection rectangle is now transparent but remains part of the image. This is done with what is called the alpha channel, which encodes information about the transparency or opacity of each pixel in a file. In this case, the erased area is completely transparent. However, any pixel can have 256 levels between 100 percent color and 100 percent transparent. This causes the Fade Out effect.

To make the images of Rowan and James stay in the background, you want them to be very transparent towards the bottom and not at all transparent at the top. This preserves their facial features while blending the images with the background image.

When working with transparency, keep in mind that shades of gray are used to determine the amount of transparency of a pixel: 100 percent black translates to 100 percent transparent; 100 percent white translates to 100 percent opaque. The 254 levels of gray between black and white represent the 254 possible levels of partial transparency. You will see how this is applied when using the Fade Out tool.

Applying Fade Out to Rowan

Using the Fade Out tool in PhotoDraw can be helpful when you want to blend pictures together. Fade Out applies a transparency in a pattern from the Start setting to the End setting. The pattern is chosen from a gallery of styles, including a normal linear pattern in various rotations (left to right, top to bottom, and so on), and some other interesting patterns. You can choose the amount of transparency at either end for a fade out effect. You can also manually set a rotation value to apply the fade.

Apply Fade Out

1 Move the image of Rowan onto the picture space, referring to the finished picture for placement.

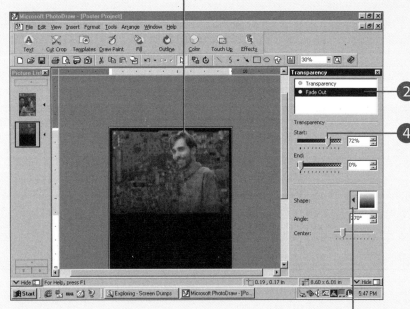

2 Click Fade Out in the Effects menu. The Fade Out Workpane appears.

4 Drag the Start slider to the right until it reaches 72 percent. This makes the bottom 72 percent transparent, which fades the top to 0 percent transparency.

3 Click the left arrow in Shape and choose the icon that says Linear With 270 Rotation in the ScreenTip (fourth from the left). The gallery closes and nothing seems to happen.

Apply Fade Out *(continued)*

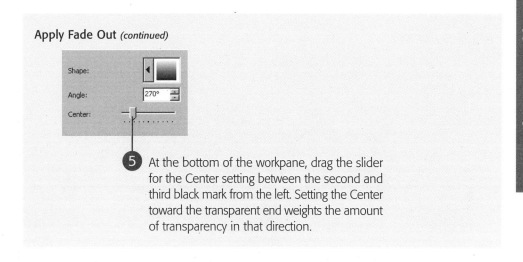

5 At the bottom of the workpane, drag the slider for the Center setting between the second and third black mark from the left. Setting the Center toward the transparent end weights the amount of transparency in that direction.

The Image of James

Next we'll work with the image of James. This will be very similar to the work we did with Rowan, but with a few differences. Notably, we'll use a different tool to cut out the image.

Erasing Using the Edge Finder

We'll use PhotoDraw's Edge Finder tool to erase the area around James. To use the Edge Finder, which appears in the Erase workpane, you first select a width, draw an edge around the object you want to cut out, and then let the edge finder figure out where the edge really is.

The Edge Finder tool works on images that have good contrast between the object that's outside the object. Usually this works best with images that have large areas of flat color (for good contrast) and few intricate lines on the outline (typically not photographs of people). However, for learning purposes we'll use it on the photograph of James.

Cut Out James

1 Insert the *james.bmp* file from the chapters/chap07 folder.

2 Click Erase from the Format menu. The Erase Workpane appears.

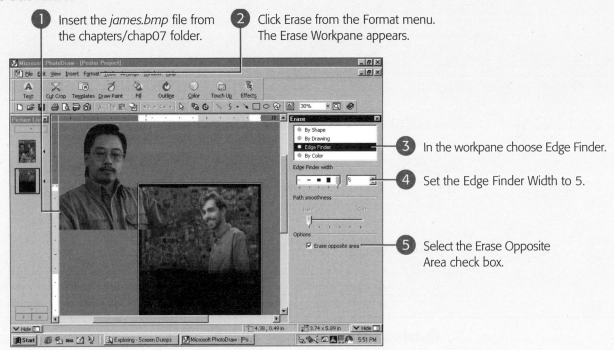

3 In the workpane choose Edge Finder.

4 Set the Edge Finder Width to 5.

5 Select the Erase Opposite Area check box.

Cut Out James *(continued)*

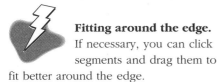

Fitting around the edge.
If necessary, you can click segments and drag them to fit better around the edge.

6 Position your cursor about one inch in from the right side of the image, just above James' sleeve. Click to set the yellow diamond start point. Move your pointer about one half-inch along the sleeve to the left and click. Keep doing this around the image of James until you reach the diamond where you started.

7 Click Finish in the floater. The area behind James is erased.

Apply Fade Out

1 Use the Blur And Sharpen Workpane, accessed from the Effects menu, to sharpen this image to a setting of 10.

2 Refer to the finished poster image and move James into position. Save your file.

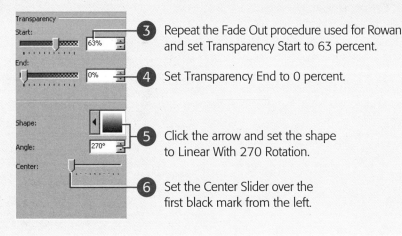

3 Repeat the Fade Out procedure used for Rowan and set Transparency Start to 63 percent.

4 Set Transparency End to 0 percent.

5 Click the arrow and set the shape to Linear With 270 Rotation.

6 Set the Center Slider over the first black mark from the left.

Amy's Image

The procedure for cutting out the background around Amy's image is identical to what we did with Rowan's image—use the Draw tool and not the edge finder. Cut out Amy's image, refer to the finished picture for position, and place Amy's image in your picture.

Borrowing from a finished image. If you're getting tired of cutting out these images, you can take a shortcut and borrow the appropriate cut out image from the *rl&a poster.mix* picture. Be careful to read the steps so you don't miss any new tricks.

Apply Fade Out to Amy's picture the same as you did with Rowan's image, except set Transparency Start is 20 percent and set Center halfway between the first and second black marks from the left side.

Stephanie's Image

Notice that applying different amounts of transparency to each image creates a feeling of proximity or distance. Rowan, who has the most transparency, is visually more distant. Amy, with the least transparency, seems closest. Even though the image of James is largest, it appears behind Amy visually because it has considerably more transparency.

There are two parts to working with the image of Stephanie. First there is the black rectangle below James and Amy that needs something to keep it from being a piece of negative space. To do that, you will use a somewhat transparent copy of Stephanie's image (complete with its background) to fill in the black area with some tone that will visually link it to the rest of the picture. A second cut out copy of Stephanie at full opacity will sit on top of the first. This fully opaque image will place Stephanie in front of the others, definitely in the foreground. Ready?

Insert and Align Stephanie's Image

1. Insert *stephanie.bmp* from the chapters/chap07 images folder on the companion CD.

2. Move the image near the bottom of the picture space then, with Relative To Picture Area active, use the Align Center and Alight Bottom tools to align the image to the center and bottom of the picture space.

3. Sharpen the image to a setting of 10.

4. Save your file.

Applying Fade Out to Stephanie

The image of Stephanie brings up a couple of design problems that PhotoDraw can solve. First, you have two images that are identical. However, one is a complete but semi-transparent image that needs to be positioned properly on the Z-order to produce the effect of blending images "above it" with the black rectangular area "below." Fortunately, PhotoDraw has a Send Backward command on the Order menu (in the Arrange menu) that does the trick nicely here.

The other problem is that the second image, which is only of Stephanie and the computer she is working on, needs to be aligned exactly on top of the first image. By aligning the duplicate image exactly with the original, it will be remain properly aligned after the Erase procedure.

Apply Fade Out to Stephanie's Image

1 Press Ctrl+D to make a duplicate of Stephanie's image and move it onto the scratch space for now so you can work on the original copy.

2 Select the original.

3 Click Blur And Sharpen on the Effects menu and set the slider to blur the image to −15.

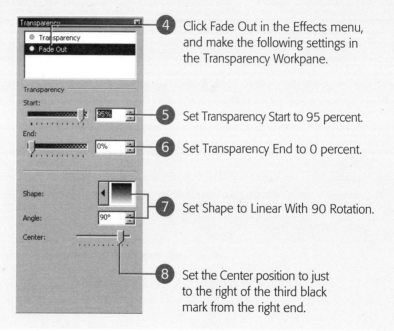

4 Click Fade Out in the Effects menu, and make the following settings in the Transparency Workpane.

5 Set Transparency Start to 95 percent.

6 Set Transparency End to 0 percent.

7 Set Shape to Linear With 90 Rotation.

8 Set the Center position to just to the right of the third black mark from the right end.

Moving the Image to the Back

The original image of Stephanie will now be placed at the bottom of the stack of employee images—in front of the image of the PC board—which is at the bottom. The Order menu, accessed from the Arrange menu, contains several items that enable you to position the selected image on the Z-order of images you are working with. We'll use Send Backward in this case.

Move the Image to the Back

1. On the Arrange menu, click Order and select Send Backward.

2. Repeat Step 1 again to send the image back one more level.

3. Save your file.

Positioning and Erasing Around the Duplicate

The second part of working with Stephanie's object involves positioning the duplicate over the original and making only the body opaque by erasing around the edge.

Position the Duplicate and Erase Around It

1. Zoom out so you can see the duplicate image you put on the scratch space. Move it onto the picture space near the bottom.

2. With Relative To Picture Area active, use the Align Center and Align Bottom tools to align this image the same way you aligned the original image of Stephanie.

Position the Duplicate and Erase Around It *(continued)*

3 Click Erase in the Cut Crop menu. In the Erase Workpane, choose By Drawing and select the Erase Opposite Area check box.

4 Draw the area around the outside of Stephanie and click Finish in the floater.

5 There is still one small area below Stephanie's arm and above the keyboard that needs to be erased. Once again use Erase By Drawing to complete the erasing for this image.

Adding 3-D Text

Now it's time to add fun, colorful 3-D text to your picture. Adding 3-D to text is an effective technique; it adds impact to your pictures, in addition to being an exciting design element. We'll go into more detail about 3-D effects in Chapter 8, but this section will give you a taste of what you can do with 3-D and text objects.

In this procedure, we'll compose the company name "RL & Associates" using three text objects. To enhance the illusion of 3-D space, we'll create the text object "RL" and rotate it to the right to look like it is moving back in space. The ampersand (&) object will face straight out from the picture, and the "Associates" object will be rotated opposite the first, so it looks as though it is coming back out of the picture.

Create the First Text Object

1 Insert a text object with the letters "RL" (in caps), set the Font to Arial Black, 72 points, bold.

2 Move this text object near the upper left corner of the picture.

3 Click 3-D Text on the Text menu. The 3-D Workpane appears. You might be asked to reinstall PhotoDraw if Direct 3-D is not installed.

4 In the workpane gallery, click the Designer 3-D 5 thumbnail. Wait until the 3-D text appears before continuing.

Changing settings. When working with the settings in the 3-D Workpane, PhotoDraw will start calculating as soon as you change the first setting. While PhotoDraw is processing the first setting, you can drag your cursor over the numbers for the next setting and change it. You will need to repeat this for however many settings you are changing.

Create the First Text Object *(continued)*

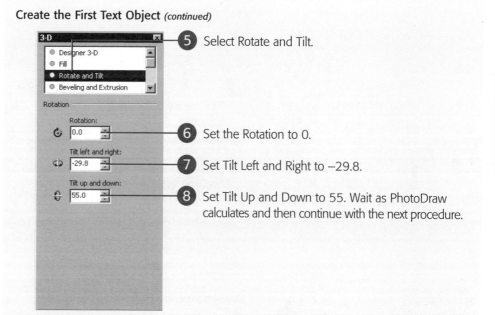

⑤ Select Rotate and Tilt.

⑥ Set the Rotation to 0.

⑦ Set Tilt Left and Right to −29.8.

⑧ Set Tilt Up and Down to 55. Wait as PhotoDraw calculates and then continue with the next procedure.

Now create the ampersand with a larger font but with no rotation or left-right tilt.

Create the Second Text Object

1 Insert another text object with the ampersand (&) character set to Arial Black, 96 points, bold.

2 Move this object to the right of the first object. Refer to the finished picture for precise placement.

3 Apply the same 3-D Text effect as for the first object.

4 In the workpane, set the Rotation to 0, set the Tilt Left and Right to 0, and set the Tilt Up and Down to 10.

Finally, create the third object with a tilt opposite to the first object.

Create the Third Text Object

1 Insert another text object and type "Associates" with a capital "A."

2 Apply the same 3-D Text effect as for the first two object. Wait for PhotoDraw to process the effects.

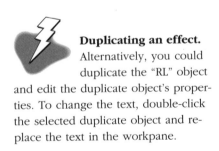

Duplicating an effect. Alternatively, you could duplicate the "RL" object and edit the duplicate object's properties. To change the text, double-click the selected duplicate object and replace the text in the workpane.

Create the Third Text Object *(continued)*

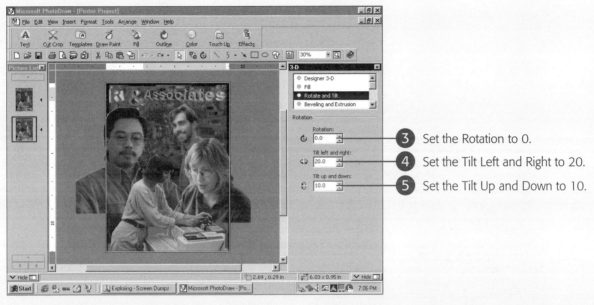

3 Set the Rotation to 0.

4 Set the Tilt Left and Right to 20.

5 Set the Tilt Up and Down to 10.

6 Position the three text objects as in the finished picture and save your file.

Adding Plain Text

The final step is to create the text that goes in the lower left corner of the picture. You don't want two objects fighting each other for attention, so we will not use 3-D. In fact, you will subdue the color a little to tone it down.

Insert Plain Text

1 Insert a text object with the words "We do" using the Arial Black Font, 64 points.

2 Make a duplicate object using the same font with the text "Networks" and make another duplicate object with the text ", etc.".

3 Move the text objects into position as in the finished picture, then select the object with the "We do" text. Group all three objects together.

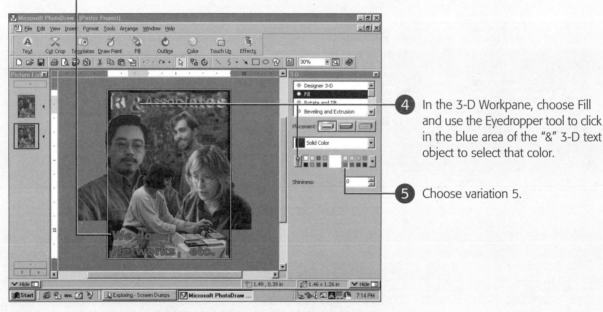

4 In the 3-D Workpane, choose Fill and use the Eyedropper tool to click in the blue area of the "&" 3-D text object to select that color.

5 Choose variation 5.

6 In the workpane, choose Outline, select the single line, make it three points wide, and then find a dark blue you like in the Active Palette.

7 Save your file.

Things To Explore on Your Own

See what happens if you apply various 3-D effects to different fonts? Try fonts with and without serifs. Try the various ways of applying transparency in the Shapes gallery on the Transparency Workpane.

Working with PhotoDraw 3-D

To gain a thorough understanding of Microsoft PhotoDraw's 3-D tools, we will take a slightly different approach in this chapter and temporarily move away from creating a demonstration project. Instead, using a variety of objects, we will deeply explore the 3-D capabilities of PhotoDraw.

About PhotoDraw 3-D Effects

3-D effects are some of the most interesting features offered by PhotoDraw. This is probably because we see objects in three dimensions in real life, so PhotoDraw's ability to render objects this way in is inherently more interesting than working with two-dimensional (flat) objects.

3-D effects are made from 2-D objects by creating an *extrusion* of the object into the z plane and then setting various 3-D properties including color fill, rotation and tilt, and lighting effects. Additionally, any 3-D object can have a bevel applied to its edge between the front and the extrusion, and the bevel itself can include several effects. You can also apply bitmap pictures onto various parts of the 3-D object or its bevel. As with other PhotoDraw features, there are plenty of styles available for 3-D effects and parameters, so you can usually quickly find something that works for you.

In this chapter, we'll visit most aspects of PhotoDraw 3-D design and gain a good understanding of what PhotoDraw 3-D can do, and more importantly, how you do it.

Three dimensions from x to z. On a three-dimensional graph, points x and y describe horizontal and vertical axes, and the z axis describes depth.

What Can Be Made 3-D?

You can apply 3-D effects to the following PhotoDraw objects:

- Text
- Lines (including outlines around graphic objects)
- Painted lines
- Shapes

For text objects, there are a couple of ways to access the 3-D tools: you can either click the 3-D Text command in the Text menu or click the 3-D command in the Effects menu. For objects other than text, use the 3-D command in the Effects menu. You can also access the 3-D function from the Formatting toolbar if it is visible. (To show the Formatting toolbar, check Formatting in the Toolbars menu, accessed from the View menu.)

Note that you cannot directly apply 3-D effects to groups of objects.

The 3-D Workpane

As with other workpanes, the 3-D Workpane has several toolsets. This illustration shows the Designer Workpane with the thumbnail gallery open and the Formatting toolbar located above the standard toolbar. We will examine all the 3-D tools in this chapter. Let's get started.

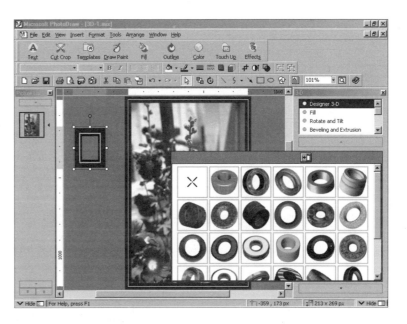

Setting Up the Picture

First you need a new picture to work with. In this chapter, we will apply 3-D effects to a graphic object (actually to the border of the graphic object) and to a shape object. Both objects will be contained in the same picture file, so you'll only need to create one.

Sizing up picture dimensions. Setting the dimensions to 800-by-1200 pixels is probably only useful for demonstration purposes such as this, as it doesn't fit any standard print or screen size.

Set Up the Project

1 Create a new picture, using the Default Picture template, with dimensions of 800 by 1200 pixels. Leave the guides locked and the color white.

2 Insert the *flowers1.bmp* file from the chapters/chap08 folder on the companion CD into your picture.

Set Up the Project *(continued)*

3 Save the file to your hard disk with a name like *3-D sample.mix* (or anything you will remember).

To use 3-D effects on a picture object such as this, you first need to give it an outline. In this case, we'll use a simple straight line outline.

Apply the Outline and Resize the Image

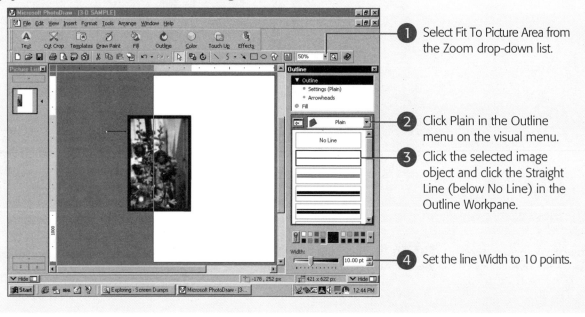

1 Select Fit To Picture Area from the Zoom drop-down list.

2 Click Plain in the Outline menu on the visual menu.

3 Click the selected image object and click the Straight Line (below No Line) in the Outline Workpane.

4 Set the line Width to 10 points.

Apply the Outline and Resize the Image *(continued)*

5 Access the Active palette and choose the color third from the left side in the top row—a dark maroon that visually pushes the flowers into the foreground. Choose variation 2 (second from the left in the top row) to make it less saturated and appear to visually recede.

6 From the Arrange menu, open the Arrange Workpane with Size and Position selected.

7 In the Size settings with Maintain Proportions selected, change the Width setting to 800 pixels (if necessary). The Height will reset automatically.

8 With Relative To Picture Area active, use the Align Center and Middle menu choices to align the image object to the picture space.

Understanding 3-D Settings

In this section, we'll visit each of the options in the 3-D Workpane and look at the effects they produce. In the next section, we'll take a little deeper look at a few more 3-D effects.

In general, to make a 2-D object into a 3-D object, you must extrude the object into the third dimension. This creates a thickness. On some objects, such as a border around an image, you must tilt the object so you aren't looking at it straight on in order to see the 3-D effect. PhotoDraw lets you tilt 3-D objects right to left and top to bottom. With other objects, such as a hollow shape, text, or a line drawing, the 3-D effect is immediately noticeable.

Choosing a Beveling and Extrusion Setting

PhotoDraw combines beveling styles with extrusion. In fact, all 3-D styles are extruded and all styles but one have beveling applied to the front edge of the object. So the Beveling And Extrusion gallery is mostly a set of bevels. In this exercise, we'll work with the one beveling-extrusion style that has no bevel. In "Using 3-D Bevels and Fills," later in this chapter, we'll look at applying beveling to 3-D objects.

Choose a Beveling and Extrusion Setting

1 Click 3-D on the Effects menu and select Beveling And Extrusion.

2 Click the Bevel Style button to open the Beveling And Extrusion gallery.

3 Click the thumbnail in the upper left corner, labeled Extrude Only (as shown in the ScreenTip). On an object with a fill such as the flowers picture, Extrude can only be seen if the object is rotated—so you won't see any effect just yet.

 Putting an image in a frame. When you want to put an image in a plain box-like frame use Extrude Only. This creates a 3-D object that has a front and sides but no fancy edges like those made when you use Bevel.

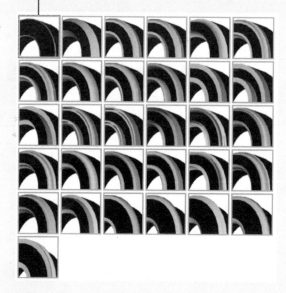

Experimenting with Rotate and Tilt

Next you are going to rotate the object to view it in 3-D. As you progress through the steps, notice that the color of the object's side changes the more that the object is rotated. This is because a light source accompanies any 3-D effect. As the object moves in the direction of the light source, its color becomes lighter. Rotating away from the light source darkens the color. We'll talk more about working with lighting sources next.

Tilt the Object

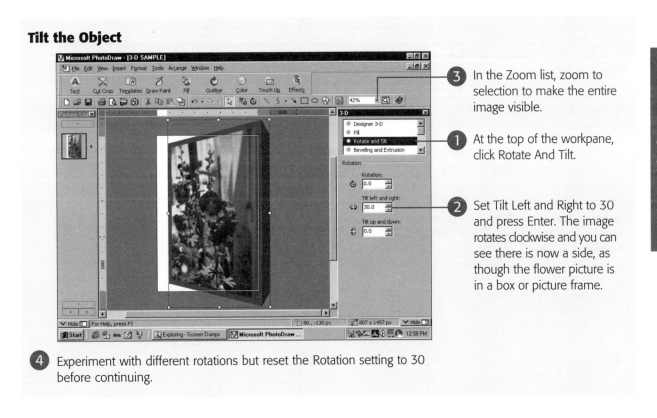

3 In the Zoom list, zoom to selection to make the entire image visible.

1 At the top of the workpane, click Rotate And Tilt.

2 Set Tilt Left and Right to 30 and press Enter. The image rotates clockwise and you can see there is now a side, as though the flower picture is in a box or picture frame.

4 Experiment with different rotations but reset the Rotation setting to 30 before continuing.

Experimenting with Lighting

Working with 3-D objects requires some understanding of lighting basics, since all 3-D effects are ultimately affected by applied light sources. PhotoDraw provides you with a main or indirect light and up to three direct lights that you can control for color and intensity. The direct lights should be set at different locations, as one might do in a photography studio. By mixing various amounts of different colored light from different positions, you can produce interesting lighting effects.

Fortunately PhotoDraw provides a gallery of lighting styles to choose from, so one of the styles will likely either match or come close to your desired effect. We'll bypass the styles for now and instead explore each of the lighting parameters so that when you choose a style you'll understand a little more about its parameters and how to tweak them if you need to.

Next, we'll look at the lighting sources that can be applied. The 3-D Lighting Workpane contains four buttons in the Settings area. One has a sun icon—this controls the indirect light; the other three have lamps—these control the direct lights. Together these create the lighting for a 3-D object.

Using lighting for effect. From a design perspective, lighting is useful in a variety of ways. You can use the color controls to make a 3-D object blend in with its surroundings creating a type of design harmony—or you can use distinctly colored lighting on an object—if you want it to stand out from the rest of the composition and attract the attention of the viewer. Once you understand the basic functions, other ways of using lighting will occur to you as you work on your own projects.

Set the Lighting Source and Color

1 In the 3-D Workpane, click Lighting and then click Settings. The Lighting Workpane appears. By default, the color in all but the Number 1 lamp should be black and the Number 1 lamp should be white.

2 Click the Number 1 lamp to make it active and click the yellow color swatch to change the current color to yellow. The image object now appears to be bathed in yellow light.

3 Click the red color box. After looking at how the object changed, choose color variation 2.

4 Click the dark blue color box and try some of the variations.

5 Click the white color box to return to the default.

Working with PhotoDraw 3-D

Experimenting with Light Direction

If you haven't applied a style from the Lighting Style gallery, the default direction of the light source comes from the front, facing into the picture space. As mentioned earlier, you can change the direction of all lights but the indirect light. Let's see how this works.

Set the Light Direction

1 With Number 1 lamp button selected, leave the current color white and change the Tilt Left and Right setting to 45. The light now appears to be coming from behind your left shoulder, shining almost directly at the *flowers1.bmp* object. The beveled side becomes dark because there is less light shining on it.

2 Now change the setting to –45 and press Enter. The beveled side becomes lighter and the image is quite dark. The light is shining from behind your right shoulder.

3 Change the setting back to 45.

Using a Second Light

In Chapter 7, we briefly covered reflected light. The 3-D lighting algorithm in PhotoDraw doesn't handle reflected light automatically because there are too many different ways you might want it to look. You can create the illusion of reflected light by adding a second light source to your 3-D object. Here's how.

Adjust the Tilt of the Second Light

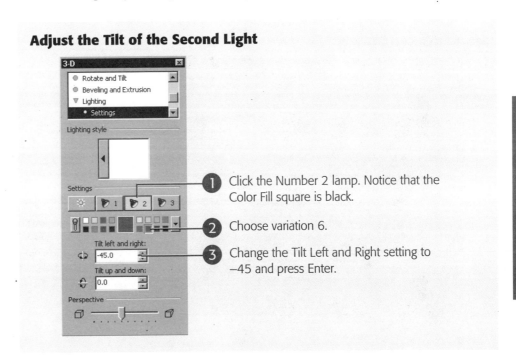

1. Click the Number 2 lamp. Notice that the Color Fill square is black.

2. Choose variation 6.

3. Change the Tilt Left and Right setting to −45 and press Enter.

Notice that the rotated front of the picture is now lighter than the edge. This is because the light at 45 degrees is white and the light at negative 45 degrees is considerably darker. Because it is easier to see the 3-D lighting effects with a hollow object than with an outlined image, we'll take a slight detour and create a simple extruded rectangle.

Create a Second Object

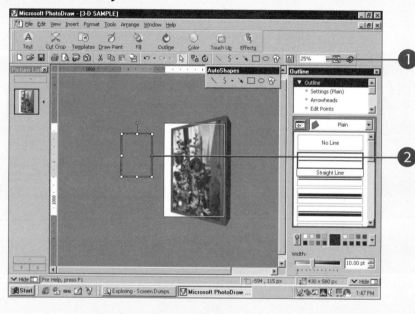

① Zoom out so you can see the scratch space to the left of the picture space. Then click Draw on the Draw Paint menu.

② Click the rectangle icon in the AutoShapes floater and drag across to make a rectangle about one-quarter the size of the flower image, with a 10-px-wide single line outline. The color doesn't matter. You will change this in the 3-D Workpane.

Create a Second Object *(continued)*

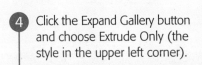

④ Click the Expand Gallery button and choose Extrude Only (the style in the upper left corner).

③ Click 3-D on the Effects menu and select Beveling And Extrusion.

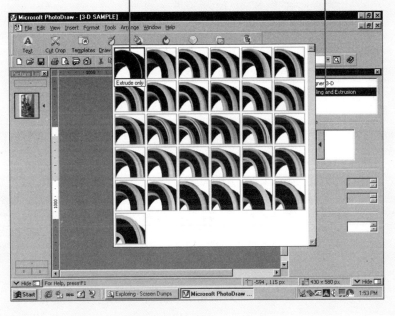

Working with PhotoDraw 3-D

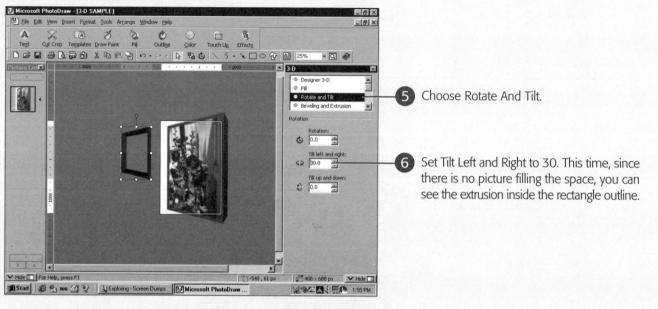

5 Choose Rotate And Tilt.

6 Set Tilt Left and Right to 30. This time, since there is no picture filling the space, you can see the extrusion inside the rectangle outline.

Setting 3-D Fill Colors

To set the color for a 3-D object, you control the color of the face, the side, and the bevel (if one is applied). There are three Placement buttons between the Fill Workpane scrolling list and the drop-down list that tell PhotoDraw which you want to set.

The Placement button on the left controls the color of an object's face, the middle button controls the bevel color, and the right button controls the color of the sides. Each button can be active or inactive. If active, a Placement button will look like it has been pressed in; if inactive, it will appear to be not pressed in. When you access the Fill Workpane, your object has the default blue color assigned to its face and a default red to the sides.

Set a 3-D Color Fill

1. In the 3-D Workpane, click Fill.

2. Set the Face and Sides Placement buttons (left and right, respectively) to be active (pressed in) and the Bevel Placement button to be inactive (not pressed in).

3. Access the Active Palette and select the color box next to last on the third row from the top.

4. Click the Face Placement button (on the left) to make it inactive.

5. Now the Side Placement button is the only one active. Click any other color box near the current Color Fill square. The sides, both inside and out, turn that color.

6. After experimenting, click Undo an appropriate number of times to return the side to the color you set in Step 3.

Working with Up and Down Lighting Angles

Let's make the sides deeper so we can see the results of the next lighting experiment.

Set the Extrusion Depth

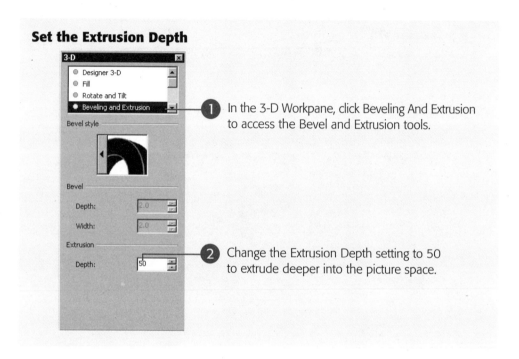

1. In the 3-D Workpane, click Beveling And Extrusion to access the Bevel and Extrusion tools.

2. Change the Extrusion Depth setting to 50 to extrude deeper into the picture space.

Notice that the inside of the top and bottom are black. This is because the light rays are shining parallel to each other, toward the object, from a position that is in the middle of the object. That means that no light rays shine up or down. Let's see how we can deal with that.

Setting the Tilt Up and Down Light Position

1 Under Settings, click the Number 2 lamp. Set the Color Fill square to black, variation 7, which is a little darker than 50 percent gray.

2 Click Number 1 lamp.

3 Set Tilt Up And Down to 60 and press the Enter key. You have made Number 1 lamp (white light) cast light coming down from above and you can see that the inside of the bottom is now better illuminated. Also, the change of angle has darkened the front face.

Illuminating the top surface. Sunlight mostly shines from above. The light in the picture comes from above and a bit from the front, so any surface that faces up will receive more light than any other surface. In this picture, the inside bottom is the only visible surface facing up, so it gets the most light. To illuminate the inside of the top surface, you need to create some reflected light to bounce up from the inside bottom surface.

Setting the Tilt Up and Down Light Position *(continued)*

④ Click the Number 2 lamp and select variation 6. This shines a little more light on everything and lightens all the faces. The inside bottom surface should be lighter than the front, however.

⑤ Click the Number 3 lamp and set the Tilt Up and Down property to −90. Change the color to black with variation 7. The inside of the top surface is no longer black and all the other surfaces have readjusted so you now have a fairly realistic depiction of how light illuminates this type of object.

About Lighting Direction

The most basic way an artist or designer looks at the direction of light is as though it were the sun. This is because sunlight is the most natural form of light. When you are standing outside in the sun, it is above your head, and depending on how you stand (or sit or lie down), the sun's rays come from the front, back, left, right, or some angle between two of these directions. Mimicking this sort of natural lighting in a picture will automatically make viewers feel that the light in your picture is "correct." An exception to this is if your picture depicts an interior scene with a table lamp or other light source. In this case you would use the light sources to determine the direction from which your light is coming. Keep in mind that most interior lighting is from above.

Working with Perspective

The concept of mechanical perspective assumes a horizon line and vanishing points into which every pair of parallel lines on a single object disappears. For purposes of design, it is often better not to have such a forced look. The Perspective property enables you to change the perspective of any object. This procedure assumes you still have the Lighting settings selected in the 3-D Workpane.

Experiment with Perspective Settings

1 Drag the Perspective slider halfway toward the right end. Notice that this makes the perspective more forced, which might be interesting under some conditions.

2 Drag the slider between the left end and the middle. The perspective becomes much less forced.

3 Select the flowers object and zoom the view to fit the selection.

4 Slide the Perspective slider halfway between the left end and the middle. The object is still rotated the same amount; however, now it feels more relaxed. Now that you know how to work with the perspective tool, you can make it do whatever you want.

Working with Tilting and Light

Photodraw lets you position a 3-D object in three ways: by rotation, tilting to the left and right, and tilting to the top and bottom. Only rotation works on 2-D objects, since it works on the *x/y* plane. The other two rotations (called tilting in PhotoDraw) use the *z* plane. In this section, we'll look at what tilting can do to an object.

Tilting an object in 3-D space will affect the amount of light that strikes the different parts and, therefore, its color as well as value. Let's see how this works by working with the rectangle object again.

Color, Hue, Value, Tint, and Tone

In the world of art and design, the terms color, hue, value, tint, and tone (or saturation) have specific meanings. Color or hue is the actual color quality, such as red, yellow, or blue. Value refers to how light or dark a color is, no matter how much saturation it has. A high value is light and low value is dark. Tint is a color mixed with white, so a tint with a high value would be a pastel color. Tone means a color with black added, so a color with a low value is a tone. Saturation means the percentage of hue compared to the amount of gray component, so a red that is almost gray would have low saturation and a strong brilliant red would have high saturation. A very bright light tends to make colors more pastel looking until the light becomes so bright that it creates pure highlights that are the color of the light source. Weak light makes even strong vibrant colors look unsaturated.

Experiment with Tilting and Light

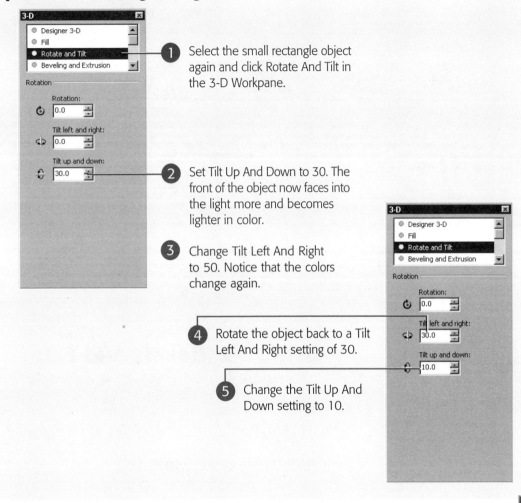

1. Select the small rectangle object again and click Rotate And Tilt in the 3-D Workpane.

2. Set Tilt Up And Down to 30. The front of the object now faces into the light more and becomes lighter in color.

3. Change Tilt Left And Right to 50. Notice that the colors change again.

4. Rotate the object back to a Tilt Left And Right setting of 30.

5. Change the Tilt Up And Down setting to 10.

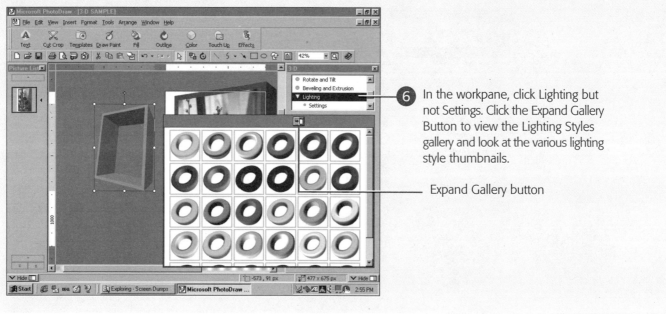

⑥ In the workpane, click Lighting but not Settings. Click the Expand Gallery Button to view the Lighting Styles gallery and look at the various lighting style thumbnails.

Expand Gallery button

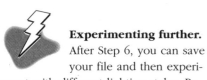

Experimenting further. After Step 6, you can save your file and then experiment with different lighting styles. Remember to click Undo to get back to where you started.

Using 3-D Bevels and Fills

You should now have a pretty good idea of how to apply a 3-D effect to an object and control the way it's lighted. Let's now turn our attention to some more interesting things you can do with 3-D effects. In this section we'll look at the use of bevels, bevel fills, and applying texture bitmaps to 3-D objects.

Working with Bevels

Bevels are rounded effects on the front of a 3-D object. PhotoDraw provides a selection of bevel styles that you can apply. These are somewhat similar to lines, in that you can choose the style and then apply various effects to the bevel, including width, depth, color fill, texture mapping, and so on.

Choosing Bevel Style, Width, and Color

We've already looked at the Bevel and Extrusion gallery in the previous section when we chose an extrusion without a bevel. Here we'll choose a beveled extrusion style and set the depth of the bevel. Then we'll visit the Fill Workpane again and set the color of the bevel.

Select Bevel Style, Depth, and Color

2 Click the Bevel And Extrusion Style gallery button to open it, and choose the second thumbnail from the left on the top row of thumbnails. The edges of the object now have an inside and outside white bevel. See Bevel 1.

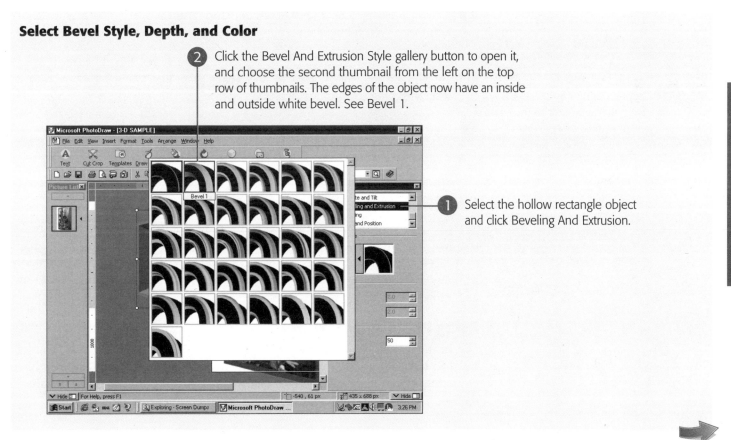

1 Select the hollow rectangle object and click Beveling And Extrusion.

Select Bevel Style, Depth, and Color *(continued)*

3 Zoom in to Selection.

4 Change the Width setting to 0.8. Notice there is more face showing now.

5 To change the color of the bevel, click Fill. Once again, you use the Placement buttons that let you control the color of the face, the bevel, and the side of your 3-D objects.

6 Set the Face and Sides buttons to inactive and press the middle Bevel button. Now you can set the color for the bevel.

7 Access the Active Palette and choose lavender, the sixth color from the left, second row from the bottom. The color is applied to the bevel.

 Applying fills. You can apply any fill type available from the Fill menu to the sides, bevel, or front face of your object—including a solid color, a texture, Designer Gradient, Two-Color Gradient, or picture.

Working with Texture and Fill

Texture mapping is one of the more stunning PhotoDraw effects—it's really dramatic in 3-D objects. With PhotoDraw, you can apply different texture bitmaps to the faces, bevel, and sides of any 3-D object. Each of the textures is actually a separate graphic file, and you can even choose your own graphic files to use as textures and fills.

Using PhotoDraw Textures

For this next exercise, we'll use the textures that come with PhotoDraw. You will need to have PhotoDraw Disc 2 in your CD drive to do this, unless you have copied the contents of CD 2 to a directory on your hard drive and have changed the File Locations in the Options dialog box to reflect that directory.

Apply Texture Bitmap Fills

1 In the 3-D Fill Workpane, adjust the Placement buttons so that only the Sides button (on the left) is active.

2 In the drop-down list, choose Texture.

3 In the Texture gallery, click the ANTIQUE texture (immediately to the right of the large X in the upper left corner). The texture is applied to the side surfaces, inside and outside.

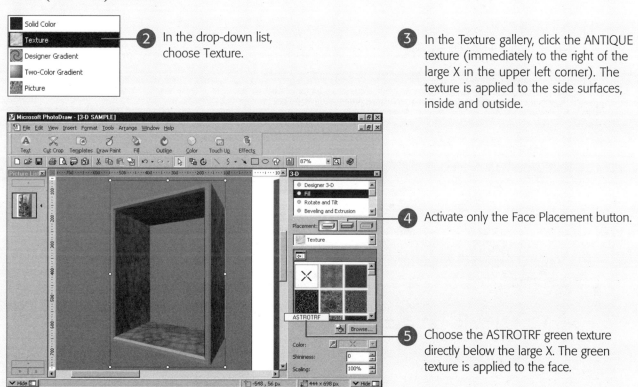

4 Activate only the Face Placement button.

5 Choose the ASTROTRF green texture directly below the large X. The green texture is applied to the face.

Using Your Own Pictures as Texture or Fill

In addition to the images in the Texture gallery, you can apply any image to an object as a texture or a picture.

Apply a Custom Texture File

1 Select the rectangle object, make a duplicate, and drag it below the original rectangle.

2 In the 3-D Workpane drop-down list, click Fill.

3 Select Texture in the Fill Type list.

4 Click the Browse button below the gallery.

5 Navigate to the chapters/chap08 folder on the companion CD and double-click the *meadow.bmp* file to apply it as a texture to the object. Depending on which Placement buttons you have selected, the image is mapped onto the parts of the object as texture. Try this with various Placement buttons active.

Apply a Custom Texture File *(continued)*

6 In the drop-down list click Picture.

7 In the chapters/chap08 folder, double-click the *forest plants.bmp* file. The picture is mapped onto the object.

8 Try using some of the pictures on the PhotoDraw CD, mapping them with different Placement buttons active. When you are done experimenting, delete the duplicate object.

Notes About Scaling

Applying 3-D effects to an object can have unexpected results. For example, look at the *flowers1.bmp* object. First select the object and use the Align Left and Align Middle tools to align it with the left side and middle of the picture space.

This image started out the same size as the picture space. However, since applying 3-D effects rotated it, the left side is now shorter and the right side is longer than the sides of the picture space (see illustration). Now if you saved your picture for use in a publication, document, or other work, the right side would be cut off at the top and bottom.

You can scale objects with 3-D effects applied to them the same way as 2-D objects—either interactively by dragging the selection rectangle control handles or in the Arrange Workpane. If this piece is to be the height of the picture space, just set the Height to 1200 pixels in the Arrange Workpane (make sure Maintain Proportions is checked first), and use the Align Center and Align Middle tools to align the object relative to the center and middle of the picture space.

Using Color, Effects and Templates

In this chapter, we'll explore several PhotoDraw tools that we haven't worked with in previous projects to round out our exploration of PhotoDraw features in this book. These include the color correction tools used for fixing up photographs and creating color effects, the touch up tools also used for repairing photographs, the distortion and transparency effects, and some designer effects. We'll also look at using templates to create a project.

Then we'll work on a project to illustrate some neat color effects, and create a postcard announcement that combines some tools we've already used. At the end of the chapter, we'll make a custom palette that enables you to create smaller graphics files useful for Web graphics.

Using Color Correction

Whether you want to fix problems or make creative adjustments to photographs, there are a considerable number of color correction tools in PhotoDraw to assist you. Often a photograph you want to use on a project might have been taken under less than ideal conditions. Or you might want to modify a picture to make it look unusual. In this chapter, you will try out and gain a basic understanding of PhotoDraw's color correction tools. Your landscape designer client is starting another business called 2Dogs AleHouse and wants you to do some work for it. He told you he has a perfect picture for their advertising and a sign over the door.

Adjusting Brightness and Contrast

The picture you were given may be perfect for advertising, but it needs a little tweaking. So first we'll fix the brightness and contrast.

Adjust Brightness and Contrast

1 Create a new picture using PhotoDraw's default blank picture choices.

2 On the Insert menu, click From File. Open the chapters/chap09 folder and insert the *2dogs.bmp* file into the picture. Drag the image object into the picture space so it is approximately centered. Save the picture to your hard drive with a name you will remember.

Judging whether PhotoDraw's Automatic corrections have done the best possible job. You must decide whether what you see is what you want the image to look like. Consider that there are endless ways an image can look "wrong" for a given purpose. PhotoDraw cannot know precisely what you need in all cases. So there will be some times when you need to make some changes yourself. The best guide is to have a clear idea of how you want an image to look. That way you are able to know which of the PhotoDraw tools will be most useful.

Aligning the 2dogs bitmap. You can also use the alignment tools on the Arrange menu to center objects in the picture space.

Adjust Brightness and Contrast

3 Drag the image onto the Picture List to create another picture that you will use for comparison later on. Save it to your hard drive. Click your original picture to make it active.

4 With the image object selected, on the Color menu, click Brightness and Contrast. The Color Workpane opens with Correct Selection highlighted and the Brightness and Contrast Effect selected.

6 Reset the Brightness to –25.

7 Reset the Contrast to 20. This helps separate the dogs from each other and from the ground.

5 Click the Automatic button. The brightness setting has changed lowering the value. In this case, the dog on the left is quite light compared to the dog on the right so Automatic did not quite work. The picture needs some additional contrast with only a moderate amount of value reduction.

Sharpening and Removing Dust and Spots

Next, we'll touch up some spots on the *2dogs.bmp* picture.

Sharpen and Remove Dust and Spots

1 On the Effects menu, click Blur and Sharpen then set the slider to 10.

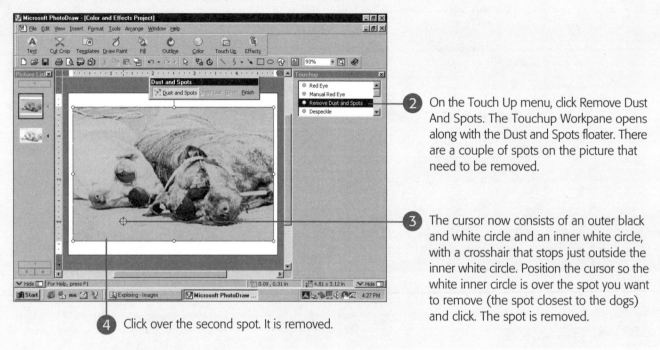

2 On the Touch Up menu, click Remove Dust And Spots. The Touchup Workpane opens along with the Dust and Spots floater. There are a couple of spots on the picture that need to be removed.

3 The cursor now consists of an outer black and white circle and an inner white circle, with a crosshair that stops just outside the inner white circle. Position the cursor so the white inner circle is over the spot you want to remove (the spot closest to the dogs) and click. The spot is removed.

4 Click over the second spot. It is removed.

Colorizing Your Pictures

The image of the two dogs was scanned from the only available photograph—a black and white print. Your client wants the dogs to have a little color, which you can do with the Colorize tool.

Colorize the Picture

1 With the image selected, on the Color menu, click Colorize. The Color Workpane appears with the Correct Selection selected.

2 Click the button at the right end of the color squares and choose More Colors. If the True Color tab is not selected, click it now. The True Color mixing controls appear.

3 You want to start with the basic color near the left side of the Hue Blackness Color Matrix (somewhere between red and yellow). Move your cursor close to the location indicated and click.

Mixing Colors

Mixing colors is accomplished in two steps. With the True Color tab selected, the More Colors dialog includes a large color area called the Hue Blackness Color Matrix, and a narrow vertical color area called the Hue Whiteness Color Matrix. In the Hue Blackness Color Matrix, choose a Hue (or color) that is close to what you want, and how much black (or neutral) is in it. Then in the Hue Whiteness Color Matrix adjust the lightness or darkness of the color. Fine-tuning can be done using the RGB controls.

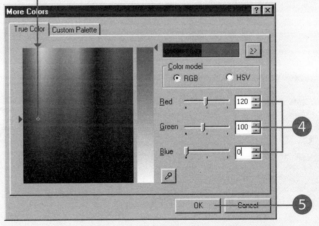

4 Fine-tune the color by changing the RGB numbers to R 120, G 100, B 0.

5 Click OK.

6 At the top of the workpane, choose Correct Selection.

7 Change the Amount slider to 100.

8 Once again, compare your picture with the original image of the two dogs. Then save your file.

Using Color, Effects and Templates

Applying Negative Color
and Adjusting Color Balance

For an upcoming office party, your client wants you to create a flyer that uses the image of the two dogs in a fun way. To create an amusing effect, we'll play with the Negative Color tool and then adjust the color balance to liven up the image and bring out the effect. Make sure the Color Workpane is active to begin this technique.

Apply Negative Color

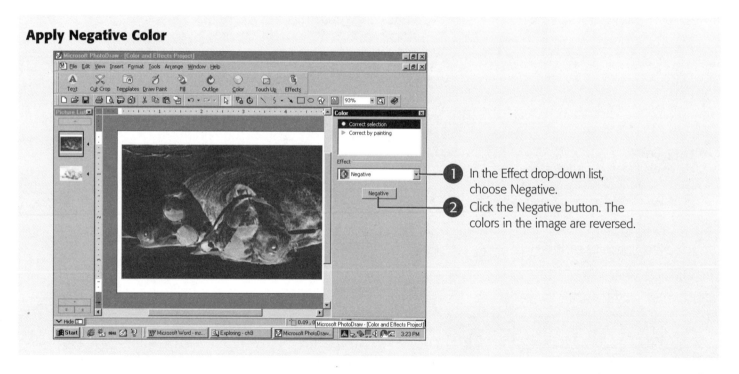

1 In the Effect drop-down list, choose Negative.

2 Click the Negative button. The colors in the image are reversed.

Adjust Color Balance

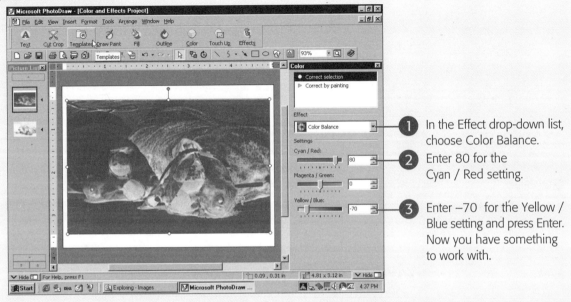

1. In the Effect drop-down list, choose Color Balance.

2. Enter 80 for the Cyan / Red setting.

3. Enter –70 for the Yellow / Blue setting and press Enter. Now you have something to work with.

Getting a different effect. To experiment a little with this picture, try cutting out the dog's sunglasses and making them different colors or adding a party announcement using the Designer Text gallery. (Click Designer Text on the Text menu when you have a text object selected.)

Working with Effects

If you've worked through the book up to this point, you've become familiar with some of PhotoDraw's effects. An effect can be defined as anything that provides enhancement to an object, so that covers a lot of ground.

On the visual menu, effects are found in the Effects menu. Shadow, Transparency, Fade Out, Blur and Sharpen, and 3-D are probably familiar to you by now. In the following section, we'll look at the Distort and Designer Effect selections from this menu. Templates can also be considered effects since they combine many other effects with a wizard approach. We'll use a couple of different templates to see how easy it is to add effects to your pictures.

Since commands in the Touch Up and Color menus enhance photographic images, these could loosely be considered effects. Earlier in this chapter, you worked with the Color menu. In a moment, we'll use some of the Touch Up menu options.

Finally, the Text menu contains several effects, such as bending text, making 3-D text, and applying Designer Text styles. You have worked with most of these in previous chapters, and we'll use them again.

Let's apply a few effects to the image of the two dogs. First we'll apply a distortion effect to the picture, then we'll cut out the image and apply negative coloration to the cut out. Following that, we'll use the Fade Out effect to add transparency, apply a design effect to emboss the picture, and finally we'll soften the edges.

Applying the Distort Effect

PhotoDraw gives you some fun distortion effects that make parts of your picture appear to bulge or warp. Let's try one of these.

On the Help menu, clicking Contents and Index will give you details about all of PhotoDraw's effects. Just click the Answer Wizard tab, type "effects" into the field, and press Enter for a list of topics.

Apply the Distort Effect

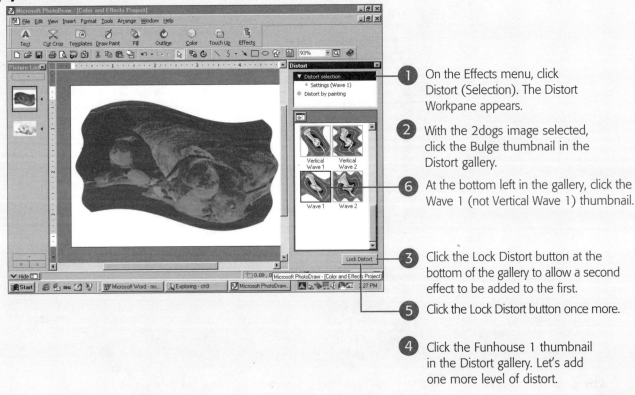

1. On the Effects menu, click Distort (Selection). The Distort Workpane appears.

2. With the 2dogs image selected, click the Bulge thumbnail in the Distort gallery.

6. At the bottom left in the gallery, click the Wave 1 (not Vertical Wave 1) thumbnail.

3. Click the Lock Distort button at the bottom of the gallery to allow a second effect to be added to the first.

5. Click the Lock Distort button once more.

4. Click the Funhouse 1 thumbnail in the Distort gallery. Let's add one more level of distort.

You can apply any number of effects to an image as long as you click the Lock button between each effect. Let's take a look at what happens when you apply an effect to a layer that has been cut out from the original.

Cut Out the Image

① On the Cut Crop menu, click Cut Out to access the Cut Out Workpane.

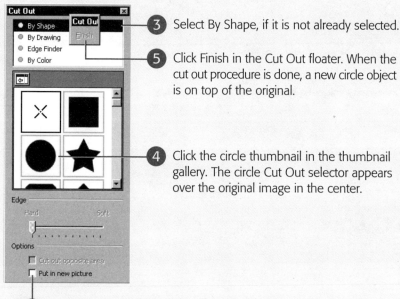

③ Select By Shape, if it is not already selected.

⑤ Click Finish in the Cut Out floater. When the cut out procedure is done, a new circle object is on top of the original.

④ Click the circle thumbnail in the thumbnail gallery. The circle Cut Out selector appears over the original image in the center.

② If the Put In New Picture check box is selected, click it to clear it.

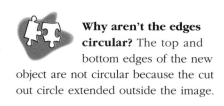

Why aren't the edges circular? The top and bottom edges of the new object are not circular because the cut out circle extended outside the image.

⑥ With the circle object selected, click Negative on the Color menu. Click the Negative button in the workpane. You now have a circle-shaped image with shades of blue over the red-orange image.

Applying Transparency

We very briefly worked with the Transparency tool earlier in the book. PhotoDraw lets you set various levels of transparency. In this case you will choose a radial Fade Out shape that applies a progressive fade out from the middle of the object outwards. By setting the Start value to 100 percent and the End value to 0 percent, the transparency is total (object not faded) in the middle and nonexistent (object completely faded) at the edges.

Apply Transparency

1 On the Effects menu, click Transparency and choose Fade Out in the workpane.

2 In the Shapes gallery, choose Radial.

3 Set Start Transparency to 100 percent and End to 0 percent.

4 Move the Center slider to approximately the second black mark from the left end.

5 When the effect is applied, choose Transparency at the top of the workpane and set it to 44. Press Enter.

Embossing and Softening Edges

The Designer Effects gallery contains over 200 design effects. Embossing is one of the parameters to these effects. You've probably seen embossing on business cards or letterheads, where an image is slightly raised from the paper. With PhotoDraw's embossing, you can even set the relief depth and the light position. Softening edges fades the outline of a picture. You can set the amount of softening.

We'll apply these to effects to our project.

Using Color, Effects and Templates

Emboss and Soften Edges

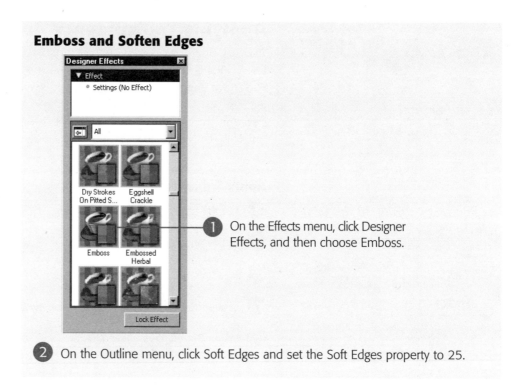

1. On the Effects menu, click Designer Effects, and then choose Emboss.

2. On the Outline menu, click Soft Edges and set the Soft Edges property to 25.

Using the Touchup Tools

The Touchup tools are useful when you are working on a photograph that is in bad shape. Each tool includes a pop-up dialog box that tells you how to use it.

Removing Scratches

PhotoDraw looks for patterns of light and dark along the path you set with the Remove Scratch tool. The quality of scratch removal depends on what the image looks like. If there is a lot of dark and light contrast along the scratch, the tool might not work so well. You will learn from experience what works and what

Why doesn't the scratch disappear? If the scratch doesn't disappear the first time, keep going over it to fill in the scratch. Note that this causes some smearing to occur, especially around any straight lines the scratch may cross.

does not. Before you begin this procedure, save and close all the pictures you have open, and then make a new picture using PhotoDraw's default settings for a blank picture.

Remove Scratches

1 Insert the *scratches.bmp* from the chapters/chap09 folder. It doesn't matter that the image size is different than the picture space—you are not going to save this file.

3 On the Touchup menu, click Remove Scratch. The Touchup Workpane appears with Remove Scratch selected and the Scratch tool floater active.

4 Leave the Width setting at 3.

5 Start with the scratch that begins in Rowan's hair. Click the point in his hair where the scratch starts, release the mouse button, and move the cursor to the other end of the scratch and click again. The scratch will be repaired.

2 There are three diagonal scratches clearly visible in this picture. Drag the image object so the scratches are in the picture space.

6 Repeat the procedure on the two remaining scratches.

7 Click Finish in the floater.

A Creative Use of Touchup

Sometimes you discover unintended uses for tools. Here is one way to use the Despeckle tool to produce an interesting effect. Let's say you want an image of a person in focus with a stylized, but recognizable background. Try this.

Customize The Despeckle Effect

1. Do a rough cut out of Rowan holding the test device and leave the new cut out where it is. Make sure Put In New Picture is unchecked in the Cut Out Workpane.

2. With the original image of Rowan selected, click Despeckle on the Touchup menu.

3. Set the Despeckle Amount to 1. After looking at the result, try setting the Amount to 2, then 3.

Using Templates

Templates are style sheets combined with wizards that give you a head start creating many common sorts of PhotoDraw projects. From the Templates icon on the visual menu, you'll find templates for Web Graphics, Business Graphics, Cards, Designer Edges, and Designer Clip Art. We'll look at the Designer Edges template and the Business Graphics template in this section.

There are a few steps to working with templates; generally, you follow the wizard from screen to screen as it guides you.

If you haven't copied the PhotoDraw Disc 2 to your hard drive, you'll need to insert that disc in your CD drive. Save and close any pictures that are currently open and open *color3.mix* from the chapters/chap09 folder.

Applying Designer Edges

Templates walk you through the process of creating a design by providing a workpane with a Next button. We'll go one step at a time as we create a Designer Edge.

 Saving time accessing PhotoDraw effects. To save time accessing PhotoDraw effects, create a directory on your hard drive and copy the contents of PhotoDraw Disc 2 to this directory. Then open the Options dialog box from the Tools menu, click the File Locations tab, and enter the directory path to the CD contents you just copied onto your hard drive. You should also clear the Prompt To insert PhotoDraw Disc 2 check box.

Apply Designer Edges—Part One

1 On the Templates menu, click Designer Edges. The Templates Workpane appears on the right and a gallery of images with Designer Edges fills the picture space and scratch space. (The program may ask for PhotoDraw CD 2.)

2 In the workpane, click Artistic.

3 In the gallery, double-click Crayon Edge. Notice that the gallery in this case does not expand or contract but fills the workspace area. Also notice that most menu items are disabled when you are using a template to create a design.

Apply Designer Edges—Part One *(continued)*

The crayon edge surrounds a temporary picture, which you will replace with your own picture in the next procedure.

Save when the wizard is finished. You cannot save your file until the wizard is finished.

Apply Designer Edges—Part Two

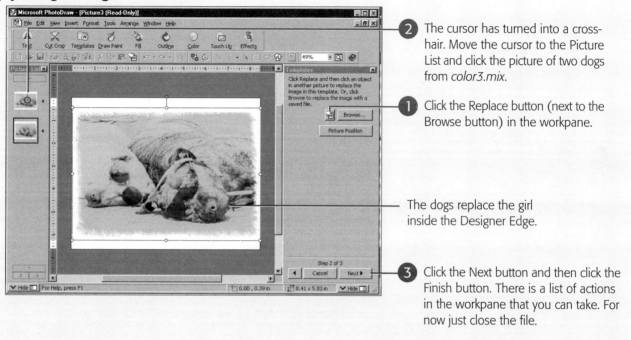

2 The cursor has turned into a cross-hair. Move the cursor to the Picture List and click the picture of two dogs from *color3.mix*.

1 Click the Replace button (next to the Browse button) in the workpane.

The dogs replace the girl inside the Designer Edge.

3 Click the Next button and then click the Finish button. There is a list of actions in the workpane that you can take. For now just close the file.

Choosing among actions in the workpane list.
The list of actions in the workpane just provide you with possible alternatives such as saving the file or printing it. You should probably always save the file first, unless you are just experimenting.

Using the Business Graphics Template

The Business Graphics template provides styles for such thing as bulletins, certificates, flyers, labels, and so on. Let's try making a flyer for advertising the 2Dogs AleHouse. Again, we'll take this one wizard panel at a time.

Using Color, Effects and Templates

Use the Business Graphics Template—Part One

1 On the Templates menu, click Business Graphics.

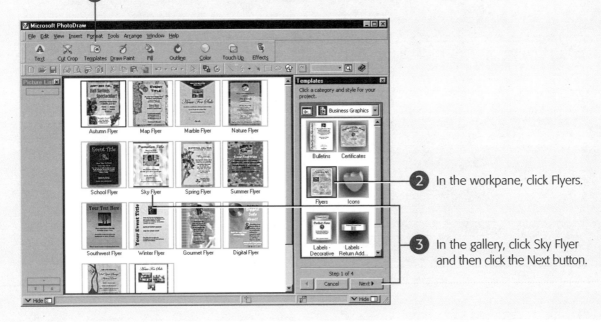

2 In the workpane, click Flyers.

3 In the gallery, click Sky Flyer and then click the Next button.

Use the Business Graphics Template—Part Two

1 Click the picture of the woman.

2 In the workpane, click the Replace button and then click the *2dogs.bmp* image in the Picture List.

3 Click the *2dogs.bmp* thumbnail in the Picture List. The *2dogs.bmp* image is resized and replaces the woman.

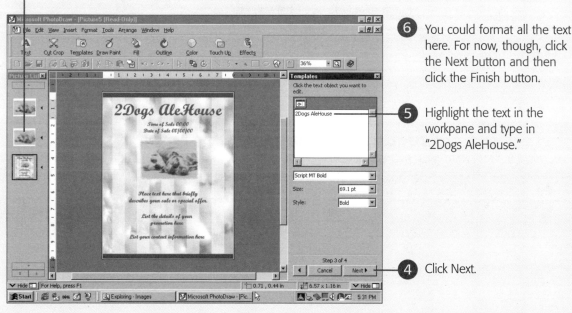

6 You could format all the text here. For now, though, click the Next button and then click the Finish button.

5 Highlight the text in the workpane and type in "2Dogs AleHouse."

4 Click Next.

Project: RL&A Postcard

The following postcard project is a "Year Two Thousand" seminar announcement for RL&Associates. In it, you will practice more ways to use some of the Effects tools. Before starting this project, close any pictures you have open.

Set Up Your Pictures

1. First, open the file *ch9.mix* in the chapters/chap09 images folder. Look at the picture a minute to see what you will create.

2. On the File menu, click New. Choose Postcard and then click OK.

3. Save the new picture to your hard drive.

Creating a Rectangle

The first thing you need to do is create the frame for the postcard.

Create a Rectangle

1 On the toolbar, click the rectangle button. The Outline Workpane with AutoShapes floater appears. The Rectangle tool is selected.

9 Choose variation 2.

8 In the Active Palette, choose a blue green—the ninth color in the second row from the bottom.

7 Choose Fill in the workpane.

6 Click the pale lavender color square that is eight from the right in the bottom row.

5 In the workpane, click the Color button and then choose Active Palette.

4 Set the Width to 14.

3 Starting about one pixel outside the upper left corner of the picture space, drag a rectangle down and to the right until it is about one pixel outside the lower right corner.

2 Zoom out so you can see all of it.

Adding Background Effects to the Postcard

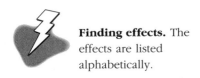

Finding effects. The effects are listed alphabetically.

You will use one of PhotoDraw's Designer Effects to create an interesting background for the postcard.

Adding Effects to the Postcard—Part One

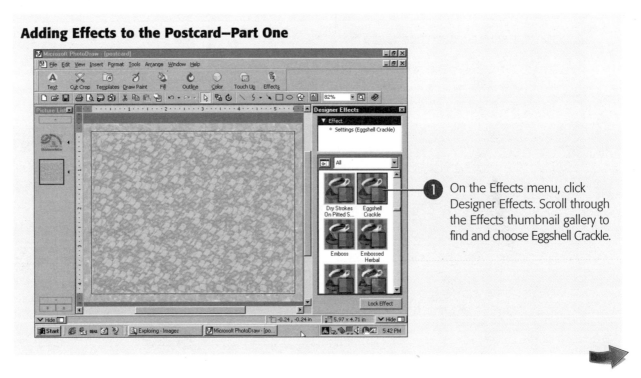

1. On the Effects menu, click Designer Effects. Scroll through the Effects thumbnail gallery to find and choose Eggshell Crackle.

Adding Effects to the Postcard—Part One *(continued)*

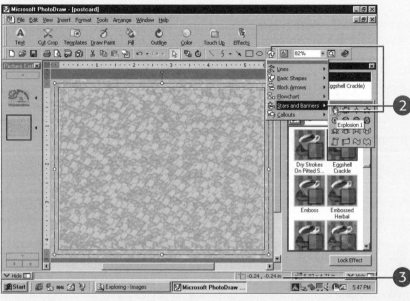

2 Click the AutoShapes button. Move the cursor down to Stars and Banners and then choose Explosion 1—the first starburst in the top row.

3 Starting in the upper left corner, drag down and to the right while watching the size information numbers on the right side of the status bar. When the numbers are at approximately 2.5 x 2.25 inches, release the mouse button.

4 Make the line Width 5 and leave the default color.

Numbers resetting. The numbers will reset to roughly 0.00, −0.02 when you release the mouse button.

Using Color, Effects and Templates

Adding Effects to the Postcard—Part One *(continued)*

⑤ Choose Fill and, in the Active Palette, choose the fourth color in the third row from the bottom—a peach color.

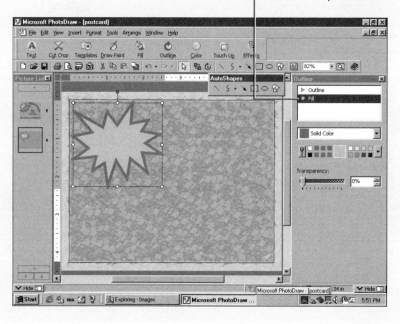

Apply an Effect

3 On the Arrange menu, click Flip.

4 Choose Flip Both.

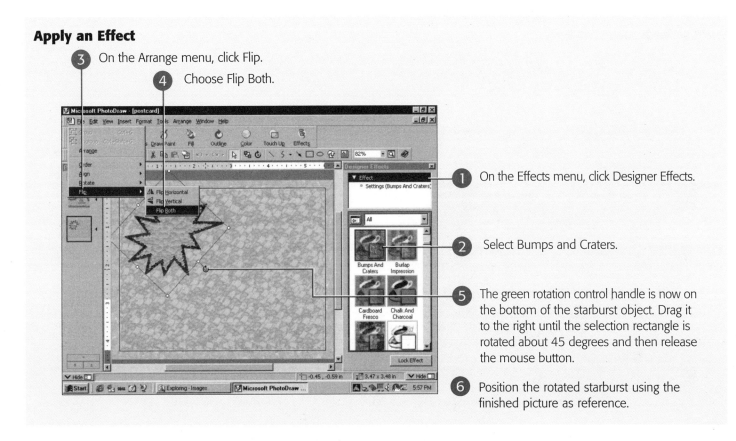

1 On the Effects menu, click Designer Effects.

2 Select Bumps and Craters.

5 The green rotation control handle is now on the bottom of the starburst object. Drag it to the right until the selection rectangle is rotated about 45 degrees and then release the mouse button.

6 Position the rotated starburst using the finished picture as reference.

Adding Text to the Postcard

The text on the postcard is a composite of three layers of text objects that create the overall effect. You will make all three layers first, then apply the effects to them, and position them for the final effect.

Add Open House Text Object

8 Make two duplicate copies and separate all three copies by the new copies up and to the right.

6 On the toolbar, click Custom Rotate. Set the Custom field to 40.

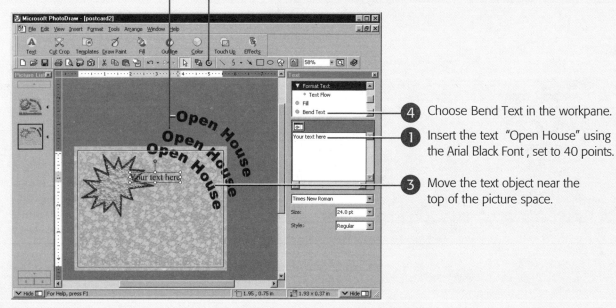

4 Choose Bend Text in the workpane.

1 Insert the text "Open House" using the Arial Black Font , set to 40 points.

3 Move the text object near the top of the picture space.

2 Make the Fill color black.

5 Under Style, choose Quarter Circle Down.

7 After the rotation is finished, move the object into position.

Getting a better view. You may want to zoom to 50 percent to get a better view of the workspace.

Now that we've created the three text objects needed to make the final "Open House" text, we need to repeat the procedure for the "January 10" and "RL&Associates" text.

Add January 10 Text Object

1 For the "January 10" text object, use the same font, 36 points, Fill black, Bend Text Quarter Circle Up, and Custom rotated 328 degrees. Make two duplicates and move them to the left onto the scratch space.

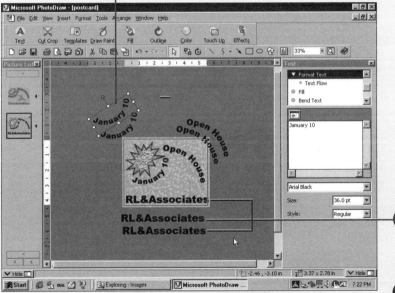

2 For the "RL&Associates" text object, use the same font, 44 points, Fill black, and no bend or rotation.

3 Position each text object as in the illustration.

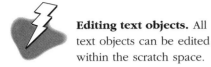

Editing text objects. All text objects can be edited within the scratch space.

Applying Effects to the Postcard

Now that all the text objects are ready, it's time to apply the effects and move them all into position.

Adding a Designer Pen

The Graphic Pen is one of the many effects available from the Designer Effects gallery. It can be applied to text as well as other objects—it makes an object look as if it has been stenciled with a pen.

Add a Designer Pen

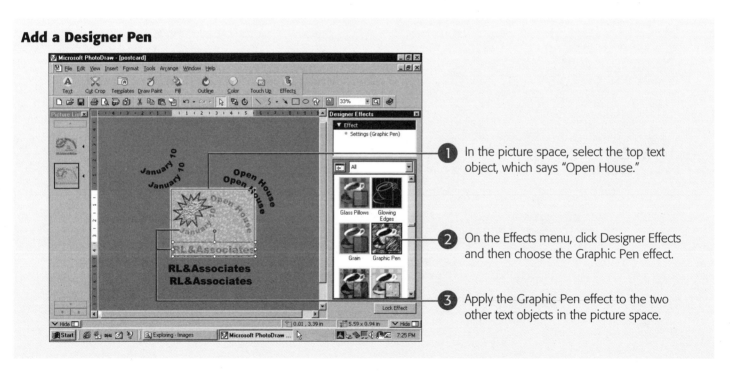

1. In the picture space, select the top text object, which says "Open House."

2. On the Effects menu, click Designer Effects and then choose the Graphic Pen effect.

3. Apply the Graphic Pen effect to the two other text objects in the picture space.

Adding Text Backgrounds

This procedure is a technique for adding a blurry background to text, which can be quite effective as a design element. Give it a try. We'll start by making the text backgrounds with the "Open House" object.

Add Text Backgrounds—First Layer

1. Move the first duplicate of "Open House" about a half-inch above the original (the one you applied the Graphical Pen to).

2. Double-click the duplicate to put it into Edit mode.

3. Choose Fill and then click the blue color square between the red color square and the large current Color Fill square. Then choose variation 6.

4. In the workpane, click Outline, then choose Straight Line. Set the Width to 5 and the color to the same as the fill.

5. On the Effects menu, click Blur and Sharpen, and set it to −40.

6. On the Effects menu, click Transparency and set the Transparency to 25 percent.

7. On the Arrange menu, click Order and then choose Send To Back. Again, on the Arrange menu, click Order and then choose Bring Forward. This places the text object below the first text object on the Z-order.

8. Move the blurry blue text object under the textured text object so that it is a little below it and to the right. Refer to the finished file for placement.

Add Text Backgrounds—Second Layer

1 Double-click the last black "Open House" text object to put it into Format Text mode.

2 Click Outline and then select Straight Line. Make the Outline 2 points, black.

3 On the Effects menu, click Blur and Sharpen and set the Blur to −30.

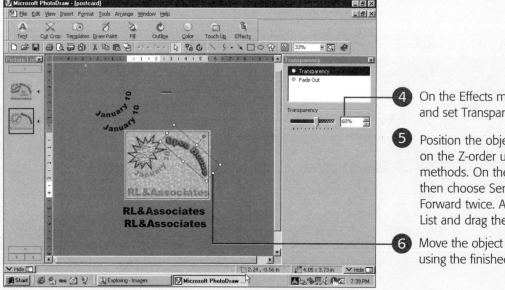

4 On the Effects menu, click Transparency and set Transparency value to 60 percent.

5 Position the object above the blue text object on the Z-order using either of the following methods. On the Arrange menu, click Order then choose Send To Back, followed by Bring Forward twice. Alternatively, open the Object List and drag the blue text object into position.

6 Move the object into position using the finished picture.

The keyboard shortcut for Bring Forward is Ctrl+Up arrow.

Choosing to use the Object List. When there are more than a couple of objects in the picture space, it may be easier to use the Object List to arrange the *z* order of objects. You will have to experiment to find the way that works best for you.

Adding "January 10" Text Object Backgrounds

We still need to add backgrounds for the remaining two "January 10" text objects. For each, repeat the above procedure, but set the values to those that follow.

For the second "January 10" blue text object:

- **Fill Color** Same as Open House blue with the same variation.
- **Outline** Straight Line, 2 points. Same color as fill.
- **Blur** -50.
- **Transparency** 40 percent.
- **Arrangement** Arrange over text on postcard. Send To Back then Bring Forward once.

For the "January 10" black text object:

- **Fill Color** Black.
- **Outline** Straight Line, 2 points. Same color as fill.
- **Blur** -40.
- **Transparency** 45 percent.

Fine-tuning the position.
Keep in mind that if you
need to fine-tune the object
positioning, you can open the Object
List, click the object you want to move,
and then click the object's selection rectangle to give it focus. Use the arrow
keys to move it 1 pixel or press the
Shift key and an arrow key for 10 pixel
increments.

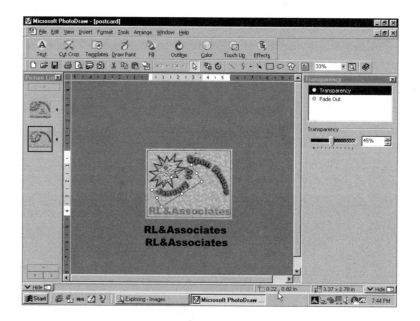

Adding the "RL&Associates" Text Object Background

The "RL&Associates" text object is slightly different. Make the finished picture active and look at that text. The blurred background is blue at the bottom, shifting to translucent lavender toward the top, and the textured text has a black, 2-point outline. Use the picture as a guide for the position of the finished objects.

Add the "RL&Associates" Text Object

1 Move the textured copy of the "RL&Associates" text object to the side.

2 Double-click the first black copy of the "RL&Associates" text object.

Add the "RL&Associates" Text Object *(continued)*

3 Choose Fill and, in the Active Palette, choose the eighth color square from the right in the bottom row—a light lavender.

4 Choose Outline, and then Straight Line and make the line 2 points. Use the same color as the fill.

5 Set Blur to −40.

6 Set Transparency to 0 percent and position the object as in the finished picture.

7 Double-click the last black text object.

8 Set the fill color to the same blue as the two other blue text background objects.

Using Color, Effects and Templates

Add the "RL&Associates" Text Object *(continued)*

9 Set the Outline to 2 points, the Blur to −40, and the Transparency to 35 percent. This object is above the lavender object on the Z-order.

10 Position as in finished picture.

11 Double-click the textured "RL&Associates" text object to select it.

12 Choose Outline, and then Straight Line, and set the Width to 2 points, black.

Adjusting Background Saturation

The background rectangle Designer Effect is so strong that it fights with the text objects, making them difficult to read. To move it back visually, lower the saturation. Lowering the saturation makes all the colors in the object more gray.

Adjusting Background Saturation

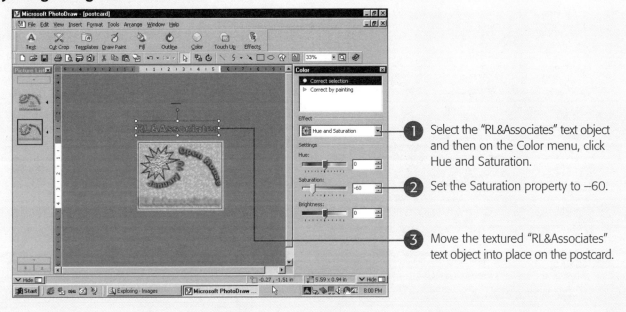

1 Select the "RL&Associates" text object and then on the Color menu, click Hue and Saturation.

2 Set the Saturation property to –60.

3 Move the textured "RL&Associates" text object into place on the postcard.

Adding a Starburst Shadow

Let's add a shadow under the starburst to give it the appearance of floating above everything else on the postcard.

Add a Starburst Shadow

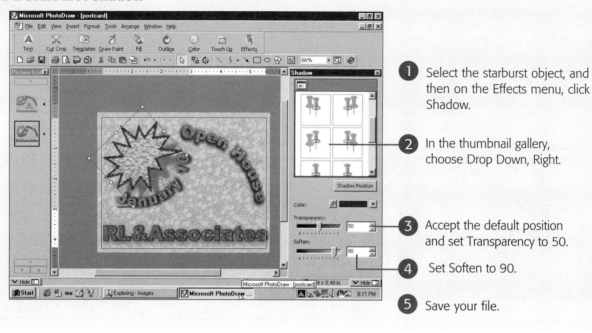

1. Select the starburst object, and then on the Effects menu, click Shadow.

2. In the thumbnail gallery, choose Drop Down, Right.

3. Accept the default position and set Transparency to 50.

4. Set Soften to 90.

5. Save your file.

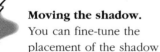

Moving the shadow.
You can fine-tune the placement of the shadow by clicking the Shadow Placement button and moving the shadow rectangle.

Add a Starburst Shadow *(continued)*

If you want, you can complete the postcard by adding the "free Y2K seminar" text in 32-point Arial Black Font. Fill it with the blue located in the Active Palette at the third row from the top, eleventh position from the right, variation 3.

Using Palletized Color

Color and shape are the two most basic elements of digital design. Ideally, all the computers in the world would be capable of displaying full 24-bit color that provides over 16 million possible colors. Unfortunately, there are still millions of computers that can display only 256 colors, and quite a few that can only display 16 colors. The color depth of your graphics card determines how many colors can be displayed.

PhotoDraw, and artwork in general on a computer, works best when you have full 24-bit capability. For those times when you know the work you are doing will not be seen in 24-bit color, PhotoDraw includes various ways to handle 256-color or 8-bit display mode. This is called palletized color. PhotoDraw enables you to make custom palettes for your pictures.

What are Palettes?

Colors displayed on a monitor are composed of red, green and blue (called RGB) primary colors. Each of these three primary colors can be displayed in any one of 256 levels of intensity that produces the various shades, tones, and tints of color. By mixing the levels of intensity of the different primary colors, over 16 million colors can be produced. Palletized pictures can only display 256 colors or less. A palette (.pal) file consists of a color lookup table that contains RGB intensity values for each of 256 colors. For instance, 256, 0, 0 represents pure red. Any picture that is palletized also has a palette color lookup table and additionally maps one of these palette colors to each pixel in the picture. If a picture displayed on your monitor uses one palette and a different palette file is loaded, the colors in the picture will change to the colors in the new palette, causing what is known as *palette flash*. It looks something like a 1960s psychedelic poster.

Why, you might ask, would anyone use palletized pictures then? There are many reasons but one very good reason is to publish them to the Web. Consider that a 24-bit image with 640 x 480 pixel resolution takes just over 900 kilobytes of storage on your hard drive. The same image reduced to 256 colors takes just over 300 kilobytes of space. That's only one-third as large. Not only does it take up less space, when downloaded from the Web, it will take only one-third or less of the time.

Creating a Custom Palette

The procedure for creating a custom palette is fairly lengthy, so it's broken into four parts. This isn't something everyone will want to do, but it's included to make things a little easier for those who do. Be sure to start with a new, blank default picture.

Create a Custom Palette—Part One

1 On the Tools menu, click Options then choose the Picture Quality tab.

6 Choose More Colors. The More Colors dialog box appears.

7 Click the Custom Palette tab. The Web Dithered palette is selected in the Color Palette drop-down list field and the colors of the Web Dithered palette are displayed in the colored squares. If anything other than Web Dithered is in the Color Palette field, click the down arrow button for that field and choose Web Dithered.

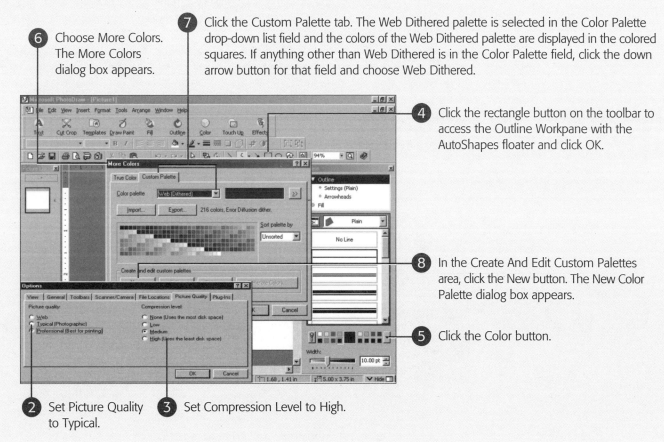

4 Click the rectangle button on the toolbar to access the Outline Workpane with the AutoShapes floater and click OK.

8 In the Create And Edit Custom Palettes area, click the New button. The New Color Palette dialog box appears.

5 Click the Color button.

2 Set Picture Quality to Typical.

3 Set Compression Level to High.

Creating a Web-Safe Palette

Notice to the right of the Export button it says "216 colors, Error Diffusion Dither." That means out of 256 possible colors in a palette, PCs running Windows and Macs have 216 common colors and 40 divergent colors. By common industry agreement, a "Web-safe" palette has been created from the 216 shared colors. This enables a content creator to produce graphics that will look the same when displayed on either platform. This palette is a fairly good general-purpose palette. However, because it contains such a diversity of colors, there are some things it does not do well. That is why the ability to make custom palettes is so useful. The colored squares in the palette represent individual items in a color lookup table. When you make a custom palette, you are creating a custom lookup table. This gets loaded into an area of memory on your graphics display card just prior to displaying the graphic image.

Create a Custom Palette–Part Two

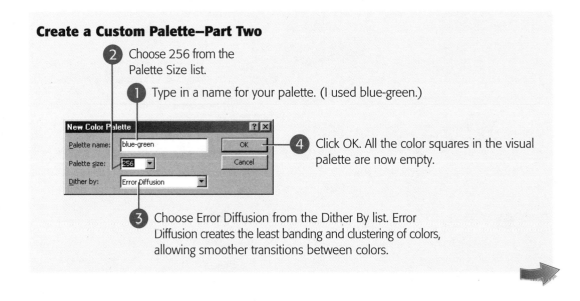

2 Choose 256 from the Palette Size list.

1 Type in a name for your palette. (I used blue-green.)

4 Click OK. All the color squares in the visual palette are now empty.

3 Choose Error Diffusion from the Dither By list. Error Diffusion creates the least banding and clustering of colors, allowing smoother transitions between colors.

Create a Custom Palette—Part Two (continued)

5 Position the cursor over the empty color square in the upper left corner—the first square of the top row and double-click. The Choose Color dialog box appears.

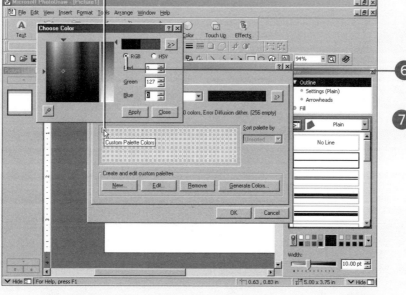

6 If the RGB button is not selected, click it to activate it.

7 Click Apply or Close to accept or reject the settings.

Creating colors in a custom palette. The custom palette you are making changes from a middle green to blue in 10 steps. For your own palettes, you can make as many or as few colors as you like, up to 236. Windows reserves 20 colors for the interface.

Create a Custom Palette—Part Three

1 In the More Colors dialog box, move the cursor to the next empty color square to the right in the top row and click.

2 In the Green field, set the value to 112.

3 In the Blue field, replace the 0 with 15.

4 Click Apply. The second square is filled with a slightly bluer green.

You will be moving to the next color square, double-clicking and changing numbers like this for the next seven squares. The procedure is identical for each square. The numbers for each square are in the following table. When you have completed these, move on to the next step.

 Colors get darker as the numbers get smaller. You will have noticed the colors getting darker as the numbers get smaller. This is how RGB color works. Lower numbers equate to darker colors and higher numbers are lighter. Another point to notice is that not all colors have equal value (lightness and darkness) when identical numbers are used. For instance, 127 blue with 0 red and green is much darker then 127 green with 0 red and blue.

Custom Palette Squares 3 – 10		
Color square no.	Green	Blue
3	87	30
4	72	45
5	57	60
6	42	75
7	37	90
8	22	105
9	7	120
10	0	150

Now that you know how to add colors to a custom palette let's continue, adding another dimension to the next ten steps. First let's see how high we need to raise the pure Blue number to make it look as light as the first Green that is 127.

Create a Custom Palette—Part Four

1 Click the next empty color square and then enter 175 in the Blue field. Leave the Red and Green numbers at 0.

2 Change the next three empty color squares to 200, 225, and 255 (respectively) in the Blue field, leaving Red and Green at 0. Somewhere between 225 and 255, the blue becomes visually as light as the original 127 Green color square.

3 Now let's briefly look at the primary and secondary colors. Double-click the next empty square and change Green to 255, and Blue to 0. Then click Apply. 255 Green is much brighter than 255 Blue.

4 Click in the next empty square and change Red to 255, Green to 0, and Blue to 0. Click Apply. Red is a very saturated color that stands out. These are the R,G,B primaries. Now let's look at the RGB secondaries: cyan, magenta, and yellow, which along with black are the colors of inks used for standard four-color printing.

5 Click the next empty square and change the numbers to Red 0, Green 255, and Blue 255. Click Apply. The result is cyan.

6 For the next square, set Red 255, Green 0, and Blue 255. The result is magenta.

7 For the last square, set Red 255, Green 255, and Blue 0. This makes yellow.

Using Color, Effects and Templates

Create a Custom Palette—Part Four *(continued)*

8 Close the Choose Color dialog box. To the right of the Export button, you see 19 Colors, Error Diffusion Dither (237 empty). That informs you that 19 colors are currently in the palette and 219 colors are unassigned.

9 Click the Export button. The Export Custom Palette dialog box appears. When you click the Export button, PhotoDraw automatically navigates to the Palettes folder.

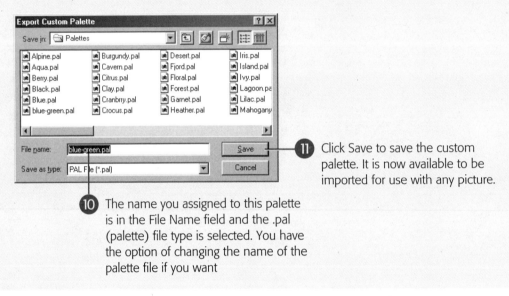

11 Click Save to save the custom palette. It is now available to be imported for use with any picture.

10 The name you assigned to this palette is in the File Name field and the .pal (palette) file type is selected. You have the option of changing the name of the palette file if you want

To use your custom palette when working on a picture, you would first access the More Colors dialog and click the Custom Palette tab. You then click the Import button, choose the custom palette you want, and click Open. The custom palette is now your Active Palette. Click OK.

PART 2

PhotoDraw Projects

Creating Web Page Graphics

The projects in this chapter guide you through the creation of several Web page graphical elements including banners, buttons, and backgrounds. You'll also find out how to create thumbnail images that link to larger pictures.

PhotoDraw contains several Web Graphic templates to get you started. We'll use templates for a banner and a button. Then we'll walk through some examples of creating banners and buttons from scratch using PhotoDraw tools you've already learned in the first part of this book.

PhotoDraw pictures are published for the Web as either JPEG (. jpeg) or GIF (.gif) files. These files are then referenced by an HTML file, also known as a Web page, which displays the pictures. The CD that accompanies PhotoDraw 2000 By Design contains sample Web pages to display the graphics you create in this chapter.

View Web pages. Browsers can view Web pages from your hard drive or CD-ROM drive as well as from a Web server.

You can double-click an HTML file in Windows Explorer to open the default browser and view that file.

About the Sample Web Pages

The graphics produced in this chapter will be used by Web pages for a fictitious resort called Desert Springs in the southwestern United States. The JPEG and GIF files you'll need for this chapter are available on Microsoft PhotoDraw 2000 CDs 2 and 3. The HTML code for these Web pages is available on the *PhotoDraw by Design* companion CD. Follow the steps in the readme.txt file on the companion CD before continuing with the project procedures in this chapter.

For the following projects, you'll create graphics with specific names that are already coded into the HTML pages. This way, when you save the file and refresh the browser, the graphic will appear on the Web page.

The following provided files make up the sample Web site:

- The home page for the Desert Springs Resort is named *index.htm*. This page displays some pictures: Ph01275k.jpg, Ph01393k.jpg, Ph02095k, and Ph01446Ja.jpg. You'll create a header graphic and a button that links to *photos.htm*.

Placeholder for banner.

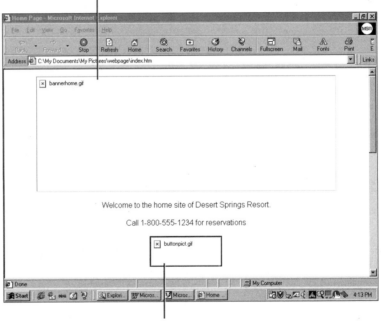

The *index.htm* home page.

Placeholder for button.

- The *photos.htm* page contains a table with thumbnail images of pictures. Each thumbnail image links to another HTML page (*picture1.htm*, for example) containing a larger version of the image in the thumbnail. The provided thumbnail graphics used in *photos.htm* are Bk0152_thumb.jpg, Bk0096_thumb.jpg, and Bk0186_thumb.jpg. You'll create the header graphic, a button that links back to *index.htm*, and you'll also create a fourth thumbnail image. In addition, you'll create a background image for this page.

Placeholder for banner.

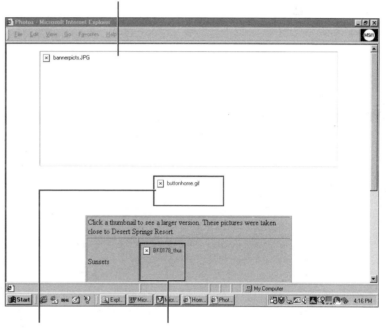

Placeholder for button.   Placeholder for thumbnail.

The *photos.htm* Web page.

◎ The file *picture1.htm* contains graphic Bk0178.jpg. Two of the buttons you create (*next.gif* and *buttonpict2.gif*) are used in this file.

@ The file *picture2.htm* contains graphic Bk0152.jpg. Three of the buttons you create (*next.gif*, *prev.gif*, and *buttonpict2.gif*) are used in this file.

@ The file *picture3.htm* contains graphic Bk00968.jpg. Three of the buttons you create (*next.gif*, *prev.gif*, and *buttonpict2.gif*) are used in this file.

@ The file *picture4.htm* contains graphic Bk0186.jpg. Two of the buttons you create (*prev.gif*, and *buttonpict2.gif*) are used in this file.

A Picture Page

Placeholder for button to previous picture.

Placeholder for button to return to *photos.htm* page.

Placeholder for button to next picture.

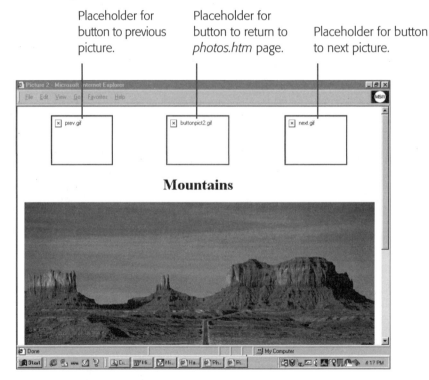

The *picture2.htm* Web page.

These are the files you'll create in this chapter and add to the Web site:

- **bannerhome.gif**   a banner used in *index.htm*
- **bannerpict.gif**   a banner used in *photos.htm*
- **buttonpict.gif**   a button used in *index.htm* (links to *photos.htm*)
- **buttonhome.gif**   a button used in *photos.htm* (links to *index.htm*)
- **Bk0178_thumb.jpg**   a thumbnail used in *photos.htm* (links to *picture1.htm*)
- **next.gif**   a button used in picture pages to link to next picture page
- **prev.gif**   a button used in picture pages to link to previous picture page
- **buttonpict2.gif**   a button used in picture pages to return to *photos.htm*

Copying the Web Files

Now that we're done taking inventory of the Web page files, let's go ahead and create the finished Web page. We'll start by copying the existing files from the accompanying CD. Then you can add the missing files to the mix.

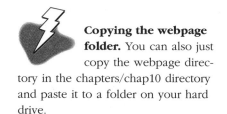

Copying the webpage folder. You can also just copy the webpage directory in the chapters/chap10 directory and paste it to a folder on your hard drive.

Copy the Files From the CD

1 Open Windows Explorer and navigate to the chapters/chap10 folder on the CD that accompanies this book.

2 Select all the files in the webpage folder and click Copy.

3 Create a folder somewhere on your hard drive named "webpage."

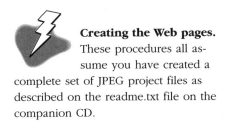

Creating the Web pages.
These procedures all assume you have created a complete set of JPEG project files as described on the readme.txt file on the companion CD.

Copy the Files From the CD *(continued)*

4 Paste the files into the webpage folder.

5 Double-click any HTML (.htm) file in the webpage folder and the Web page should open, displaying the graphics created as part of the JPEG project files. You'll see empty places for the graphics you will create.

Create a Banner

Web page banners are usually located at the top of a page—they provide the main graphical statement for the page. They generally contain text elements along with a logo, sort of like a business card or letterhead.

Because Web pages are displayed on varying sizes of screen resolution, you should design them for the lowest resolution they might encounter. This is currently considered to be 640 by 480 pixels. A banner is typically centered at the top, so a 640-pixel-wide banner will work for the smallest or largest display resolution the Web page might encounter. The height of the page isn't quite as critical (that is, not strictly restricted to 480 pixels), but most navigation buttons should appear at the top so users don't have to scroll down to jump from one page to another. A link that jumps to the top of the page is often included at the bottom of a page to minimize scrolling.

Creating a Banner Using a Template

The first banner we'll create is *bannerhome.gif*, used in the home page file *index.htm*. For this banner, we'll use a template. All template banners in PhotoDraw are 640 by 240 pixels when using Typical picture quality. You may find the height to be a little larger than you want. (It takes up half of a 640-by-480-pixel screen.) If so, you can resize the graphic later. For this exercise, we'll simply use the default. First, we'll create the banner and save it. The save operation is detailed in this procedure because you need to remember to save the graphic both as a PhotoDraw file and a GIF file. In all other parts of this project, this is assumed.

Creating the Banner

When you create a new project with a template, the Template Wizard walks you through four steps, during which you can substitute graphics and text components of the banner.

Create a Banner Using a Template—Step 1

1 Open PhotoDraw. In the opening dialog box, click the Design Template button and click OK. If PhotoDraw is already open, on the File menu, click New Template. (You might have to load PhotoDraw CD 2.)

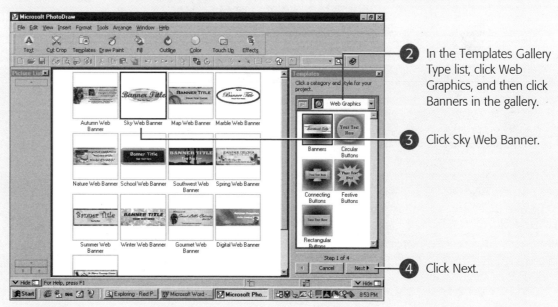

2 In the Templates Gallery Type list, click Web Graphics, and then click Banners in the gallery.

3 Click Sky Web Banner.

4 Click Next.

Create a Banner Using a Template—Step 2

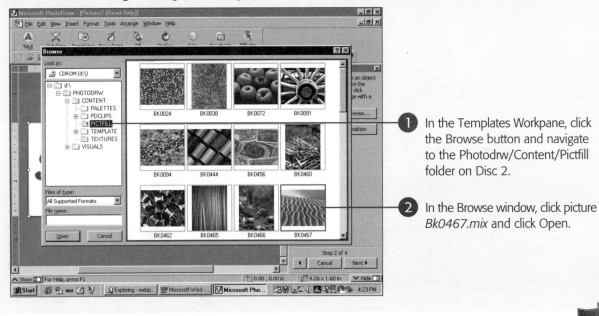

1 In the Templates Workpane, click the Browse button and navigate to the Photodrw/Content/Pictfill folder on Disc 2.

2 In the Browse window, click picture *Bk0467.mix* and click Open.

Replacing images. In this step of the wizard, you can replace the image in the banner by browsing to select another picture or you can replace any component of the picture using objects in the Picture List. For this exercise, we'll use the Browse option. Later, we'll replace the component using the Picture List.

Create a Banner Using a Template—Step 2 *(continued)*

3 Click the Position button and position the picture behind the text as shown.

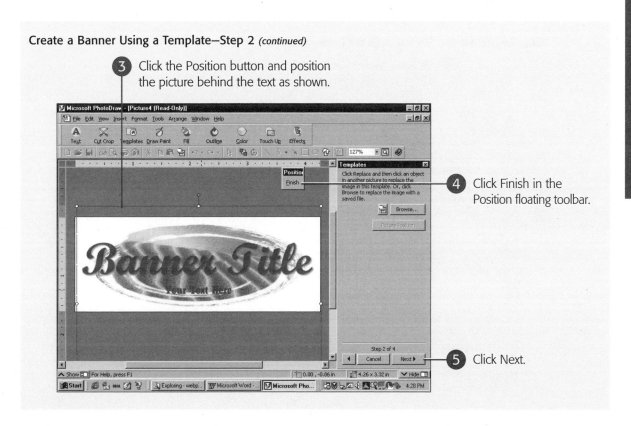

4 Click Finish in the Position floating toolbar.

5 Click Next.

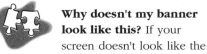

Why doesn't my banner look like this? If your screen doesn't look like the illustration, you might have selected one of the text objects before importing the picture. If so, click the back arrow button to return to the previous step and start over.

Create a Banner Using a Template–Step 3

1 Replace "Banner Title" with "Desert Springs" and change the font size to 48 points.

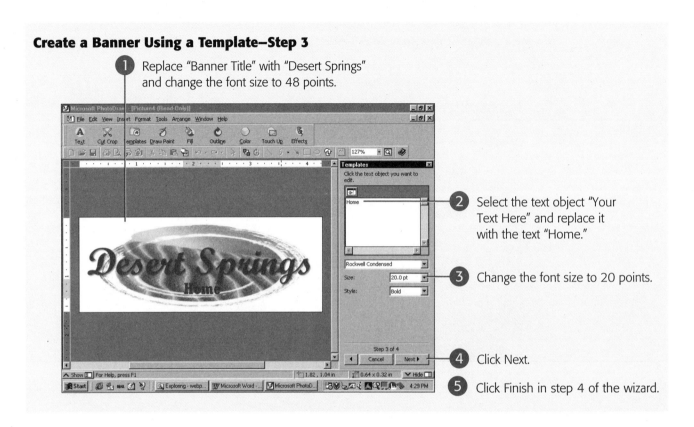

2 Select the text object "Your Text Here" and replace it with the text "Home."

3 Change the font size to 20 points.

4 Click Next.

5 Click Finish in step 4 of the wizard.

Setting Up Picture Resolution

To be safe, you should check the picture quality settings for your current PhotoDraw session. This affects the ultimate size of the graphics files.

The size of the file saved to disk depends on the picture quality setting you use in PhotoDraw and the type of file you save it as (GIF or JPEG). The Picture Quality tab in the Options dialog box offers three types of resolution. Normally you should leave this set at Typical (Photographic), which produces 150 pixels per inch. Setting this to Web provides 96 pixels per inch resolution—this creates smaller graphics files with lower resolution.

When using a banner template, however, the size of the banner or button is predetermined in inches and assumes the Typical picture quality setting. For example, banners should be 640 pixels wide and are therefore created at 4.27 inches by default (4.27 inches multiplied by 150 pixels per inch is 640 pixels). If you choose Web picture quality, the width will be only 410 pixels (4.27 inches multiplied by 96 pixels per inch). If you choose Typical picture quality, you can always create smaller pictures when you save as GIF or JPEG files; however, you cannot save at a larger resolution than the picture quality you have chosen.

Set Up Picture Resolution

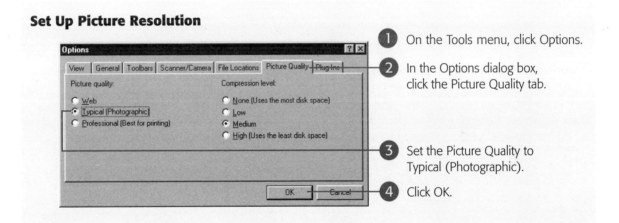

1. On the Tools menu, click Options.

2. In the Options dialog box, click the Picture Quality tab.

3. Set the Picture Quality to Typical (Photographic).

4. Click OK.

Saving the Template Banner

You should always save a Web graphic as both the file for the Web page and as a PhotoDraw (.mix) file so you can make changes to individual components later. In this case, we'll use the name *"bannerhome.gif"* for the home page banner created in this project. This filename is used in our sample Web page, so if you save your banner with that name, you can view it by pointing your browser to *index.htm*.

Save the Banner as a GIF File

1 On the File menu, click Save As.

2 In File Name, replace the default name with "bannerhome."

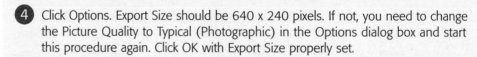

3 In Save As Type, select GIF (*.gif).

4 Click Options. Export Size should be 640 x 240 pixels. If not, you need to change the Picture Quality to Typical (Photographic) in the Options dialog box and start this procedure again. Click OK with Export Size properly set.

5 Click Save. (Click Yes again when the Warning dialog box appears.)

Viewing your banner in a Web page. To see your banner in a Web page, open the *index.htm* file (in the webpage directory you created) with your browser.

Save the Banner as a MIX File

1 On the File menu, click Save As.

2 In the Save As dialog box, navigate to the webpage folder. (It should be visible by default.)

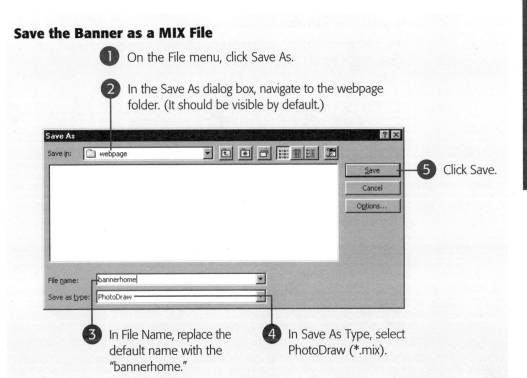

5 Click Save.

3 In File Name, replace the default name with the "bannerhome."

4 In Save As Type, select PhotoDraw (*.mix).

Save the Banner as a MIX File *(continued)*

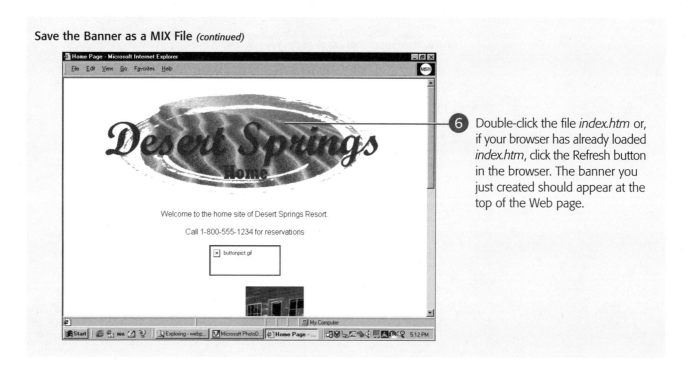

6 Double-click the file *index.htm* or, if your browser has already loaded *index.htm*, click the Refresh button in the browser. The banner you just created should appear at the top of the Web page.

Resizing and Positioning a picture. To quickly resize and position the picture, click Arrange on the Arrange menu, clear the Maintain Proportions check box, and enter a height of 250 pixels and a width of 650 pixels. Then use the align tools to center the graphic.

Creating Custom Banners

Technically, you create a custom banner every time you use a template and modify it. However, we'll use the term "custom banner" to mean a banner you create without using a template. It's quite easy to create banners from scratch with PhotoDraw, since they are essentially just text and pictures. There is even a Banner picture type in the Picture dialog box. The banner we're about to create is fairly simple but there are many ways you can create banners. For some ideas, see "Creating Custom Buttons" later in this chapter. Banners are larger and generally more complex than buttons, but the same sorts of techniques apply to creating both—they use many of the PhotoDraw tools and tricks you've encountered so far in this book.

Creating the Banner

The default Banner picture type is 600 by 64 pixels. We'll make this the same size as the custom banner for consistency, then add a picture, add a fade effect to the picture, and add text. This banner file—*bannerpicts.jpeg*—is used in *photos.htm*.

Create the Graphic

1 On the File menu, click New and click Banner in the Picture dialog box.

2 On the File menu, click Picture Setup, set the Width to 640 pixels, the height to 240 pixels, and click OK.

3 On the Insert menu, click PhotoDraw Content. Navigate to the Photodrw/Content/Pdclips/Textures/Stone folder on Disc 2 and insert the picture labeled TX0257.MIX.

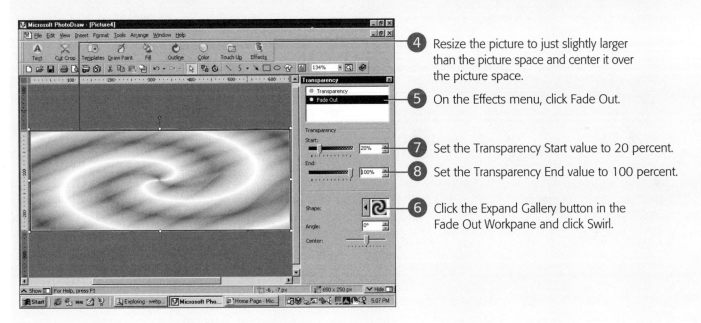

4 Resize the picture to just slightly larger than the picture space and center it over the picture space.

5 On the Effects menu, click Fade Out.

7 Set the Transparency Start value to 20 percent.

8 Set the Transparency End value to 100 percent.

6 Click the Expand Gallery button in the Fade Out Workpane and click Swirl.

Add Text

1 In the Picture List, open the Object List for *bannerhome.mix*.

4 Double-click Home and change the text to "Pictures."

2 Drag the "Desert Springs" text object into the picture and position it just above the middle.

3 Drag the "Home" text object into the picture and position it just below "Desert Springs."

Saving in different formats. Saving a graphic as a GIF creates a file with a smaller number of colors (based on the Web palette). This creates files that are smaller than uncompressed JPEG files, which use higher color depth. However, JPEG files can be compressed and GIF files cannot. Experiment with saving files as both file types (using different JPEG compression settings) to find the best compromise between file size and picture quality.

 Seeing your banner in a Web page. To see your banner placed in a Web page, open the *photo.htm* file (in the webpage directory you created) with your browser. Or, if *index.htm* is already loaded, click the *buttonpic.gif* button in the center of the page. (There is no graphic for this button yet.)

Saving the Banner

Saving this banner is similar to saving the template banner—with one exception. This banner looks better as a JPEG file than when saved with a Web palette.

Save the Banner

1 On the File menu, click Save As.

2 In the Save As dialog box, navigate to the webpage folder you created earlier.

5 Click Save. (Click Yes again when the Warning dialog box appears.)

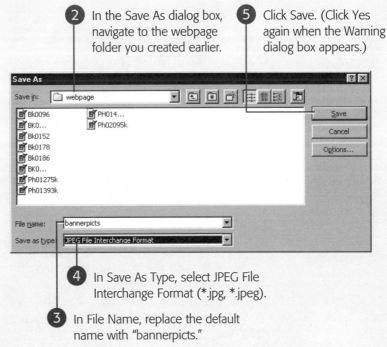

4 In Save As Type, select JPEG File Interchange Format (*.jpg, *.jpeg).

3 In File Name, replace the default name with "bannerpics."

6 Save your file a second time as a PhotoDraw (*.mix) file with the name "bannerpics.mix."

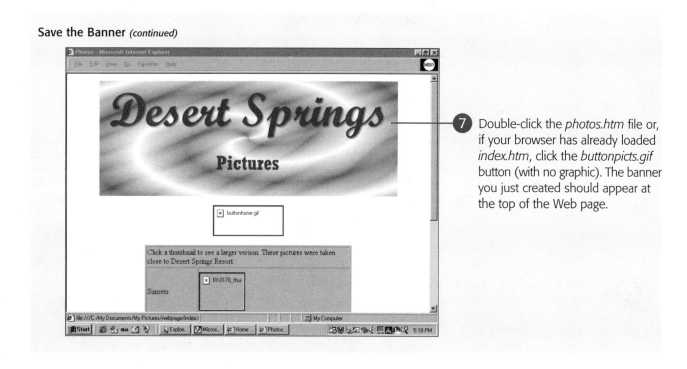

⑦ Double-click the *photos.htm* file or, if your browser has already loaded *index.htm*, click the *buttonpicts.gif* button (with no graphic). The banner you just created should appear at the top of the Web page.

Create a Background

As with the custom banner, we'll use the pictures page (*photo.htm*) to display the background. Background images are tiled on a Web page. You can create an image larger than your Web page to avoid the tiling effect, but that will create a larger file that takes longer to download. In this example, we'll use a smaller image, saved as a JPEG file to maintain color depth. We'll apply fade out to make the tiled pictures blend together better and stand out less from the background.

The *photo.htm* file is already coded to look for a background file named *backgrnd1.jpg*, so any file we create with that name will be applied as the background image. Feel free to experiment with different backgrounds by creating any mix file and saving it in the webpage directory as a JPEG file named *backgrnd1.jpg*.

Create a Background Image

1 Create a new default picture in PhotoDraw, then open the Picture Setup dialog box, and set the Width to 300 pixels and the Height to 200 pixels.

2 On the Insert menu, click PhotoDraw Content. Navigate to the Photodrw/Content/ Pdclips/Nature folder on Disc 2 and insert the cactus picture labeled "BK0160.MIX."

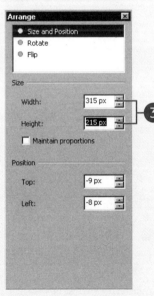

3 On the Arrange menu, click Arrange and set the size of the image to 315 by 215 pixels. (Make sure Maintain Proportions is not selected.)

4 Center the picture over the picture space using the Align Center and Align Middle tools.

Create a Background Image *(continued)*

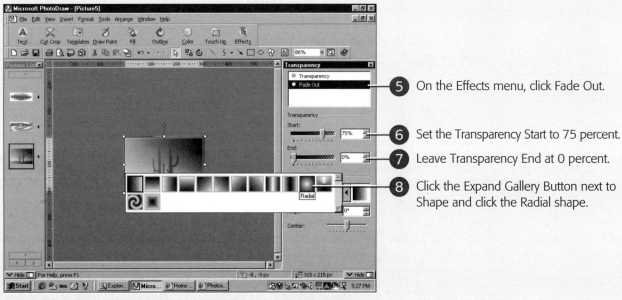

⑤ On the Effects menu, click Fade Out.

⑥ Set the Transparency Start to 75 percent.

⑦ Leave Transparency End at 0 percent.

⑧ Click the Expand Gallery Button next to Shape and click the Radial shape.

⑨ Save the file as *"backgrnd1.mix"* and then again as a JPEG file named *"backgrnd1.jpg"*.

Refresh your browser.
To see your background on the Web page, refresh the browser.

Create Buttons

This project uses two different button types. The two main HTML pages—*index.htm* and *photos.htm*—each have buttons that link to each other. We will begin by creating these two buttons—one with the text "Home," used in *photos.htm* to jump to *index.htm*, and the other with the text "Pictures," used in *index.htm* to jump to *photos.htm*. We'll use the Rectangle button template to create these two buttons.

The other set of buttons can be found in the picture files. Picture files (*picture1.htm*, *picture2.htm*, and so on) are linked to the *photo.htm* page by thumbnails. Each of the picture files contains a large version of the picture along with navigation buttons at the top that enable a viewer to return to the *photo.htm* file, go to the next picture file, or go to the previous picture file. You will create these three buttons (*next.gif*, *prev.gif*, and *buttonpict2.gif*) using AutoShapes, a two-color gradient fill, and text.

Creating Buttons Using Templates

First we'll create rectangular buttons for the *index.htm* and *photo.htm* pages. This procedure is very similar to the way we created the banner template, so we will not go into as much detail as we did earlier.

Create a Button Using a Template

1 On the File menu, click New Template and in the Templates Gallery Type list, click Web Graphics, then click Rectangular Buttons in the gallery.

2 Click Southwest Rectangle Button, then click Next.

3 Click Next in Step 2 of the wizard.

Create a Button Using a Template *(continued)*

④ Replace "Your Text Here" with the word "Home" and set the font size to 20 points. Click Next and then click Finish.

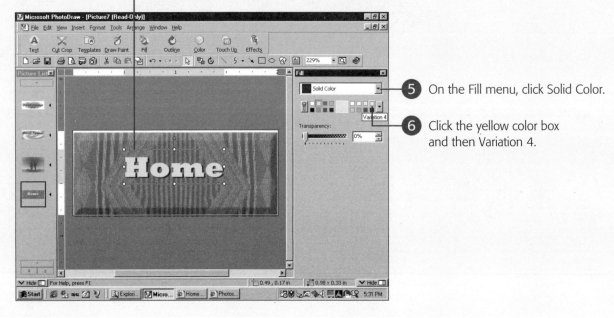

⑤ On the Fill menu, click Solid Color.

⑥ Click the yellow color box and then Variation 4.

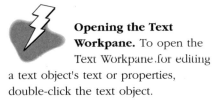

Opening the Text Workpane. To open the Text Workpane for editing a text object's text or properties, double-click the text object.

Save the Home Button File

1 On the File menu, click Save As.

3 Select GIF (*.gif) as the file type, and then click the Options button.

2 Type in "buttonhome" as the file name.

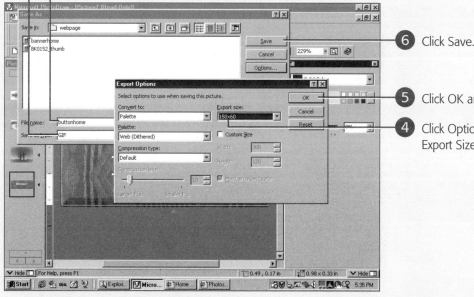

6 Click Save.

5 Click OK and then click Yes.

4 Click Options and set the Export Size to 150 x 60.

7 Save the picture again as "*buttonhome.mix*".

Save the Home Button File *(continued)*

The Home button on the *photos.htm* page.

Viewing the button.
You can see the button by viewing the *photo.htm* file. Refresh the browser if this file is already loaded.

If your button isn't showing up on the Web page it may be because of a simple typing error. The *photos.htm* file is coded to look for a file named *buttonhome.gif* in the same folder as *photos.htm*. Open Windows Explorer and make sure your button file has the correct name and resides in this folder. Be sure to refresh the browser to pick up your changes.

Create and Save the Pictures Button

1 Double-click the word "Home" in the *buttonhome.mix* file to open the text editor.

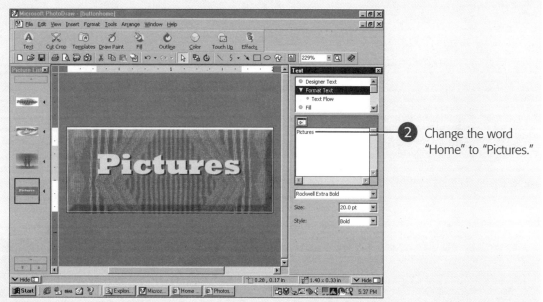

2 Change the word "Home" to "Pictures."

3 Save the file as *"buttonpict.mix"*.

4 Save the file again as *"buttonpict.gif"*, using the same procedure as for the previous button.

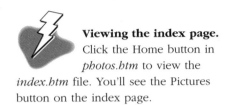

Viewing the index page.
Click the Home button in
photos.htm to view the
index.htm file. You'll see the Pictures
button on the index page.

Create and Save the Pictures Button *(continued)*

The Pictures button on the *index.htm* home page.

Creating Custom Buttons

The two buttons you just made were almost too easy, since you used a button template and used the default picture. You won't always be that fortunate, however, and you'll probably need to create buttons from the ground up at some point. There are as many ways to create buttons for Web pages as there are tools in the PhotoDraw arsenal. Some of the most common approaches to creating buttons in PhotoDraw are listed below. All of these techniques work equally well for banners:

@   Place a photograph or piece of clip art over a rectangular picture space and add text.

@   Use AutoShapes to create a shape that surrounds text, then use an interesting fill and text.

@   Use Cut Out or Erase to cut an interesting shape from a picture, put it into the picture space, and add text.

@   Use text (instead of a picture), but make the text colorful or artistically styled (for example, use 3-D text or Designer Text). Make the background a two-color gradient fill.

@   Add effects to any of the above techniques to create unique buttons.

In the next part of this project, we'll use AutoShapes and text to create three button graphics to go in the picture files. The files we will create are:

@   **next.gif**   a right-pointing arrow that links to the next picture file

@   **prev.gif**   a left-pointing arrow that links to the previous picture file

@   **buttonpict2.gif**   an arrow, pointing up, that links to the *photo.htm* file to return to the picture list

In the next three procedures, you'll create *next.gif* from scratch, modify *next.gif* and save it as *prev.gif*, and then modify *prev.gif* and save it as *buttonpict2.gif*. As you modify each button to make the next, make sure you save the changes as the new name and not the old.

Create the Next Button

1 Create a new default picture in PhotoDraw. Open the Picture Setup dialog box, set the Width to 130 pixels and the Height to 100 pixels, then click OK. Zoom to Fit Picture Area.

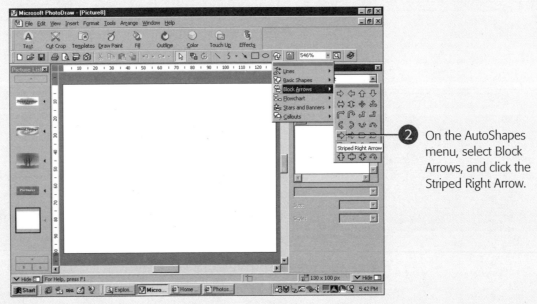

2 On the AutoShapes menu, select Block Arrows, and click the Striped Right Arrow.

3 In the Outline Workpane, select Plain menu, Straight Line, and set the line Width to 1 point

Create the Next Button *(continued)*

4 Draw an arrow that just fills the picture space.

6 Add two text objects, one each with the words "Next" and "Picture" in a 10-point, Verdana regular text and arrange them as shown.

5 Click Fill at the top of the Outline menu and select Two-Color Gradient. Set the Start color to Yellow and the End color to Red.

7 Save the file as both *next.gif* and *next.mix*.

Create the Previous Button

① Select the arrow object.

② On the Arrange menu, click Flip and then click Flip Horizontal. The button now faces the opposite direction.

③ Double-click the word "Next" and change it to "Previous."

Why should I wait to save in the final step?
You'll save the changes you're making to this file as a new file name in the final step. Saving before then will overwrite the current file with these changes.

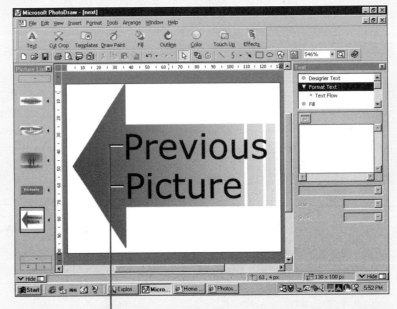

④ Align the words as shown so that the first letters of each word line up with the back of the arrowhead.

⑤ Save the file as both *"prev.gif"* and *"prev.mix"*.

Create the Return to Pictures Button

1 On the Arrange menu, click Rotate Right.

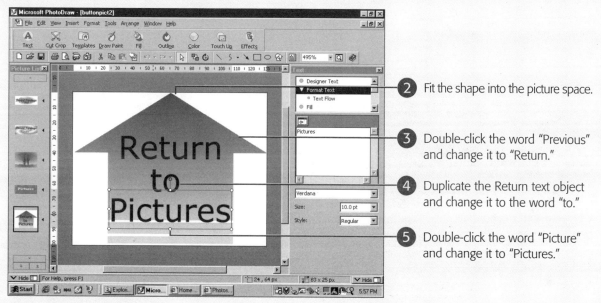

2 Fit the shape into the picture space.

3 Double-click the word "Previous" and change it to "Return."

4 Duplicate the Return text object and change it to the word "to."

5 Double-click the word "Picture" and change it to "Pictures."

6 Position the words as shown.

7 Drag the diamond handle on the shape to make the base of the arrow wide enough for the widest word ("Pictures").

8 Save the file as both *"buttonpict2.gif"* and *"buttonpict2.mix"*.

Create the Return to Pictures Button *(continued)*

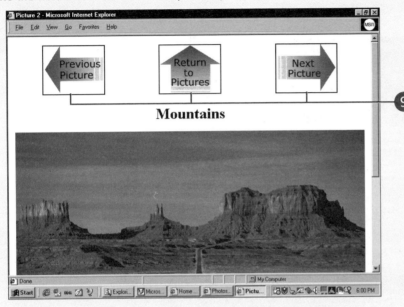

9 If your browser has already loaded *index.htm*, click the *buttonpict.gif* button in the browser, then click the second thumbnail picture (Bk0152_thumb.gif) to open *picture2.htm*. You should see the three buttons you just created at the top of the Web page.

Create Thumbnails

The final project in this chapter is fairly simple. By now you've seen and used the thumbnails in *photos.htm* and you've probably noticed that one is missing. PhotoDraw makes it very easy to save a thumbnail-sized image using the Save For Use In Wizard.

When should I use the Save For Use In Wizard?
Use this wizard any time you don't know exactly how you want to save your Web graphic. It analyzes your graphic and provides you with information about possible compression and file type choices.

Saving a Picture as a Thumbnail Image

The missing thumbnail is the first one in the Picture List (Bk0178_thumb.jpg) on the *photos.htm* page. This thumbnail links to *picture1.htm*, which imports the file Bk0178.jpg. In this procedure, you'll open Bk0178.jpg and use the Save For Use In Wizard to save it as a thumbnail.

Save the Picture as a Thumbnail

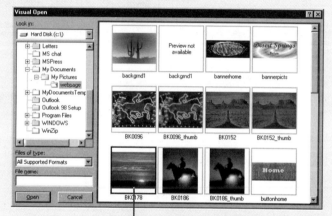

1 On the File menu, click Visual Open and double-click the sunset picture (Bk0178.jpg) in the webpage directory to open the file.

2 On the File menu, click Save For Use In.

3 Select the option labeled On The Web as a thumbnail and click Next.

Save the Picture as a Thumbnail *(continued)*

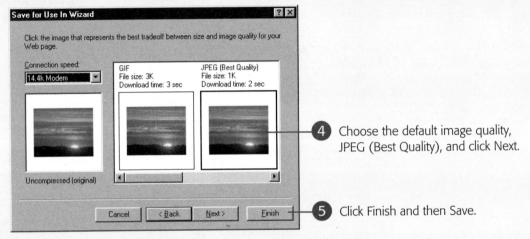

④ Choose the default image quality, JPEG (Best Quality), and click Next.

⑤ Click Finish and then Save.

⑥ In the File Name box, change the name "Bk0178" to "Bk0178_thumb" and click Save.

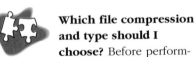

Which file compression and type should I choose? Before performing Step 6, take a look at the possible options. A thumbnail is a small graphic so there isn't much difference between the file sizes of the various options; for larger graphics you'll notice distinct differences between file sizes.

Save the Picture as a Thumbnail *(continued)*

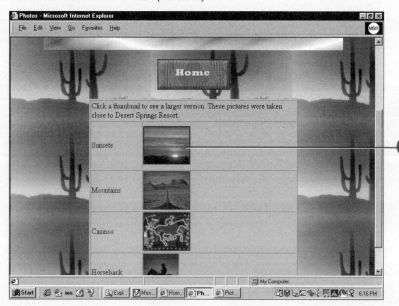

7 To view the thumbnail, open *photos.htm*. (Click Return To Pictures if your browser is still viewing *picture2.htm*.)

Creating Personal Office Supplies

In this chapter, we will make several styles of personalized stationery and office supplies. We will create:

@ Letterhead stationery using decorative fonts

@ Disk labels

@ Watermark stationery and matching envelopes

@ A ToDo list

The techniques demonstrated in this chapter can be used to create an entire collection of matching stationery, envelopes, invitations, grocery lists, and so on.

Create a set of watermark stationery, envelopes, mailing labels, or ToDo and grocery lists as gifts for friends. Organize your household floppy disks by creating a set of labels for each person. As a family activity, children enjoy being included in the design choices for their label.

Personalizing stationary. Your personalized stationery can include favorite quotes or a graphic. Businesses can feature logos, slogans, current sale items, or other topical information. And, once created, the stationery can be changed on demand and is available immediately—no need to reorder from a commercial source.

Creating Letterhead Stationery

In this project, we'll create a letterhead on letter-sized paper. This project has many applications as well as almost endless design possibilities. And, as is true with most Microsoft PhotoDraw projects, it can be easily changed to suit new situations, such as changing seasons or special events.

This project uses a mixture of fonts. The user's name is created with a designer font while the address and other information are in a simpler, smaller font.

Create the Letterhead Stationery

1 Open PhotoDraw. On the File menu, click New and select Letter. A blank letter form appears.

2 Insert a text object with information for the first line only—use your name for this example.

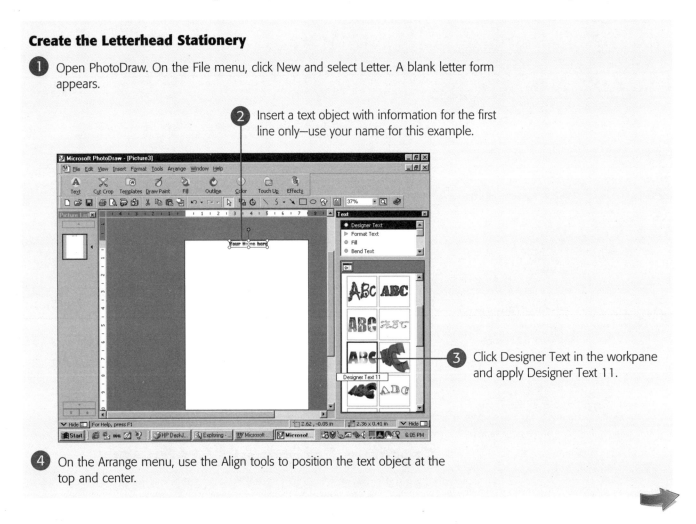

3 Click Designer Text in the workpane and apply Designer Text 11.

4 On the Arrange menu, use the Align tools to position the text object at the top and center.

5 Create a second text object with your address.

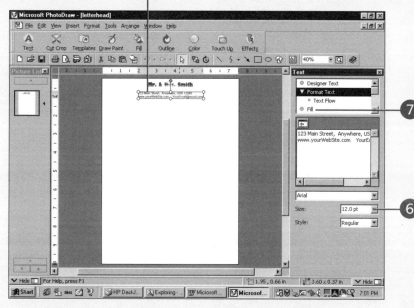

7 With the second text object selected, click Fill in the workpane. Apply a color to the text object that matches the name object. This example used variation 6 of yellow.

6 Set the size of the font to 12 points and position this object below the first object.

8 Adjust the size and position of the two text objects by using the handles and Align tools. Group the two text objects together and nudge them down from the top twice (to allow for the printer margin) using the arrow keys.

9 Save your .mix file with a unique name.

Creating a Personalized Disk Label

Personalized disk labels are useful when you have disks for several projects and need to identify them quickly. Personalized labels can also be handy to identify and separate disks belonging to family members. They are also handy when distributing information to friends or customers. To aid in the identification of disks that belong to different projects or people, you can insert unique graphics for each project. Once you have created the basic framework for the disk label, it is easy to change the name or image.

This project is easy and quick to do using built-in PhotoDraw tools. We will use the 3.5-inch disk size and a selection from the Decorative Labels template to create a personalized disk label for someone who likes frogs.

The template to create a disk label takes you through the process in just a few steps. After you select the type of label and the background, you insert a graphic and then the text. The graphic can be of your own creation or one of PhotoDraw's images. The text can be anything you want. Once the wizard has finished, you can modify the text, the graphic, and the background as you need.

For this project, you will need Avery disk labels for your printer.

Create a Personalized Disk Label

To find out what type of label you need, click Print Reprints on the File menu. The Reprints template appears. This project uses Avery 8196 labels for ink-jet printers. You can exit the wizard by clicking Cancel.

Using the Business Graphics Wizard

The wizards available in PhotoDraw provide powerful timesaving tools to create many types of office supplies. This project uses a built-in style to quickly create a personalized disk label.

Use the Business Graphics Wizard

1 Select New Template on the File menu.

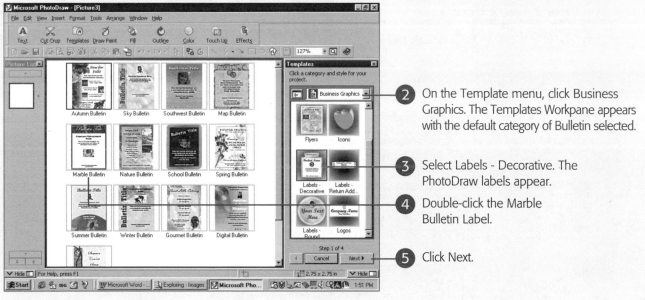

2 On the Template menu, click Business Graphics. The Templates Workpane appears with the default category of Bulletin selected.

3 Select Labels - Decorative. The PhotoDraw labels appear.

4 Double-click the Marble Bulletin Label.

5 Click Next.

Use the Business Graphics Wizard *(continued)*

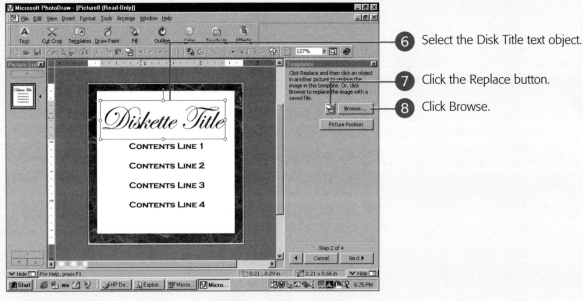

6. Select the Disk Title text object.

7. Click the Replace button.

8. Click Browse.

9. Insert PhotoDraw Disc 2 and navigate to the Photodw/Content/Pdclips/Animals folder.

10. Click the frog picture then click Open. The image of the frog replaces the text.

11. Click Next. At this point, you can edit the text objects if you want. You will make further adjustments to the image, the background, and the text later—so for now just click Next and then click Finish.

Changing the Background Color of the Label

Now we will change the background to a pale green color by inserting a rectangle and using the Eyedropper tool to tint it with green from the border. You can change the background color of the picture space instead of inserting and tinting the rectangle, but we want the color to match the border.

Change the Background Color

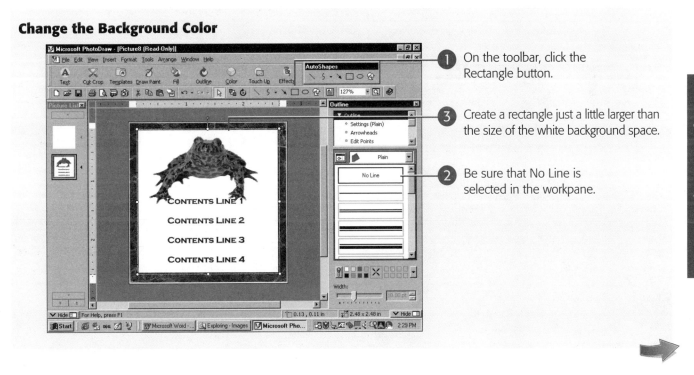

1 On the toolbar, click the Rectangle button.

3 Create a rectangle just a little larger than the size of the white background space.

2 Be sure that No Line is selected in the workpane.

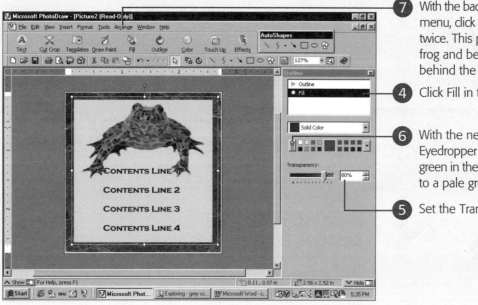

7 With the background selected, on the Arrange menu, click Order then click Send Backwards twice. This puts the background behind the frog and behind the text object, but not behind the base of the label.

4 Click Fill in the workpane.

6 With the new rectangle selected, click the Eyedropper tool to select it, then click a light green in the frame. The background changes to a pale green.

5 Set the Transparency to 80 percent.

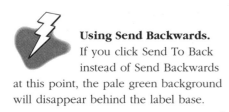

Using Send Backwards. If you click Send To Back instead of Send Backwards at this point, the pale green background will disappear behind the label base.

Changing the Label Text

This label is intended for the use of a family member, so it only needs the person's name and a couple of lines on which the contents can be written. The name and the contents lines will be two separate text objects, which will allow us to apply different effects to each element.

Change the Text on the Label

1 Double-click the text object. The Text Workpane opens. Change the text as you want; in this case, type "Property of Bobby."

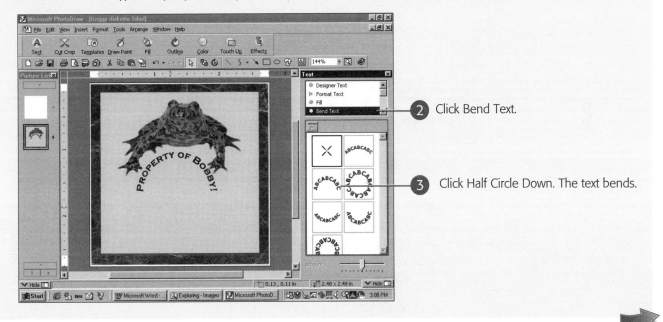

2 Click Bend Text.

3 Click Half Circle Down. The text bends.

Creating Personal Office Supplies

Change the Text on the Label *(continued)*

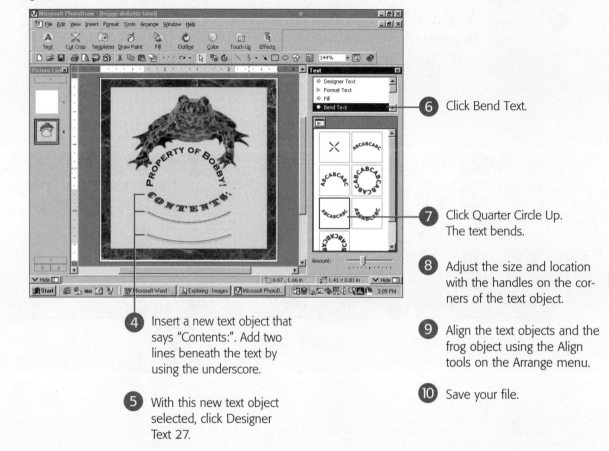

⑥ Click Bend Text.

⑦ Click Quarter Circle Up. The text bends.

⑧ Adjust the size and location with the handles on the corners of the text object.

④ Insert a new text object that says "Contents:". Add two lines beneath the text by using the underscore.

⑤ With this new text object selected, click Designer Text 27.

⑨ Align the text objects and the frog object using the Align tools on the Arrange menu.

⑩ Save your file.

Printing the Disk Label

Now you are ready for the final alignment of objects on the disk label. Then you can print your label using the Reprints Wizard.

Print the Disk Label

1 On the File menu, click Print Reprints. The Reprints Wizard appears. Do not put your disk printer paper in the printer yet. We will print a test sheet first.

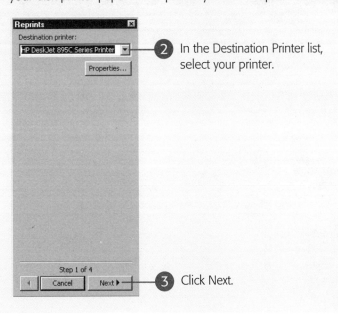

2 In the Destination Printer list, select your printer.

3 Click Next.

Print the Disk Label *(continued)*

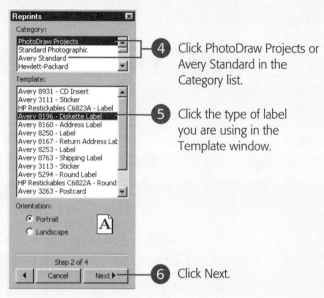

④ Click PhotoDraw Projects or Avery Standard in the Category list.

⑤ Click the type of label you are using in the Template window.

⑥ Click Next.

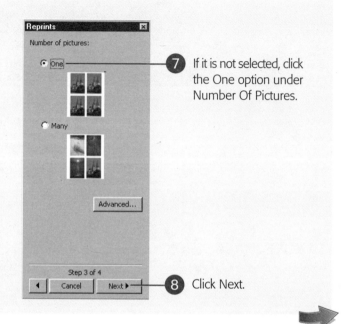

⑦ If it is not selected, click the One option under Number Of Pictures.

⑧ Click Next.

Choosing labels. This project uses Avery 8196, but you should use labels that match your printer.

9 Double-click the thumbnail of the disk label you created and drag the image to the picture space. (Keep the Object List closed.) The picture automatically fills in all the squares.

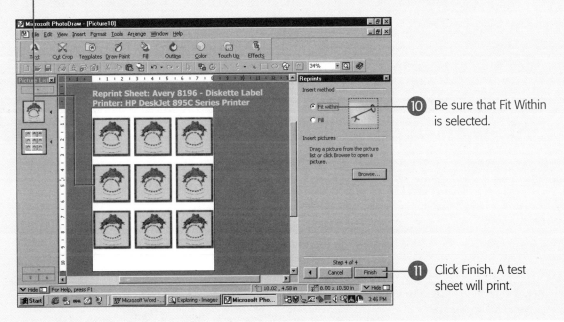

10 Be sure that Fit Within is selected.

11 Click Finish. A test sheet will print.

When you are satisfied with the label, save the file with a unique name such as "*froggy label printer.mix*". Then insert the label sheets into your printer and print. (Be sure the paper is oriented correctly.) When you need labels in the future, you do not need to run the Reprints Wizard again. Just open the file that you saved from the Reprints Wizard (*froggy label printer.mix*), insert paper into your printer and print. (Notice that the exact label paper you need is listed at the top of the page, as is the printer.)

Creating Watermark Stationery

In this section, we will create watermark stationery sheets and matching envelopes. Once the watermark has been created for the stationery, it's quick and easy to create the matching envelopes by reusing the art from the stationery sheets. The return address created in this project can also be used on the envelopes.

The graphic choices for a watermark are almost limitless. In this example, we'll create a soft floral watermark on the default letter size, but virtually any design you can think of can be used as a watermark. The watermark in this project is full-page size, but the size is really up to you. For example, it could be a centered design, a border, a top or bottom banner, or just a corner.

You can use clip art and PhotoDraw pictures as the source of the watermark, as well as bitmaps or scanned personal photographs. In other words, any image that you can insert into PhotoDraw can be the source of your watermark.

Creating Watermark Stationery Sheets

The first step is to decide on an image to use. If you don't already have a specific image in mind, spend a moment browsing the PhotoDraw pictures and clip art. This project uses a PhotoDraw picture of apple blossoms

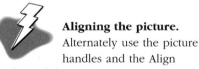

Saving your file. While you're working, remember to save your project with a descriptive file name that will be easy to remember later.

Aligning the picture. Alternately use the picture handles and the Align tools until the picture is centered to your liking.

Create Watermark Stationery Sheets

1 Open PhotoDraw. On the File menu, click New and select Letter. A blank letter form will appear.

2 On the Insert menu, click PhotoDraw Content. Insert a picture of your choosing by double clicking it.

3 Resize the blossom image to be slightly larger than the page by selecting one of the handles in the corner and stretching.

Create Watermark Stationery Sheets *(continued)*

④ On the Cut Crop menu, click Erase.

⑤ Select By Color and erase the dark branch parts and any unwanted background. See the sidebar for more information on erasing by color.

Zooming in for more precision. We will remove the dark branch from this picture, leaving the blossoms as our watermark. You may want to zoom in to erase those areas immediately adjacent to the parts you wish to keep for finer precision.

Erasing Large Areas by Color

There are two ways to erase large areas by color. You can click the different colors in the area and zoom in to clear the edges. This can be time-consuming and require a lot of clicking if the area is very large and has a lot of different colors, as is the case with our branch.

To clear a large area quickly, using Erase By Color, click one section and while holding down the right mouse button, drag the cursor across the field you want to erase.

Erasing Large Areas by Color *(continued)*

A line will appear. When you release the mouse button, all the areas containing the colors your line touched will be erased. Be sure not to touch any areas you don't want to erase.

Note that if you use Undo after erasing, it will undo everything you have erased, not just the last bit of erasure.

Creating the Watermark

The watermark is created by applying Designer Effects to the apple blossom image and then making the image transparent.

Create the Watermark

1 On the Effects menu, click Designer Effects.

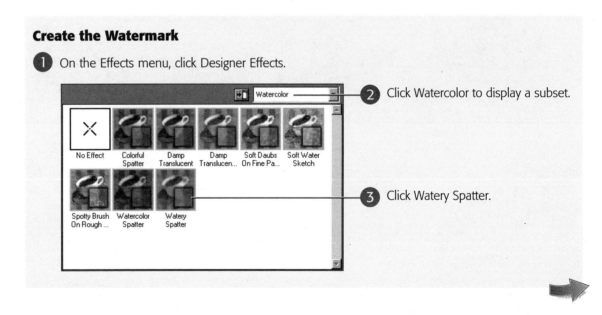

2 Click Watercolor to display a subset.

3 Click Watery Spatter.

Create the Watermark *(continued)*

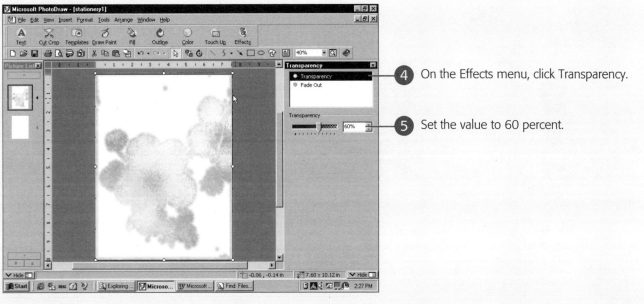

④ On the Effects menu, click Transparency.

⑤ Set the value to 60 percent.

⑥ Save your file with a unique name like *"stationery1.mix"*.

Setting transparency. By making the watermark as transparent as possible, any typing or writing on the paper will be easier to see. You may want to try several degrees of transparency to find one that suits you best, but usually a transparency between 60 percent and 80 percent works quite well.

Creating the Return Address

The return address should be easy to read and proportioned to the letter size. This example places it on the front in the upper left corner, but it could be placed at the bottom or centered.

Create the Return Address

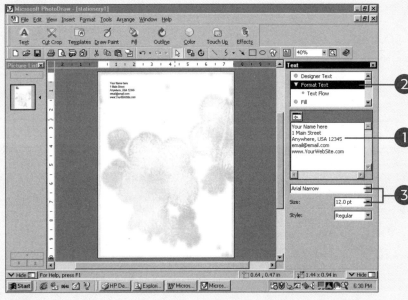

2 On the Text menu, click Format Text.

1 Insert a text object with the heading information, such as your name and address. Position the text object.

3 Choose a font size and style appropriate for your overall design. This project uses 12-point, Arial Narrow.

4 Select Fill and open the Active Palette. Click a color you like. This project uses a dark burgundy.

5 When you are satisfied with the appearance of your stationery, save your file.

Trying out fonts. Experiment with different font colors for the return address on different paper colors.

Testing first. Be sure to print out a test page for a final critique.

Printing Your Stationery

Most printers have a minimum margin setting. This means that there will be a white border around all the stationery from your printer. Usually this isn't a problem; however, if you want to minimize this effect, use the Fade Out tools from the Effects menu.

Creating a Watermark Envelope

We will now create an envelope to match our stationery sheets. We will reuse the watermark created earlier by inserting it into this project.

Create a Watermark Envelope

1 From the File menu, click New. The New dialog box appears. There are three choices of envelope size. Choose the one you want and then click OK. This project uses Envelope #10.

2 On the Insert menu, click Visual Insert. Navigate to the directory that contains your watermark stationery project. Insert the file.

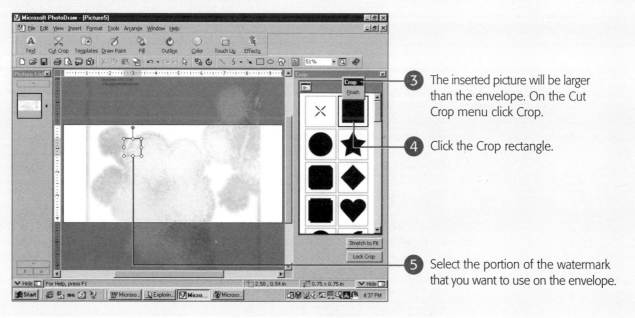

3 The inserted picture will be larger than the envelope. On the Cut Crop menu click Crop.

4 Click the Crop rectangle.

5 Select the portion of the watermark that you want to use on the envelope.

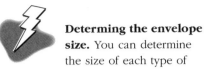

Determing the envelope size. You can determine the size of each type of envelope by selecting each one, clicking OK, and then opening the Picture Setup dialog box. You will be presented with the measurements of each type.

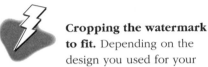

Cropping the watermark to fit. Depending on the design you used for your watermark, you may want to crop an area larger than the envelope and shrink the cropped image to fit the envelope.

Create a Watermark Envelope *(continued)*

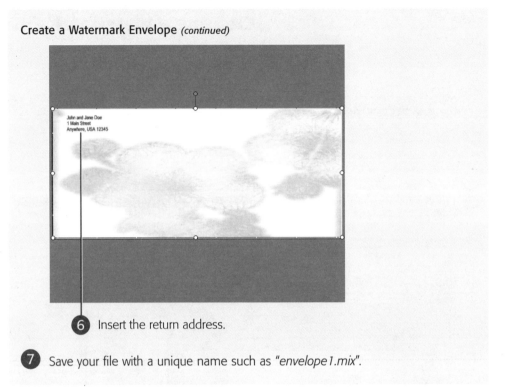

John and Jane Doe
1 Main Street
Anywhere, USA 12345

6 Insert the return address.

7 Save your file with a unique name such as *"envelope1.mix"*.

Creating a ToDo List

In this useful but simple project, we will create a ToDo list. The project is broken into two sections. In the first section, we'll create a grid—a set of lines—for the background. In the second part of this project, we'll create the ToDo list using the lines, decorative text, and graphics.

Creating Lines for the ToDo List

For elements such as lines, grids, tables, and so on, it is helpful to create a form and reuse it in different projects. The ToDo list requires a set of lines, so we'll create these as a separate project. If you'd prefer to use a the finished version of this project for your ToDo lines rather than creating them yourself, you can use *grid1.mix* in the chapters/chap11 folder of the accompanying CD and skip this procedure.

Create Lines for the ToDo List

1 Open PhotoDraw. From the File menu, click New and click Letter in the New dialog box and click OK.

2 On the View menu, click Snap To Grid. This will allow you to align the lines accurately.

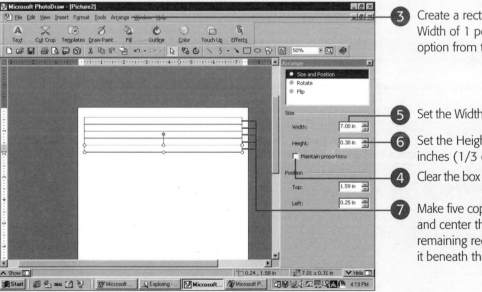

3 Create a rectangle of any size with a line Width of 1 point and select the Arrange option from the Arrange menu.

5 Set the Width of the rectangle to 7 inches.

6 Set the Height to about .33 inches (1/3 of an inch).

4 Clear the box marked Maintain Proportions.

7 Make five copies of the rectangle. Position and center the first rectangle. Grab each remaining rectangle in turn and position it beneath the first rectangle.

Creating Personal Office Supplies

Create Lines for the ToDo List *(continued)*

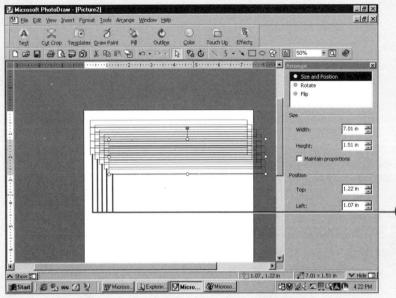

8 Group the rectangles together and make three or four duplicates of the group. Arrange the groups just as you did the individual rectangles.

9 When you are satisfied that everything looks right, be sure to print a test page before proceeding. If one of the groups is not exact, make fine adjustments from the Arrange selection on the Arrange menu.

10 Save this file with a unique name such as *"grid1.mix."* You can open this later and remove sections if you want to add a header or add text.

Leaving room at the top. Leave a couple of inches for a header, if you wish. Be sure to center each rectangle while it is the active object.

Making open-ended lines. If you want open-ended lines, make the rectangles wider than the page.

Create Lines for the ToDo List *(continued)*

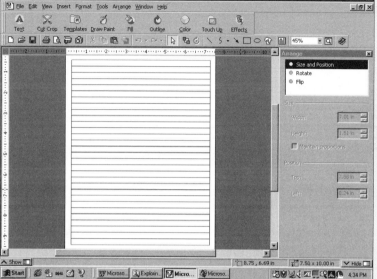

Your line form will look something like this.

Creating the List Using a PhotoDraw Picture and Lines

Now let's create the actual ToDo list. You could also create a camping list or a list of yearly gardening tasks using graphics to represent the tasks to be accomplished.

Create a ToDo List Using a PhotoDraw Picture and Lines

1 Open PhotoDraw. On the File menu, click New and open a new letter-sized picture.

2 If you want lines on your page, either create lines using the steps outlined in the previous procedure, or insert the *grid1.mix* file from the chapters/chap11 folder on the CD that accompanies this book.

3 Save this project under a new name, such as *"ToDo.mix"* to prevent overwriting your *grid1.mix* file.

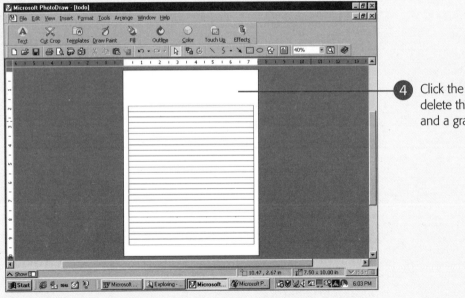

4 Click the top group of lines and delete them to make room for text and a graphic that we will add.

Create a ToDo List Using a PhotoDraw Picture and Lines *(continued)*

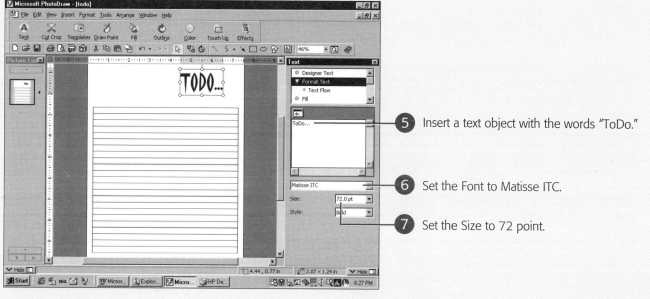

5 Insert a text object with the words "ToDo."

6 Set the Font to Matisse ITC.

7 Set the Size to 72 point.

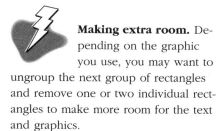

Making extra room. Depending on the graphic you use, you may want to ungroup the next group of rectangles and remove one or two individual rectangles to make more room for the text and graphics.

Create a ToDo List Using a PhotoDraw Picture and Lines *(continued)*

8 Insert a graphic from the selections that accompanies PhotoDraw or, for a truly personalized ToDo list, insert your own image, such as a scanned photograph from a vacation. Resize and position the images and text as shown.

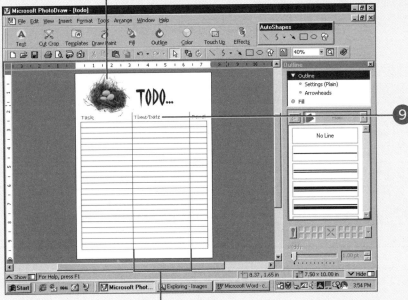

9 Make column headers by inserting a single new text object for all three columns, typing in the name of each column header, and separating each header with spaces or ellipsis (…). Center this text item.

10 On the toolbar, click the Straight Line tool and add dividing lines.

11 Save your file.

 Making dividing lines. For the dividing lines, make one vertical line the length you want and then duplicate it.

 Creating column titles. Suggestions for the column headers include: Notes, Phone numbers, Need to Take, People to Meet, and so on.

Creating Photograph Displays

People have always used art and pictures to decorate their living and working spaces. These days, your work and play environments often include your computer, so this chapter features projects to make your favorite pictures into Windows background art so you can enjoy them every day.

The first project displays multiple pictures on the screen at once, formatted as a photo album page. The second displays a single picture, framed and matted as if it were hanging on a wall.

Create a Photo Album Page

This project demonstrates how to mount a group of pictures in a textured paper background. The target is a Windows background wallpaper file, but you could apply this same technique to other uses, such as printing photo album pages for a loose-leaf book or publishing groups of pictures on the Internet.

Setting Up the Picture

For this project, use a picture space the size of your screen. We'll start with 800 by 600 pixels, which provides a fair amount of room to display pictures. However, in the project, you'll resize all of the pictures as you arrange them so you can fit them to your own display resolution. First we'll build a background that appears to have the texture of paper.

Sizing the picture to your display. You can create a new picture with your screen size by clicking Full Screen in the New dialog box.

Finding Disc 2 files. If you have previously copied the contents of Disc 2 to your hard drive, navigate to that directory instead of inserting the CD.

Create a Picture and Insert a Frame

1 Open PhotoDraw and create a new picture the dimensions of your computer screen with the units in pixels. (As mentioned, we'll use 800 by 600 pixels high.)

2 Insert PhotoDraw Disc 2 in your CD drive.

3 On the Insert menu, click Insert PhotoDraw Content and navigate to the Content/Pdclips/Textures/Paper folder.

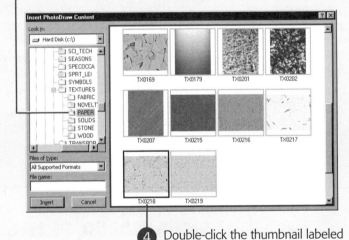

4 Double-click the thumbnail labeled TX0218 to insert it into your picture.

5 On the View menu, click Fit All to view the entire texture picture.

Create a Picture and Insert a Frame *(continued)*

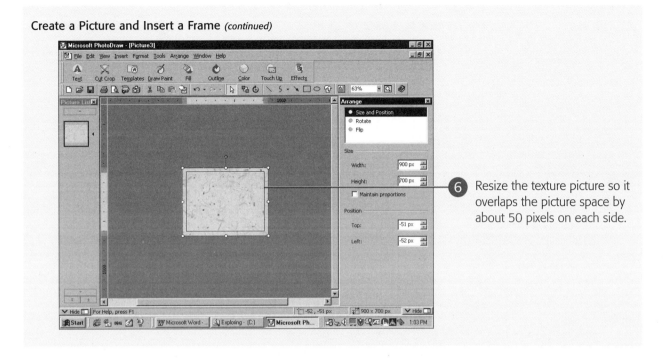

6 — Resize the texture picture so it overlaps the picture space by about 50 pixels on each side.

Resizing and centering. On the Arrange menu, click Arrange and set the texture image size to 900 by 700 pixels. Then use the Align Center and Align Middle tools on the Align menu to center the texture over the picture space. (Make sure Relative To Picture is active.)

Inserting the Pictures

The next step is to insert four pictures that you want to display on your screen. Remember that you can make several photo album pages and display different pages from time to time. For this project, we'll use some pictures from PhotoDraw Disc 2 so you can get the idea.

Insert the Pictures

1 On the Insert menu, click PhotoDraw Content and navigate to the Content/Pdclips/People folder on the CD.

2 Double-click the picture labeled BK0203 (the skier). The picture is inserted.

3 Click any corner handle of the picture and resize it to a little less than one-fourth the size of the picture area.

 You can use your own pictures. We're using PhotoDraw samples but go ahead and substitute your own if you want.

Just get it close. Don't worry too much about exact size and placement at this point. You can make adjustments this later.

Insert the Pictures *(continued)*

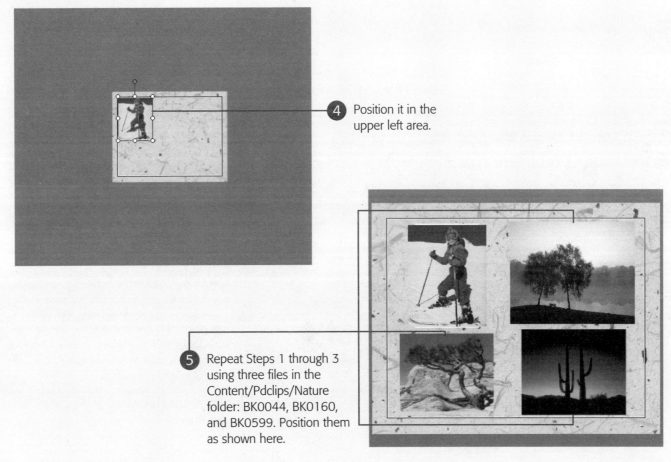

④ Position it in the upper left area.

⑤ Repeat Steps 1 through 3 using three files in the Content/Pdclips/Nature folder: BK0044, BK0160, and BK0599. Position them as shown here.

Mounting the Pictures

Erasing the cut out area.
Make sure the paper texture image (and only that image) is selected when performing these erase procedures.

We'll make the pictures appear to be mounted behind the paper texture image by cutting out areas of the paper texture to fit the images that will be placed underneath.

There are a number of ways to make the cut outs fit the pictures and also to arrange the cut outs properly on the page. In this technique, we'll erase the texture behind the picture so we can use the picture as a guide.

Make a Cut Out for the Skier Picture

1 Click the paper texture image to select it.

2 On the Cut Crop menu, click Erase. The Erase Workpane opens with By Shape selected as the erase mode.

5 On the Erase toolbar, click Finish. You cannot yet see the crop.

4 Position the erase shape over the skier and resize the erase shape so that all sides are inside the skier picture. (Since the paper texture is selected, it will be erased, not the picture.)

3 In the Erase shapes list, click Photo Corners.

Make a Cut Out for the Skier Picture *(continued)*

6 To see the effect, on the Arrange menu, select Order and then click Bring To Front.

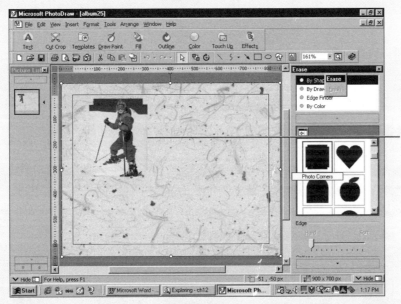

The paper moves in front of all the pictures and the skier shows through.

7 If you need to, select the picture of the skier and move it or resize it slightly to make sure no white spaces show.

Making an Emblem Cut Out

There are many erase shapes to choose from. Try to find a shape that complements the picture. The Angled Corners or Photo Corners work well for the photo-album-page look, but sometimes you'll want more unusual effects. For example, the tree in the upper right corner of the picture space has a central round figure that will work well with the Emblem erase shape.

Make a Cut Out for the Round Tree Picture

1 Select the paper texture image again and click Order on the Arrange menu and then Send To Back.

2 Select the tree in the upper right corner and position it so the middle of the tree is aligned with the middle of the skier picture and is balanced in the upper right part of the picture.

3 Select the paper texture image again.

Positioning the picture. Make sure the picture you are cutting out is positioned properly so the cut out will appear balanced on the page. After you make the cut out, you cannot move it.

Watch what's selected. Make sure only the paper texture image is selected when performing erase procedures.

5 Position the erase shape over the trees and resize and reposition it so that all sides are inside the picture and the tree is framed by the round area of the emblem shape.

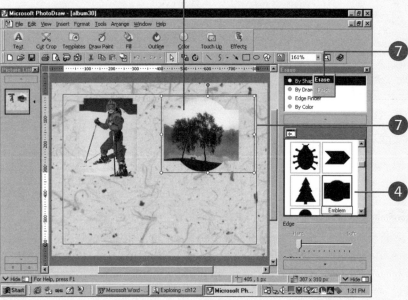

7 On the Erase toolbar, click Finish. To see the effect, on the Arrange menu, select Order and then click Bring To Front.

7 If you need to, select the tree picture and move it or resize it slightly to make sure no white spaces show around it.

4 In the Erase shapes list, click Emblem.

If you need to, select the tree picture and move it or resize it slightly to make sure no white spaces show around it.

Making a Cut Out with Photo Corners

For this exercise, we'll use the same erase shape as for the skier but we'll use a picture of a cactus. This time, the cactus image will be sent to the back so you can see the cut out area above the picture. This allows you to center the cut out better. You can try this same technique with the other pictures you are mounting.

Make a Cut Out for the Cactus Picture

1. Select the paper texture image again and send it to the back of the order.

6. Position the erase shape over the trees and resize and reposition the erase shape so that the erase shape is centered inside the picture.

7. On the Erase toolbar, click Finish.

8. To see the effect, on the Arrange menu, select Order then click Bring To Front.

2. Select the tree picture in the upper right and send it to the back of the order. This will help you see the previous cut out so you can better position the new one.

5. In the Erase shapes list, click Photo Corners.

3. Select the cactus picture in the lower right corner and position it so it is centered below the tree picture.

4. Select the paper texture image again.

Making a Cut Out with Angled Corners

This procedure is the same as the previous three. However, this time we'll try to make the cut out line up with the other three cut outs. We'll use another tree image for this one—a wind-swept tree growing from rocks. Remember, you can resize the picture behind the cut out, so don't worry if it doesn't quite fit this tree picture—it's more important to place the cut outs so the overall arrangement looks balanced. In other words, you can adjust the picture size and placement later to fit the cut out but you can't adjust the cut out after you make it.

Make a Cut Out for the Rock Tree

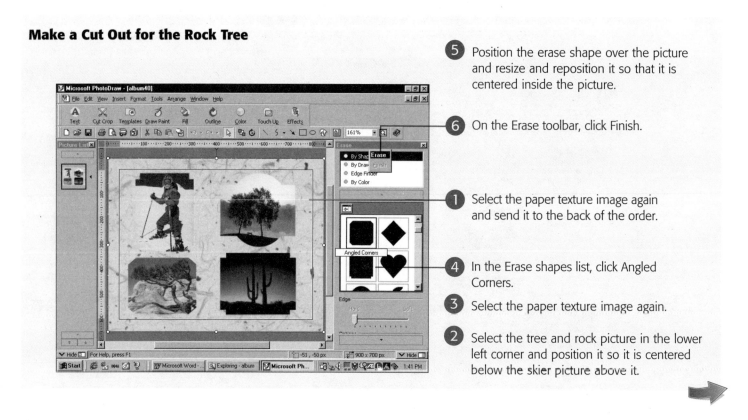

5 Position the erase shape over the picture and resize and reposition it so that it is centered inside the picture.

6 On the Erase toolbar, click Finish.

1 Select the paper texture image again and send it to the back of the order.

4 In the Erase shapes list, click Angled Corners.

3 Select the paper texture image again.

2 Select the tree and rock picture in the lower left corner and position it so it is centered below the skier picture above it.

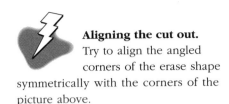

Aligning the cut out.
Try to align the angled corners of the erase shape symmetrically with the corners of the picture above.

Make a Cut Out for the Rock Tree *(continued)*

7️⃣ To see the effect, on the Arrange menu, select Order then click Bring To Front.

Adding Shadows

To give some depth to the page, we'll add a shadow effect to the paper. Make sure the paper image is still selected.

Add a Shadow Effect

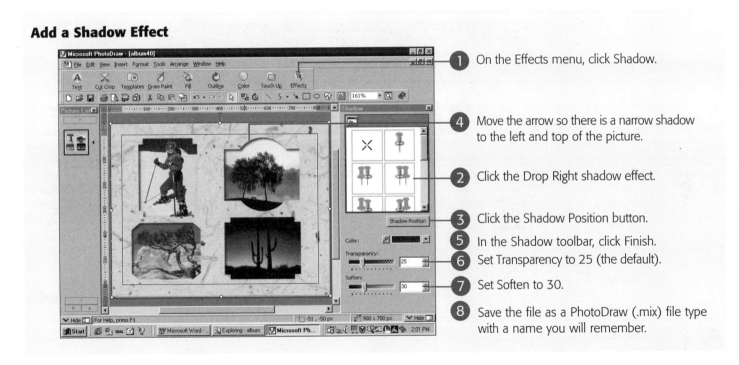

1️⃣ On the Effects menu, click Shadow.

4️⃣ Move the arrow so there is a narrow shadow to the left and top of the picture.

2️⃣ Click the Drop Right shadow effect.

3️⃣ Click the Shadow Position button.

5️⃣ In the Shadow toolbar, click Finish.

6️⃣ Set Transparency to 25 (the default).

7️⃣ Set Soften to 30.

8️⃣ Save the file as a PhotoDraw (.mix) file type with a name you will remember.

Creating Photograph Displays

Defining a bitmap. A bitmap is a Windows image file format. The background wallpaper uses a bitmap (.bmp) image that you can specify.

Making a Windows Bitmap

The last step is to save the file as a bitmap and select it as the background for your computer. This procedure assumes you are using Windows 95 or Windows 98 and that the previous project remains open in PhotoDraw.

Create the Bitmap

1 On the File menu, click Save As.

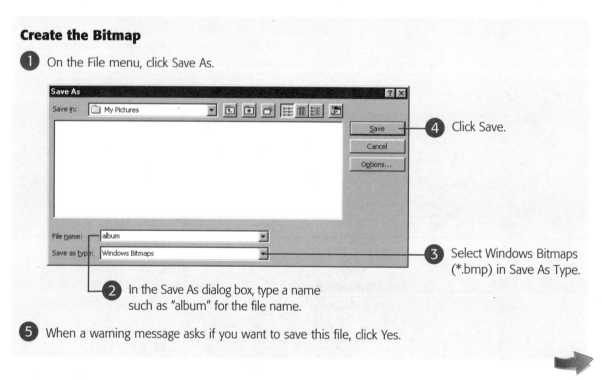

4 Click Save.

3 Select Windows Bitmaps (*.bmp) in Save As Type.

2 In the Save As dialog box, type a name such as "album" for the file name.

5 When a warning message asks if you want to save this file, click Yes.

Saving the bitmap. You can save this file in the Windows directory if you want quicker access to the background bitmap should you decide to change it.

Opening the Display Properties dialog box. To open the Display Properties dialog box, click Start on the Microsoft Windows taskbar. Then point to Settings, select Control Panel, and double-click Display. You can also right-click the Windows desktop and choose Properties from the shortcut menu to access this dialog box.

Create the Bitmap (continued)

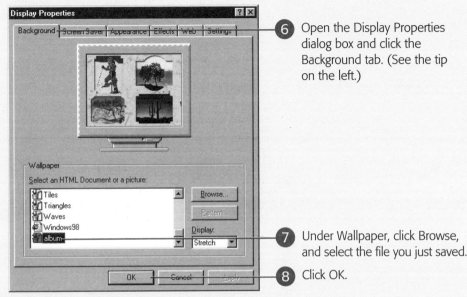

6 Open the Display Properties dialog box and click the Background tab. (See the tip on the left.)

7 Under Wallpaper, click Browse, and select the file you just saved.

8 Click OK.

Create a Framed Picture

This project uses PhotoDraw 3-D effects on a wood panel image to create a frame for a picture. A mat for the picture is created using Designer Effects and then it's beveled and shadowed to produce a realistic-looking picture frame. We'll make this into a Windows background bitmap, but you could use this in any number of ways—in cards, calendars, Web pages, or you can even print it out and put on your wall.

Setting Up the Picture

As in the previous project, we'll assume a background screen size of 800 by 600 pixels, but you can size the picture to fit your display resolution.

Create the Picture and Insert a Wood Image

1 Open PhotoDraw and create a new picture the dimensions of your computer screen with the units in pixels (in this case, 800 by 600 pixels).

2 Insert PhotoDraw Disc 2 into your CD drive.

3 On the Insert menu, click PhotoDraw Content and navigate to the folder Content\Pdclips\Textures\Wood.

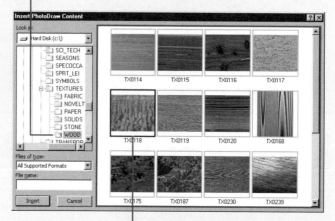

 Allowing extra room. An extra 100 pixels on each side allows you some room if, for example, you want to shrink the frame later or enlarge the picture space. Also, because we'll bevel this frame (and beveling is applied to both inside and outside), you don't want the outside bevel to show in the picture.

4 Double-click the burl wood thumbnail labeled TX0118 to insert it into your picture.

Create the Picture and Insert a Wood Image *(continued)*

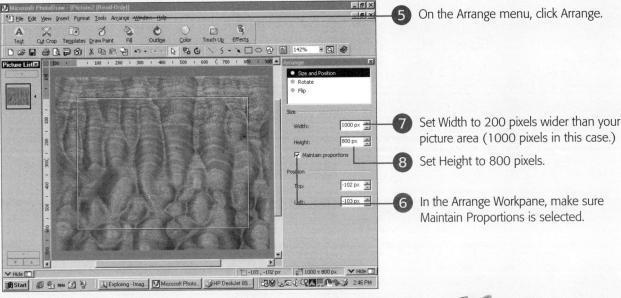

5 On the Arrange menu, click Arrange.

7 Set Width to 200 pixels wider than your picture area (1000 pixels in this case.)

8 Set Height to 800 pixels.

6 In the Arrange Workpane, make sure Maintain Proportions is selected.

9 On the Arrange menu, use the Align menu commands Align Center and Align Middle to center the burl picture over the picture area.

10 On the View menu, click Fit To All to view the entire texture picture.

Press Alt+R, Alt+A, and then Alt+C to align center. Press Alt+R, Alt+A, and then Alt+M to align middle.

Making the Frame

To make a frame, you must first erase a section from the middle of the wood image. It's helpful to use the coordinate indicators on the status bar to make sure the erase square is centered properly. Then you apply a beveled 3-D effect, and finally, you map the wood image to the beveled side to make it appear as a wooden bevel.

Erase the Center

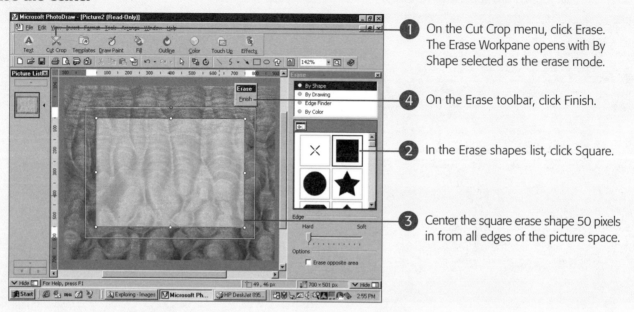

1. On the Cut Crop menu, click Erase. The Erase Workpane opens with By Shape selected as the erase mode.

4. On the Erase toolbar, click Finish.

2. In the Erase shapes list, click Square.

3. Center the square erase shape 50 pixels in from all edges of the picture space.

Using status bar indicators. Use the location coordinates on the status bar for the upper left coordinates (50, 50) and use the object size coordinates on the status bar for the size (100 less than the picture space width and height—700, 500 in this case). You can be a few pixels off.

Apply the 3-D Effect

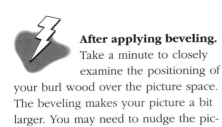

After applying beveling. Take a minute to closely examine the positioning of your burl wood over the picture space. The beveling makes your picture a bit larger. You may need to nudge the picture a few pixels with the arrow keys to center it.

1 On the Effects menu, click 3-D.

2 At the top of the 3-D Workpane, click Beveling and Extrusion.

3 Click the Expand gallery button.

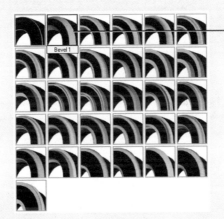

4 Click the Bevel 1 style.

5 Set Extrusion Depth to 0.

Apply the Wood Picture to the Bevel

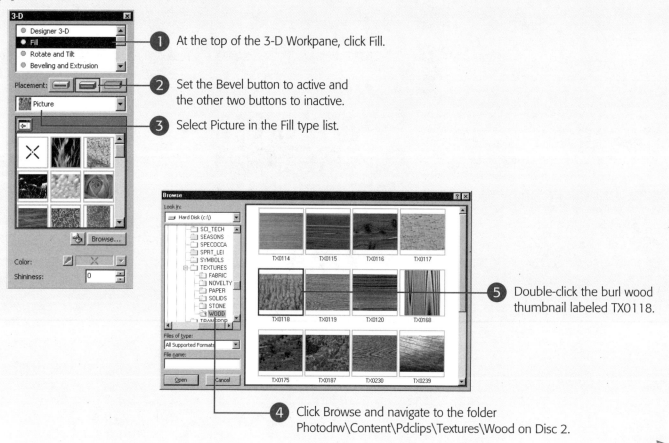

1. At the top of the 3-D Workpane, click Fill.

2. Set the Bevel button to active and the other two buttons to inactive.

3. Select Picture in the Fill type list.

5. Double-click the burl wood thumbnail labeled TX0118.

4. Click Browse and navigate to the folder Photodrw\Content\Pdclips\Textures\Wood on Disc 2.

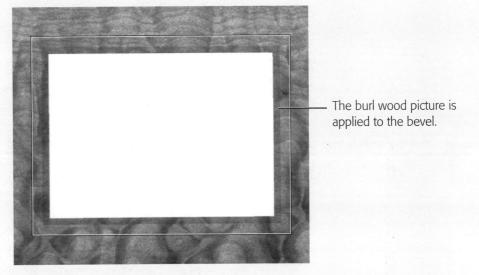

The burl wood picture is applied to the bevel.

Adding the Mat and Picture

In the final steps of this project, we'll add a matting rectangle, and insert the picture to be framed. Then we'll erase a rectangle in the mat so the picture shows through and apply beveling to the mat.

The mat we'll use is a color-filled rectangle to which we'll apply a Designer Effect. We could just as well use many other elements to make a mat, including a texture bitmap, for example. The bevel used for the mat is an interesting curved one, which adds a nice effect to the picture. Again, play with different bevels if you'd like to see what you can come up with.

Creating Photograph Displays

Add the Mat Rectangle

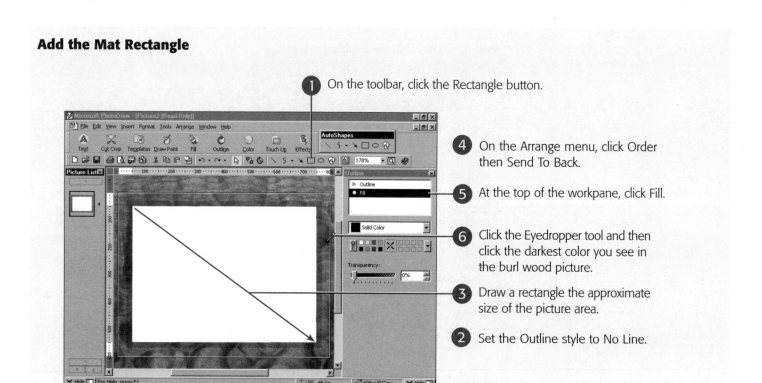

1 On the toolbar, click the Rectangle button.

4 On the Arrange menu, click Order then Send To Back.

5 At the top of the workpane, click Fill.

6 Click the Eyedropper tool and then click the darkest color you see in the burl wood picture.

3 Draw a rectangle the approximate size of the picture area.

2 Set the Outline style to No Line.

Next, you'll apply a Designer Effect to this image. At that point, you can use the Eyedropper tool to try different colors from the burl wood or the picture you insert.

Add Effects to the Mat

1 On the Effects menu, click Designer Effects.

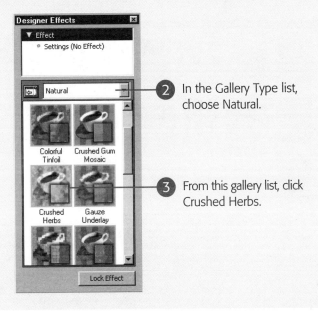

2 In the Gallery Type list, choose Natural.

3 From this gallery list, click Crushed Herbs.

Insert the Picture

1 On the Insert menu, click PhotoDraw Content and navigate to the folder Photodrw\Content\Pdclips\Bldg_arc.

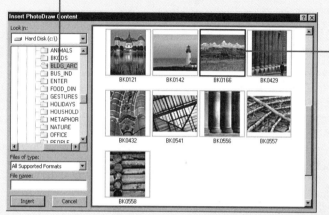

2 Double-click the barn thumbnail labeled BK0166 to insert it into your picture.

3 On the View menu, click Fit To All.

Sizing the picture. This image will be placed behind the matting, so make it larger than the part you want showing.

4 Resize and center the picture in the frame. In this case, make it about 600 by 480 pixels.

Figuring the Coordinates

Use the location coordinates on the status bar for the upper left coordinates of the erase square. For this project (at 800 x 600 pixels), a coordinate of approximately 108, 108 puts the erase square just inside the picture. Then, try to center the right and bottom sides in the frame using the size coordinates on the status bar. Since the matting rectangle is the picture size, to figure the erase square dimensions, subtract the offset amount multiplied by 2 (one for each side) from the picture size dimensions (2 x 108 = 216). In this case, it should be 584 pixels wide (800 – 216) by 384 pixels high (600 – 216).

Making adjustments. You can move the picture around to better center it after making the cut. If you don't like the placement of the cut out, use the Undo list to try it again.

Erase the Rectangle

1 Click the matting rectangle to select it.

2 On the Cut Crop menu, click Erase.

3 In the Erase shapes list, click Square.

4 Center the square erase shape over the picture to cut out the center of the matting.

5 On the Erase toolbar, click Finish.

6 Click the barn picture to select it.

7 On the Arrange menu, click Order then Send To Back.

At this point, your picture should look like this.

Apply Bevel to the Mat

① Select the mat rectangle.

② On the Effects menu, click 3-D.

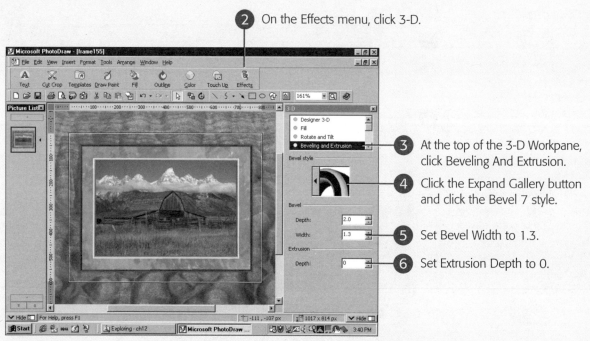

③ At the top of the 3-D Workpane, click Beveling And Extrusion.

④ Click the Expand Gallery button and click the Bevel 7 style.

⑤ Set Bevel Width to 1.3.

⑥ Set Extrusion Depth to 0.

⑦ To make a backup copy, save the file as a PhotoDraw picture (.mix) with a name you will remember.

Backing up. In the last stage of this project, you'll save the file as a Windows bitmap. It's always a good idea to save *backup .mix* file in case you later decide to make changes to the image.

Making a Windows Bitmap

This procedure is exactly like the one used in the previous project in this chapter. Here are the steps as a reminder, or in case you are creating this project first.

Saving the bitmap. You can save this in the Windows directory if you want quicker access to change the background bitmap.

Create the Bitmap

1 On the File menu, click Save As.

2 In the Save As dialog box, type a name such as "album" in the File Name box.

3 Select Windows Bitmaps (*.bmp) in Save As Type.

4 Click Save.

5 When a warning message asks if you want to save this file, click Yes.

6 Open the Display Properties dialog box and click the Background tab.

7 Under Wallpaper, click Browse, select the file that you just saved, and click Apply.

Creating Cartoons
and Greeting Cards

I n this chapter, you'll find two projects that use clip art to create cartoons. The first project walks you through a stand-alone cartoon with a single callout. The second project creates a two-panel cartoon formatted as a greeting card.

While the definition of humor is subjective (that is, you may or may not find these cartoons *funny*), the basic techniques will allow you to create cartoons with your own personal style.

Create a Cartoon Using Clip Art

Creating cartoons can be fun, but sometimes your humorous ideas can be made even better with the services of a good artist. That's where Microsoft PhotoDraw and clip art can lend a hand. In this project, you'll create a cartoon using clip art, callout shapes, and a couple of rectangles (and of course some text). With all due respect to the professionals that create cartoons from scratch, you'll be surprised at how far you can go using this approach to cartooning.

Setting Up

Let's get the picture started. We'll use the default dimensions and draw a border to frame the cartoon.

Create a Picture and Insert a Frame

① Open PhotoDraw and create a new picture with the default dimensions.

② Zoom in or out of the window to fit the picture space. (Select Fit Picture Area in the zoom box.)

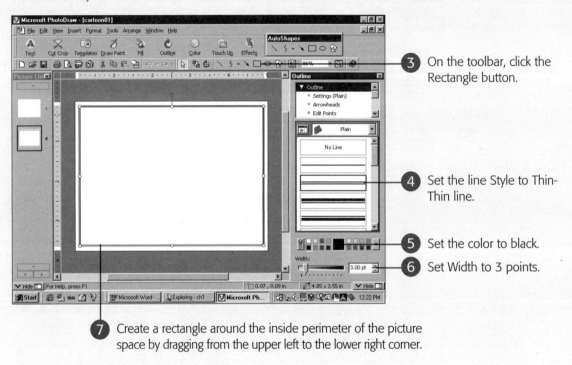

③ On the toolbar, click the Rectangle button.

④ Set the line Style to Thin-Thin line.

⑤ Set the color to black.

⑥ Set Width to 3 points.

⑦ Create a rectangle around the inside perimeter of the picture space by dragging from the upper left to the lower right corner.

Inserting and Positioning the Clip Art

Now we'll insert the clip art, size it, and position it correctly within the picture.

At this stage we'll insert two clip art objects into the picture. We'll add a third one later—purely for background—so we don't clutter the picture too much at first.

Find and Insert a Bird Cartoon

1 On the Insert menu, click Clip Art.

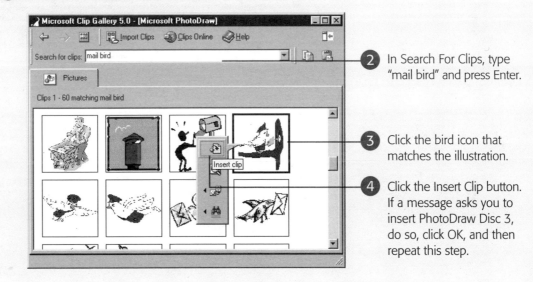

2 In Search For Clips, type "mail bird" and press Enter.

3 Click the bird icon that matches the illustration.

4 Click the Insert Clip button. If a message asks you to insert PhotoDraw Disc 3, do so, click OK, and then repeat this step.

Find and Insert an Airplane

1 On the toolbar, click Insert, and then click Clip Art.

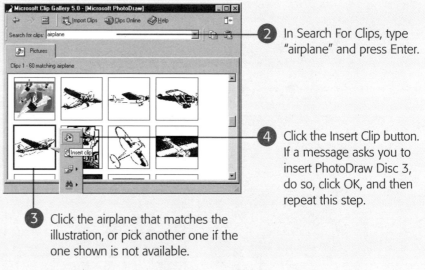

2 In Search For Clips, type "airplane" and press Enter.

4 Click the Insert Clip button. If a message asks you to insert PhotoDraw Disc 3, do so, click OK, and then repeat this step.

3 Click the airplane that matches the illustration, or pick another one if the one shown is not available.

5 Leave the Clip Gallery open and switch to PhotoDraw.

Resize and Position the Clip Art

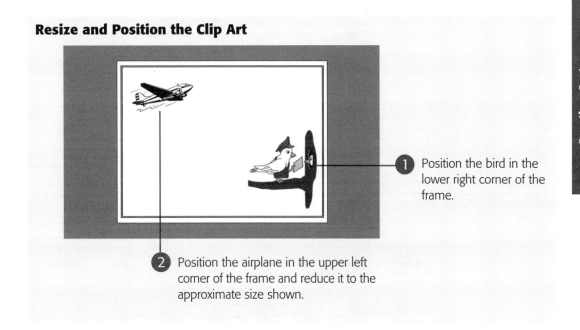

1. Position the bird in the lower right corner of the frame.

2. Position the airplane in the upper left corner of the frame and reduce it to the approximate size shown.

Adding the Text Balloon and Creating Clouds

Now we'll work with the callout shapes. The first callout will hold text. We'll use other callout shapes to create clouds.

Adding the Text Balloon

The text balloon is a simple oval callout. The blue color in the bird clip art will work nicely with the default blue line color, so you just need to set the line width and draw the callout using the AutoShapes Oval Callout tool.

Add a Text Balloon

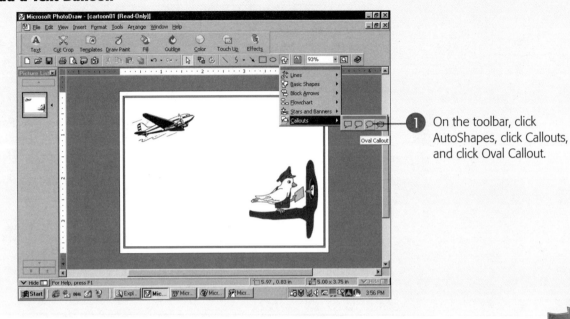

1 On the toolbar, click
AutoShapes, click Callouts,
and click Oval Callout.

Add a Text Balloon *(continued)*

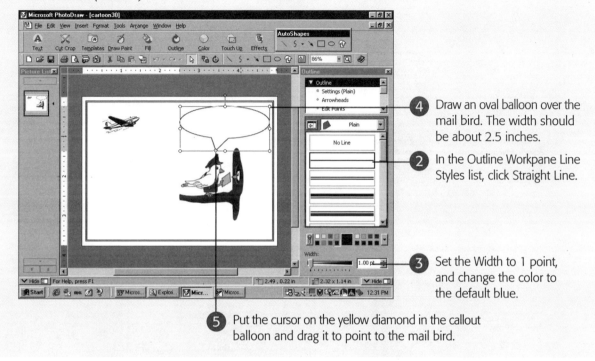

4 Draw an oval balloon over the mail bird. The width should be about 2.5 inches.

2 In the Outline Workpane Line Styles list, click Straight Line.

3 Set the Width to 1 point, and change the color to the default blue.

5 Put the cursor on the yellow diamond in the callout balloon and drag it to point to the mail bird.

Creating and Positioning the Clouds

Clouds can be difficult objects to draw. Here's a technique that may save you time. Since PhotoDraw already has a cloud callout balloon, we'll use that and simply remove the extension bubbles below the balloon. Then we'll make a duplicate cloud, resize and position the clouds, and put everything in the correct front-to-back order.

Add a Second Text Balloon

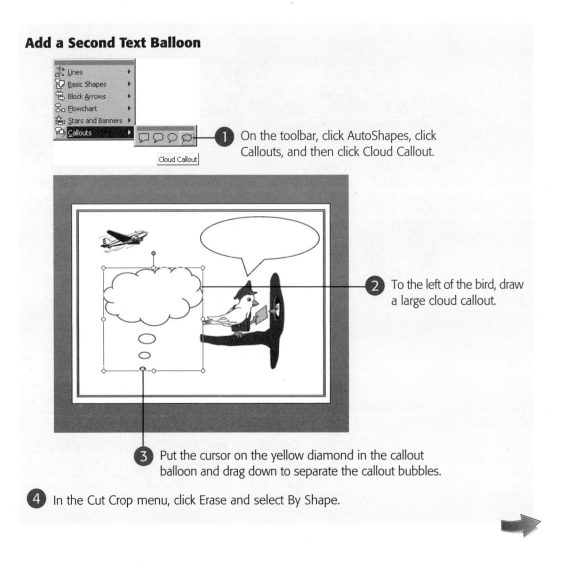

1 On the toolbar, click AutoShapes, click Callouts, and then click Cloud Callout.

2 To the left of the bird, draw a large cloud callout.

3 Put the cursor on the yellow diamond in the callout balloon and drag down to separate the callout bubbles.

4 In the Cut Crop menu, click Erase and select By Shape.

Add a Second Text Balloon *(continued)*

5 In the Erase Workpane, click the erase Square.

7 Click Finish on the Erase toolbar.

6 Adjust the erase square to encompass the three bubbles that extend below the cloud.

Finish the Clouds

① Select the cloud and press CTRL+D to duplicate the cloud.

② Reduce the size of the duplicate cloud and position it at the top of the picture.

③ Select the larger cloud and click Solid Color on the Fill menu.

④ Click the white color square in the Fill workpane.

 Why do my balloon bubbles reappear after I erase them? You'll find that after erasing the balloon bubbles, they reappear if you drag the callout handle outside the area that was erased, so you'll need to watch this when resizing.

⑤ Move the larger cloud so it just covers the airplane.

⑥ On the Arrange menu, select Order and click Send To Back. The cloud is now behind the airplane.

⑦ Select the smaller cloud and click Solid Color on the Fill menu.

⑧ Click the white color square in the Fill Workpane.

⑨ On the Arrange menu, select Order and click Send To Back.

Add Text

1 Insert a text object with the words "Looks like your frequent flier miles came through." using Comic Sans MS font at 10 points. Note that you will need to put a line feed (press Enter) after the word "flier."

2 Position the text inside the oval callout. Adjust the size of the callout if necessary.

3 Select the oval callout and click Solid Color on the Fill menu.

4 Click the white color square in the Fill Workpane.

Adding Final Touches

The cartoon already gets the joke across, but you might want to spruce it up a bit. You can complete the tree trunk and then add some background scenery with clip art. Finally, you can add a blue-sky background and fade the scenery into the distance.

Completing the Tree Trunk

To complete the tree trunk, we'll create a rectangle and fill it with the same color as the tree in the bird clip art.

Finish the Tree Trunk

1 On the toolbar, click the Rectangle button.

2 In the Outline Workpane, make sure No Line is selected.

3 Create a rectangle extending from the top to the bottom of the outer border, with the left edge lined up with the left edge of the tree trunk and the right edge just outside the callout.

4 On the Fill menu, click Solid Color.

5 In the Fill Workpane, click the Eyedropper tool and then click any brown spot in the tree.

Finish the Tree Trunk *(continued)*

6 On the Arrange menu, select Order and click Send To Back.

7 The tree rectangle moves behind the clip art and appears to be part of it.

Adding Background Scenery

The clip art collection has several rural scenes to choose from for a background image. We'll pick one to give the scene some depth. This is probably a more complex background than you'd normally find in a cartoon drawn by hand, but it adds a nice touch. Later, we'll fade this background scene to move it more into the background.

Add Background Scenery Clip Art

1 On the Insert menu, click Clip Art, or switch to the Microsoft Clip Gallery.

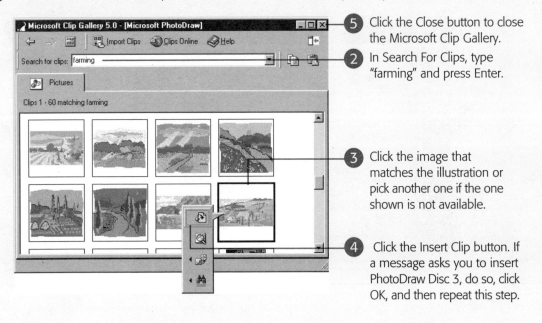

5 Click the Close button to close the Microsoft Clip Gallery.

2 In Search For Clips, type "farming" and press Enter.

3 Click the image that matches the illustration or pick another one if the one shown is not available.

4 Click the Insert Clip button. If a message asks you to insert PhotoDraw Disc 3, do so, click OK, and then repeat this step.

Add Background Scenery Clip Art *(continued)*

6 In PhotoDraw, position and resize the farm clip art to fill the lower half of the frame.

7 Send the clip art to the back of the Z-order using Send To Back on the Order menu. (Point to Order on the Arrange menu.)

Adding Color Fill

Next we'll use a color fill for the background frame and pick the same color as the farm clip art sky. The sky color will then be made 40 percent transparent, because we'll fade the clip art in the final procedure.

Add Color Fill to the Background

1 Select the outer rectangle and click Order on the Arrange menu.

4 Click the blue at the top of the farm clip art.

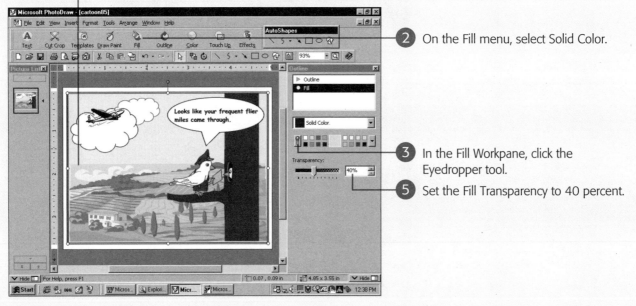

2 On the Fill menu, select Solid Color.

3 In the Fill Workpane, click the Eyedropper tool.

5 Set the Fill Transparency to 40 percent.

6 Then click Send To Back to send it to the back of the Z-order.

Fading the Clip Art

To give the illusion of perspective and to keep the farm picture from grabbing your attention, we'll fade the farm from bottom to top.

Fade the Clip Art

1 Select the farm clip art.

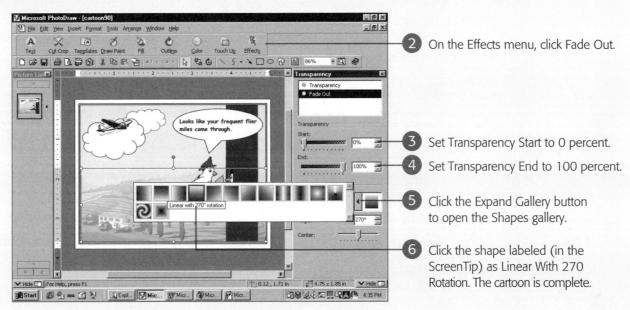

2 On the Effects menu, click Fade Out.

3 Set Transparency Start to 0 percent.

4 Set Transparency End to 100 percent.

5 Click the Expand Gallery button to open the Shapes gallery.

6 Click the shape labeled (in the ScreenTip) as Linear With 270 Rotation. The cartoon is complete.

Create a Greeting Card with a Cartoon

You've seen how to create a cartoon using clip art. Now we'll use similar techniques to create a greeting card with a cartoon. In some ways, this is easier, because greeting card art tends to be sparse.

For a professional-looking card, we'll need to print two sides of the same card stock. (Use thick paper if your printer won't handle card stock.) Therefore, we'll create two separate cartoon graphics—one for the outside of the card and one for the inside. This project is based on a standard card size of 5 by 7 inches. Since we'll fold it in half, the total width of the card needs to be 10 inches. Of course, you can use any size you want, just adjust the sizing in the procedures accordingly.

Making the Outside Graphic

The outside graphic is a single piece of clip art with a callout. We'll use a canine theme. To get the idea for the cartoon, I looked over the available clip art and then thought of an appropriate joke. If you look at cartoon greeting cards in stores, you'll find it's often the surprise factor of the punch line that provides the humor rather than the art. Even so, there are quite a few clip art pictures in the Microsoft Clip Gallery that lend themselves to humorous captions. Just browse the Clip Gallery and be creative.

Setting Up

To begin with, we'll create a picture that's 10 by 7 inches. The size at which you print the card will depend on the paper you choose and your printer, but this will be our starting size.

We'll add a rectangle to divide the picture in half. The rectangle provides a frame in which to compose your picture. You can remove this rectangle before printing, or use it during print tests to visually align the front and back of the paper. You can use it as a guide for trimming the card if your paper is larger than 10 by 7 inches.

Create the Picture and Frame

1 Open PhotoDraw and create a new picture 10 by 7 inches.

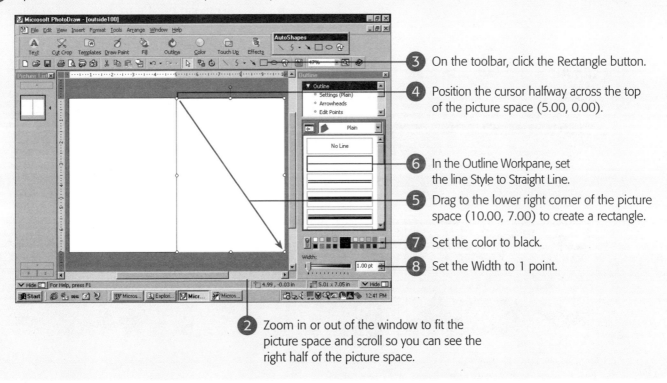

3 On the toolbar, click the Rectangle button.

4 Position the cursor halfway across the top of the picture space (5.00, 0.00).

6 In the Outline Workpane, set the line Style to Straight Line.

5 Drag to the lower right corner of the picture space (10.00, 7.00) to create a rectangle.

7 Set the color to black.

8 Set the Width to 1 point.

2 Zoom in or out of the window to fit the picture space and scroll so you can see the right half of the picture space.

Setting the standard size. The default letter size is 7.5 by 10 inches, given standard margins. Create this card size by clicking Letter in the New dialog box when you create a new picture. Then set the picture to Horizontal in the Picture Setup dialog box to make it 10 by 7.5 inches.

Adding the Clip Art

The front of the card shows a worried dog. This particular piece of clip art is a good setup for a punch line—you could add almost any caption to lead into a joke. (You'll add the caption later.) To make the figure stand out, we'll add a shadow effect.

Add Clip Art and Create a Shadow

1 On the Insert menu, click Clip Art.

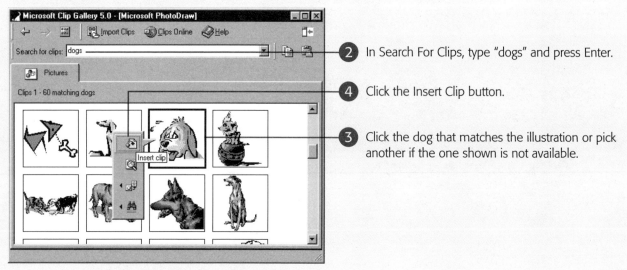

2 In Search For Clips, type "dogs" and press Enter.

4 Click the Insert Clip button.

3 Click the dog that matches the illustration or pick another if the one shown is not available.

Add Clip Art and Create a Shadow *(continued)*

5 Leave the Clip Gallery open and switch to PhotoDraw.

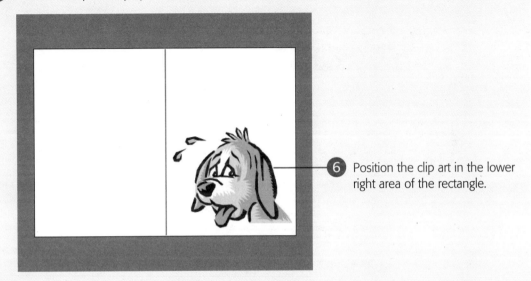

6 Position the clip art in the lower right area of the rectangle.

Create the Shadow

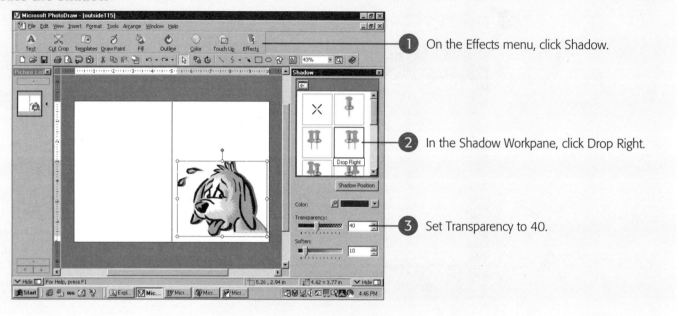

1 On the Effects menu, click Shadow.

2 In the Shadow Workpane, click Drop Right.

3 Set Transparency to 40.

Adding the Text Balloon

Adding the text callout is straightforward. Just use the AutoShapes Callouts menu and draw the callout. Then put text into the callout. To achieve a hand-drawn effect, we'll apply an artistic brush to the outline of the callout.

Add Callout

① On the toolbar, click AutoShapes, click Callouts, and the click Rounded Rectangular Callout.

② Draw a rectangle in the top half of the larger rectangle.

Add Callout *(continued)*

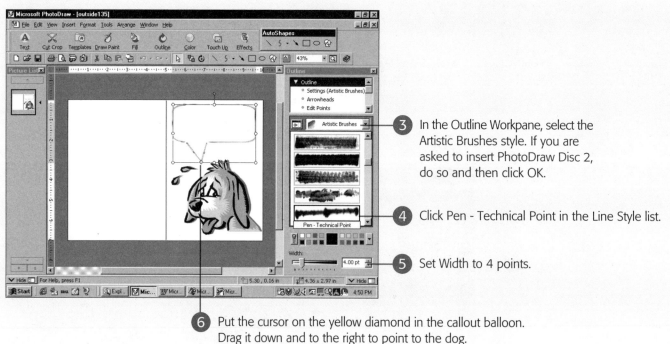

3 In the Outline Workpane, select the Artistic Brushes style. If you are asked to insert PhotoDraw Disc 2, do so and then click OK.

4 Click Pen - Technical Point in the Line Style list.

5 Set Width to 4 points.

6 Put the cursor on the yellow diamond in the callout balloon. Drag it down and to the right to point to the dog.

Add a Text Object

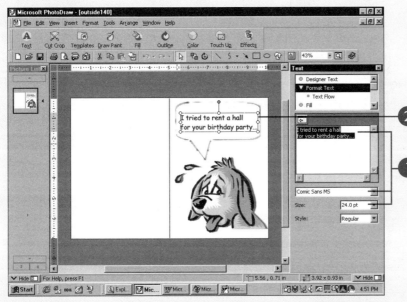

2 Position the text inside the callout balloon.

1 Insert a text object that says "I tried to rent a hall for your birthday party...", using 24-point Comic Sans MS font. Note that you will need to put a line feed (press Enter) after the word "hall."

3 Save this picture as a PhotoDraw picture (.mix) with the name "outside.mix" in any convenient directory.

4 Select the frame rectangle and drag it onto the Picture List to use in the next part of this project.

You can delete the frame, or you might want to leave the rectangle in the picture to help you figure out print positioning. You can delete it before you print the final card.

Making the Interior Graphic

The inside graphic doesn't require a callout. The punch line appears as a simple centered line of text below the graphic. Following the punch line is the Happy Birthday salutation. The fun of creating your own cards, of course, is that you can add any greeting you want and customize the card for any occasion.

Setting Up

We will create the inside picture frame exactly as we did the outside. In this case, however, we already have a sized rectangle on the Picture List that we can use.

Create the Picture and Frame

1 Create a new picture 10 by 7 inches.

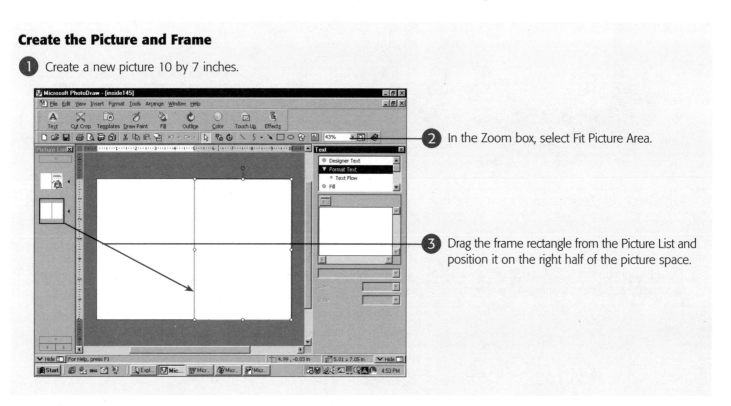

2 In the Zoom box, select Fit Picture Area.

3 Drag the frame rectangle from the Picture List and position it on the right half of the picture space.

Adding the Clip Art and Text

 How can I quickly find the image if I closed the Clip Gallery? If you closed the Clip Gallery, click Insert Clip Art on the PhotoDraw Insert menu, type "dogs" in the Clip Gallery Search For Clips box, and press Enter.

One nice thing about the Clip Gallery is that you can search for art by concept. In this case, the group of dogs that we saw earlier also contains a dog for the inside of the card. You'll simply need to position this dog and resize it to fit the page.

Adding text is also simple for this type of card. You can get as fancy as you want with text, of course, but sometimes simple text works better, especially when the picture should be the focal point.

Add Clip Art

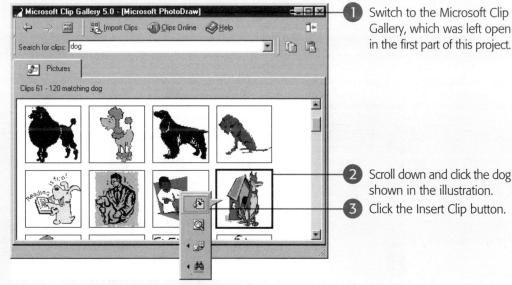

1. Switch to the Microsoft Clip Gallery, which was left open in the first part of this project.

2. Scroll down and click the dog shown in the illustration.

3. Click the Insert Clip button.

4. Close the Clip Gallery and switch to PhotoDraw.

Add Clip Art *(continued)*

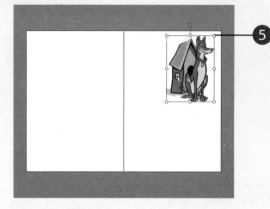

5 Reduce the clip art by grabbing the corner handle and moving it inward and position it in the upper right area of the rectangle.

Add Text

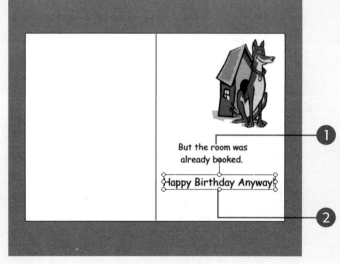

But the room was already booked.

Happy Birthday Anyway!

1 Insert a text object that says "But the room was already booked." using 24-point Comic Sans MS font. Note that you will need to put a line feed (press the Enter key) after the word "was."

2 Create another text object that says "Happy Birthday Anyway!" using 28-point Comic Sans MS font.

Creating the second object. To create the second object, you can duplicate the first object, edit the text, and change the font size.

Centering the graphic. When printing to standard 8.5-by-11-inch paper size, try choosing Fit To Page to center the graphics on each size. This reduces the page to 9.6 by 6.7 inches.

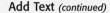

Add Text *(continued)*

3 Position both text objects as shown.

4 Optionally, select the outside rectangle and delete it. You may want to leave the rectangle in the picture to help you figure out the print positioning.

5 Save the file with the name "inside.mix" in a convenient directory.

Printing the Card

To print this card, you will need either card stock or the thickest paper your printer will handle. Since it is 7 by 10 inches, a normal letter-size sheet will work if you trim the edges to fit. Print *outside.mix* first, then turn the cardboard sheet over and upside down, and print *inside.mix*. Fold it in half and trim it to the folded size of 5 by 7 inches.

Because of the many different paper sizes and printers available, a description of exact printing steps is beyond the scope of this book. Just work with your printer and the Position tab in the Print dialog box to get the pictures on the front and back to line up when you fold the page.

Creating Advertisements

Microsoft PhotoDraw is not limited to hobbyists. Businesses can create excellent advertisements and fliers with PhotoDraw. For homes, churches, and other organizations, PhotoDraw is an excellent tool for composing literature for advertising events such as garage sales, raffles, bake sales, and the like.

This chapter shows how to put together a simple garage sale advertisement for a home project. Many of the techniques and ideas demonstrated in this project can be easily applied to other advertisements you may have in mind.

Creating a Basic Garage Sale Advertisement

The garage sale advertisement uses a few tricks to grab the attention of readers and convey information. It uses PhotoDraw's Designer Text to produce first-class typography. It uses a map graphic and pointer to show the location of the sale, and it uses clip art and PhotoDraw pictures to convey the idea of a garage sale.

Finding a Map

The most important point of a garage sale advertisement, or any sale for that matter, is location, location, location. With the advent of World Wide Web map sites and the proliferation of map software in stores, it's fairly easy to find a map that leads prospective buyers to your location. In this case, the map was retrieved from the *http://www.expediamaps.com* Web site.

Using content from the Internet. Content on the Internet is often copyrighted. Be sure to respect any copyrighted graphic before using it.

Using map software. If you are using map software, such as Microsoft Streets, find your sale location using the software and then use the copy command (either from the menu or by typing Ctrl+C) to copy the map to the clipboard. Then paste it (Ctrl+V) into PhotoDraw.

This graphic will go at the bottom of the advertisement, below the address. If you don't want to use a map like this, you could use a picture of your house or some notable item you are selling. You can also draw a simplified map using PhotoDraw's drawing tools.

Note that the following instructions may be inaccurate if the Web site changes, as Web sites often do. The important part to remember, regardless of the Web site, is that once you find a map to your address, using your browser, right-click and then click Save Picture As from the shortcut menu. This saves the map graphic to your hard drive.

Obtain a Map to Your House

1 Use your Internet service provider and favorite browser to connect to the World Wide Web.

2 Go to *http://www.expediamaps.com* and click the Address Finder button, or go directly to *http://www.expediamaps.com/Addressfinder.asp*.

3 Type your address and click Go.

4 If more than one matching address is found, click the one that matches.

5 Increase the map to a suitable resolution. (Click Make Map Larger on the Web page.)

6 Right-click inside the map area and click Save Picture As to save the map graphic to your hard drive. Save it with a name like *"salemap.gif"*.

7 Close the browser.

Creating the Picture and Inserting the Map

The garage sale sign we'll create will be printed on a standard letter-sized page. This can be delivered as a flier or posted on bulletin boards or in other public places.

Create the Picture and Insert the Map

1 Open PhotoDraw or click New from the File menu if PhotoDraw is already open.

2 Click Letter in the Pictures tab and click OK.

3 Insert the map graphic. If you saved it as a graphic file, click From File on the Insert menu and navigate to the file. If you copied it to the clipboard, click Paste on the Edit menu.

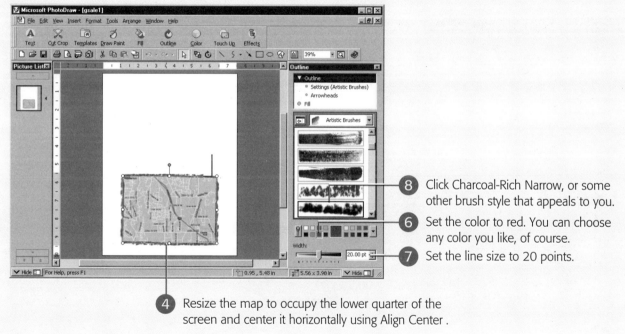

8 Click Charcoal-Rich Narrow, or some other brush style that appeals to you.

6 Set the color to red. You can choose any color you like, of course.

7 Set the line size to 20 points.

4 Resize the map to occupy the lower quarter of the screen and center it horizontally using Align Center .

5 On the Outline menu, click Artistic Brushes to open the Outline Workpane. Insert PhotoDraw CD 2 if the program asks for it.

Adding Text

There are four text objects in this advertisement. The first, at the top, is a Designer Text object that says "Garage Sale." We'll bend it slightly for effect. The three other text objects display the day, time, and location.

Add Garage Sale Text

1 Insert a text object with the text "Garage Sale."

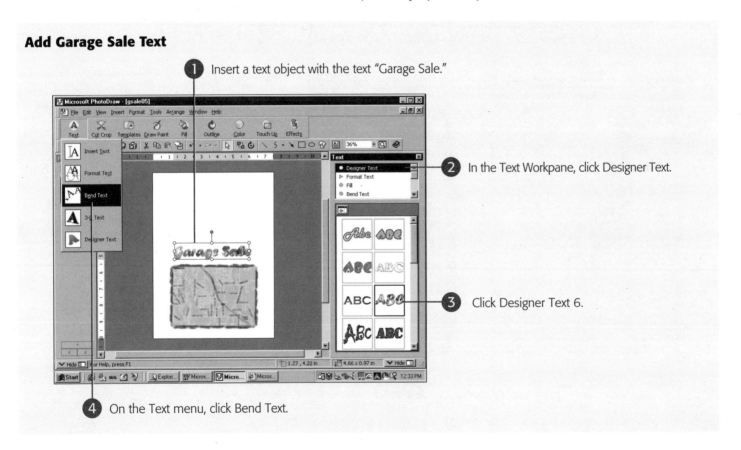

2 In the Text Workpane, click Designer Text.

3 Click Designer Text 6.

4 On the Text menu, click Bend Text.

Add Details Text

6 Position the text at the top of the picture space and center it using the Align tools on the Align submenu of the Arrange menu.

5 Click Quarter Circle Down in the Text Workpane.

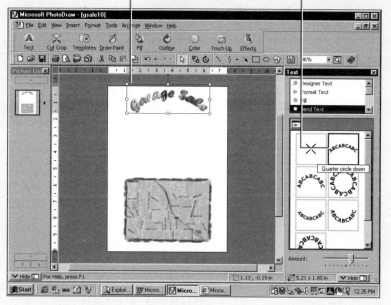

Add Details Text *(continued)*

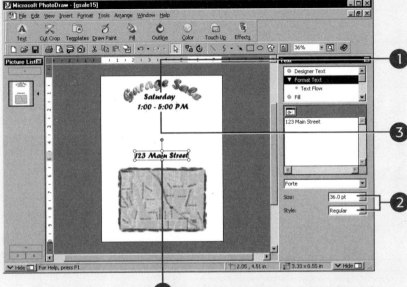

1. Insert a text object with the text "Saturday" (or the day or days of your garage sale), and center it below the "Garage Sale" text object.

3. Duplicate the text and change the words to indicate the time (1:00 - 5:00 PM in this case). Center this below the previous text object.

2. Set the Font to 36-point Forte, or any style you like.

4. Duplicate the currently selected text object, change the text to the address of your sale, and place this text just above the map.

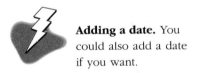

Adding a date. You could also add a date if you want.

Adding a Pointer

To help potential buyers locate your sale location, you can add a pointer to the location on the map using the Curve Line tool and the Arrowheads style.

Add a Pointer to the Location

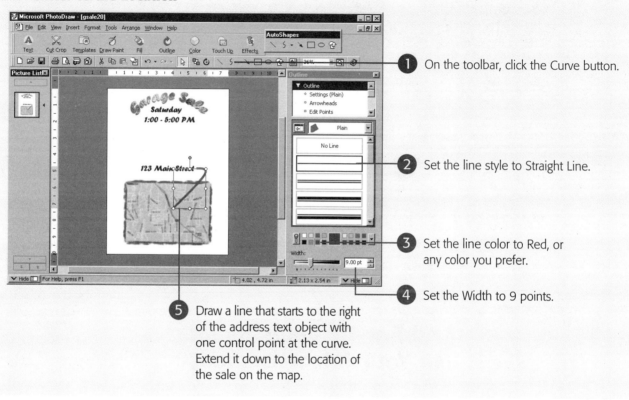

① On the toolbar, click the Curve button.

② Set the line style to Straight Line.

③ Set the line color to Red, or any color you prefer.

④ Set the Width to 9 points.

⑤ Draw a line that starts to the right of the address text object with one control point at the curve. Extend it down to the location of the sale on the map.

How can I quickly fix my line? If you don't get this right the first time, click Edit Points, right-click the image to get the shortcut menu, and adjust the curve to look something like the illustration.

Add a Pointer to the Location *(continued)*

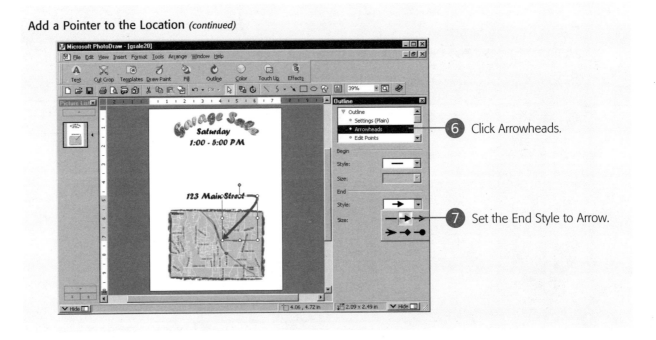

6 Click Arrowheads.

7 Set the End Style to Arrow.

Adding Embellishments to Your Advertisement

After you've created the basic advertisement, you can further embellish it to distinguish it from other ads. You can add clip art cartoons, fun backgrounds, and photographs—for starters.

Adding a Clip Art Cartoon

You can find some clip art in the Microsoft Clip Gallery that will help spruce up any advertisement, and garage sales are no exception. In this case, there is only one drawing that exactly matches a garage sale, but it's a pretty good one. We'll add this in the middle of the flier.

Adding Clip Art

1 On the Insert menu, click Clip Art.

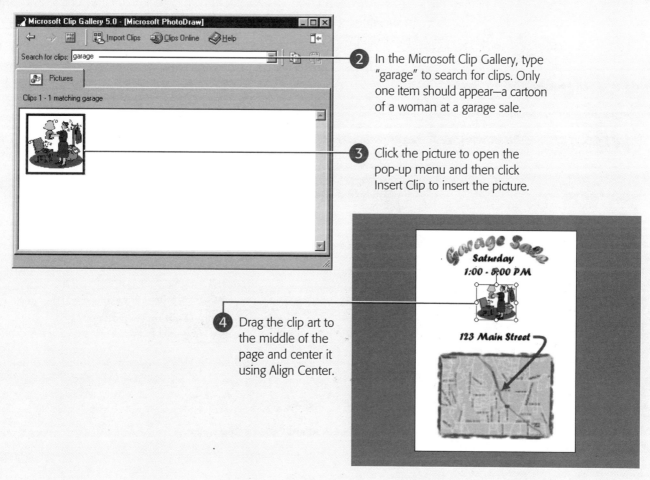

2 In the Microsoft Clip Gallery, type "garage" to search for clips. Only one item should appear—a cartoon of a woman at a garage sale.

3 Click the picture to open the pop-up menu and then click Insert Clip to insert the picture.

4 Drag the clip art to the middle of the page and center it using Align Center.

Adding a Background

The advertisement works well so far. However, you can enhance it by adding a background. Probably the easiest background to produce is one composed of text. In this case, we'll add the text "Sale!" and replicate it several times for use as a faded backdrop.

Adding a Background Using Text

① Insert a default text object.

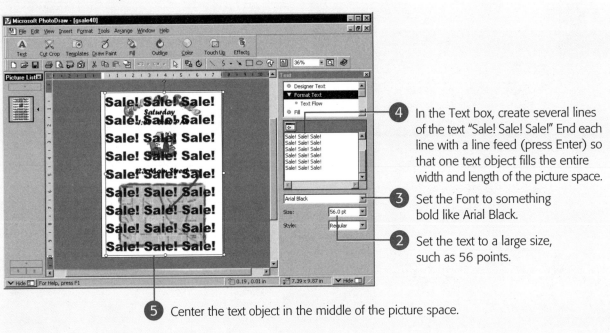

④ In the Text box, create several lines of the text "Sale! Sale! Sale!" End each line with a line feed (press Enter) so that one text object fills the entire width and length of the picture space.

③ Set the Font to something bold like Arial Black.

② Set the text to a large size, such as 56 points.

⑤ Center the text object in the middle of the picture space.

Adding a Background Using Text *(continued)*

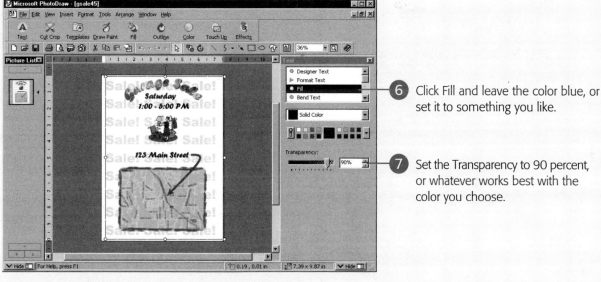

⑥ Click Fill and leave the color blue, or set it to something you like.

⑦ Set the Transparency to 90 percent, or whatever works best with the color you choose.

⑧ On the Arrange menu, click Order and then Send To Back.

Adding Photographs

To finish this garage sale advertisement, we'll insert several photographs of items you're likely to find at a garage sale. This helps to immediately communicate the nature of the sale. We'll add, resize, and place these at different angles around the border of the picture.

Adding Photographs Around the Border

1 On the Insert menu, click PhotoDraw Content and navigate to the Household folder.

2 Scroll down and double-click the antique television picture—CT0727.

Selecting more than one item. When selecting more than one item from a folder, you can hold down the Ctrl key while clicking on different objects. Each object you select will be outlined with a blue border. When you have finished selecting pictures, click Open and all pictures will be inserted at once.

Making an image transparent. You can make these images more transparent if you like or place them behind the map on the Z-order if they overlay some important marker on the map.

Adding Photographs Around the Border (continued)

3 Resize and position the picture as shown and use the rotate handle to angle it.

4 Repeat Steps 2 through 4 to insert and position other pictures from the Household folder:

The typewriter (CT0565)

The stained glass window (CT0641)

The red wagon (CT0205)

The lawn mower (CT0752)

5 Repeat Steps 2 through 4 to insert and position the picture of the baseball glove (CT0211) from the Sprt_lei folder.

Creating a Personalized Calendar

By creating a calendar that contains the dates of special events—birthdays, anniversaries, annual events, and holidays, you will create something of special value that any family member will appreciate. This would be a great way to use family photographs that relate to the different seasonal events.

There are many different formats for calendars. You could create one page for each month and put the pages in a binder. In this example, one page is created for each season with a seasonal picture at the top and the corresponding months at the bottom. We'll use standard letter-sized paper (7.5 by 10 inches with 1-inch margins).

You'll want the ability to add appointments throughout the year, as well as making notes, so we will include a note section at the bottom and enough room to jot down an appointment or two.

This project is broken into two parts. In the first part, we create a calendar framework that can be reused. In the second part, we create a calendar for the winter months.

For this project, you will need the following:

Hang the calendar on your refrigerator. By using standard weight paper, the calendar can be hung on the refrigerator with a magnet.

@ A list of the dates you want to include.

@ A copy of a calendar for the year you are creating as a reference.

@ The pictures you want to use for your calendar pages.

@ If you want to use legal-sized paper, you will need some of that, too.

This chapter references the *calendarFrame.mix* file included on the *PhotoDraw 2000 by Design* companion CD. This PhotoDraw file is a completed 3-month calendar framework ready for you to use. If you choose to use this file, you can skip the "Creating the Calendar Framework" section, unless you want to learn how to make the frame file.

Creating the Calendar Framework

In this section of the project, we'll create a framework that can be reused to create the individual pages of our calendar. We will create a blank picture area at the top and four smaller areas at the bottom—three that represent the months and one area for notes.

Creating the Picture Area

This procedure simply creates a picture area at the top of the picture space. We'll add the picture later.

Create the Picture Area

1 From the File menu, click New and then click Letter in the New dialog box to open a new letter-sized picture.

2 Be sure Snap To Grid is not selected on the View menu.

Create the Picture Area *(continued)*

3 On the toolbar, click the Rectangle button. Select the line and set the thickness to 3.

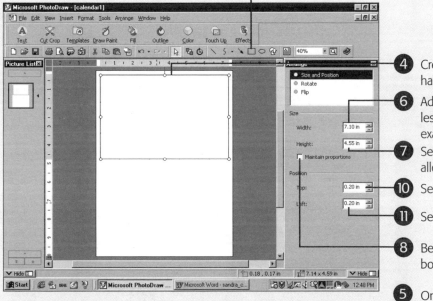

4 Create a rectangle that takes up about half of the top area of the picture space.

6 Adjust the final size of this rectangle to be just less than half the size of the letter. In this example, set the Width to 7.10 inches.

7 Set the Height to 4.55 inches. This will allow for border area.

10 Set the Top margin to 0.20 inches.

11 Set the Left margin to 0.20 inches.

8 Be sure the Maintain Proportions box is not selected.

5 On the Arrange menu, click Arrange.

9 Position the rectangle as shown.

12 Save your file with a unique name such as *"calendar1.mix"* or *"calendarBase.mix"*.

Saving with meaningful names. Saving your file at this point will save time and effort later. When you create the calendar pages for each season, load this file, make changes, and then resave each season's calendar under a new name such as *"calendarWinter.mix"*, *"calendarSpring.mix"*, and so on.

Creating the Grid for the Days and Weeks

Now we will create grids to hold the days and weeks. We will create one and then duplicate it for the other two months. Then we'll add column grids to each to represent the days of the week.

Create Grids for the Days and Weeks

1 Create another rectangle about one-fourth the size of the remaining space.

2 On the Arrange menu, click Arrange

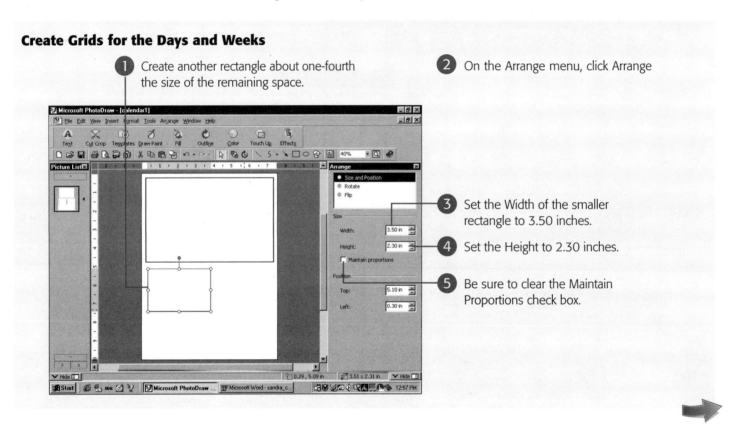

3 Set the Width of the smaller rectangle to 3.50 inches.

4 Set the Height to 2.30 inches.

5 Be sure to clear the Maintain Proportions check box.

Create Grids for the Days and Weeks *(continued)*

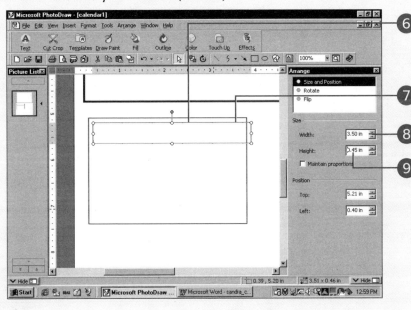

6 With the smaller rectangle selected, click Selection in the Zoom drop-down list box to zoom to the selected area. Now we will create the areas for the days and the weeks.

7 Create a new rectangle with a thickness of 1 point.

8 Set the Width of the rectangle to 3.50 inches.

9 Set the Height to .45 inches.

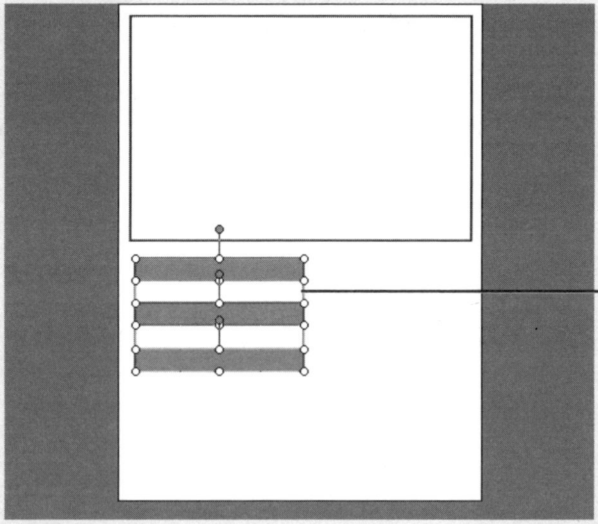

10 Create two duplicates for a total of three smaller rectangles. On the View menu, check the Snap To Grid box and align the squares as shown. (To emphasize the placement, the picture shows all three smaller rectangles shaded.)

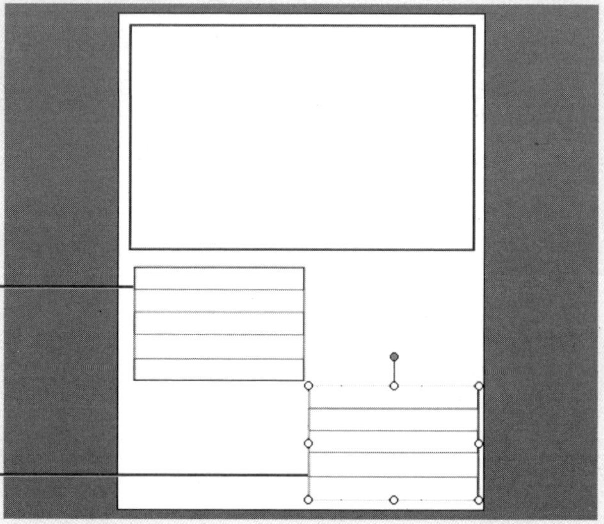

11 Select the three smaller rectangles and the surrounding rectangle (hold Shift down while clicking these objects) and group them together (Ctrl+G).

12 Make one duplicate of the group and set it off to the side. This will be the notes area.

Create Grids for the Days and Weeks *(continued)*

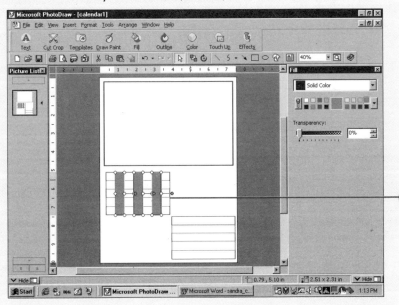

13 Create the columns for the days of the weeks following the previous example, only make the rectangles vertical instead of horizontal. Make three rectangles .50 by 2.3 inches and position them as shown. (To emphasize this point, the vertical rectangles are shaded.)

Snapping to the grid. You may have to snap the larger rectangle to grid first.

Grouping for placement and duplication. Grouping these objects together is essential for placement and duplication.

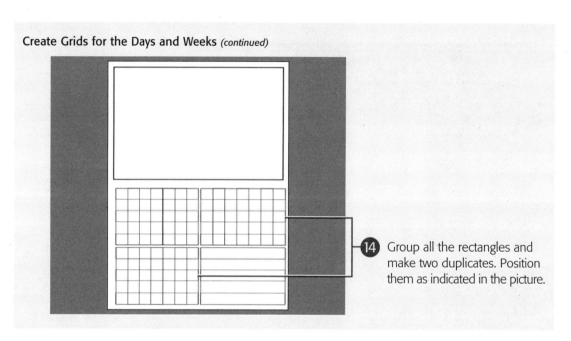

Create Grids for the Days and Weeks *(continued)*

14 Group all the rectangles and make two duplicates. Position them as indicated in the picture.

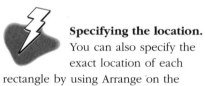

Specifying the location.
You can also specify the exact location of each rectangle by using Arrange on the Arrange menu.

Creating the Days of the Week Text Object

Next we will create a text object with the abbreviated days of the week, duplicate it, and position it.

Create a Days of the Week Text Object

1 Insert a text object that lists the abbreviated days of the week. Position it at the top of the upper left month grid and adjust the spacing so that it fits across the top.

What if some of the rectangles extend beyond the boundary?

If you notice that some of the rectangles overextend the rectangle that encloses the calendar, increase the line size of the rectangle slightly.

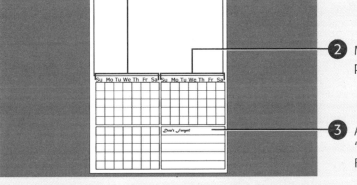

2 Make a duplicate and position it as shown.

3 Add a new text object with the word "Notes" or, as in this example, "Don't Forget!" Position it as shown.

4 Save your completed calendar framework.

Creating a Winter Calendar Using the Calendar Framework

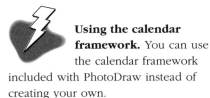

Using the calendar framework. You can use the calendar framework included with PhotoDraw instead of creating your own.

Now that the framework has been created, we will use it to create a personalized calendar. To accomplish this, we'll insert a picture, add beveling and color to the border, and edit the text for the days of the week. Then we'll add the dates for the months and finish by highlighting personal dates.

Inserting the Picture

A great benefit of using PhotoDraw to create your calendar is that you can personalize it with your own pictures. This procedure uses a picture from PhotoDraw Disc 2, but you can use any image.

Insert the Picture

1 Open PhotoDraw. On the File menu, click Visual Open and insert either the calendar framework file you just created or the *calendarFrame.mix* file in the chapters/chap15 folder on the companion CD. Then save the file with a unique name, such as *"calendarWinter.mix"*.

2 Select the largest rectangle.

3 On the Insert menu, click PhotoDraw Content, navigate to the Seasons folder and insert BK0101.BMP. Or if you are using your own picture, click Visual Insert, navigate to the location of your picture, and insert it.

4 Resize the picture file to fit inside the picture area either by using the Arrange menu or by using the corner handles. Make it only a little smaller than the frame.

Applying Beveling and Color to the Picture Frame

To add some depth to the picture, you can add a beveled frame and change the outline color. Note that this slightly increases the size of the picture, so some adjustments may be needed either to the picture or to the text below it. We'll adjust the text after this procedure, but you could also readjust the beveled picture to fit.

Experimenting to find the right mix. Experiment with bevel colors to find the best one to match your picture. You also might want to experiment with the Artistic and Photo Brush effects on the Outline menus.

Apply Beveling and Color to the Picture Frame

1 With the largest rectangle selected, on the Outline menu, click Plain.

2 Set the Width to about 10 and choose a border color that looks good with your picture. This example uses variation 7 of the color red.

3 On the Effects menu, click 3-D and select Beveling And Extrusion. Try different styles of bevels. As shown, this example uses Bevel 1 with the Extrusion Depth set to 5.

Resizing the Days of the Week Text Object

If adding the bevel to the picture extended it into the text area, you'll need to resize the days of the weeks text object.

Resize the Days of the Week Text Object

1 Double-click one of the "Su Mo Tu..." text areas and change the font size to 12 points. Add spacing between the days as necessary.

2 Change the color if you want to better match the colors in the picture.

3 Make a duplicate, and replace the other text object containing days of the week with the new one.

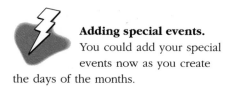

Adding special events. You could add your special events now as you create the days of the months.

Adding the Dates for the Month

Using your existing calendar as a guide, enter the days of the month. This example shows January 1999.

Add the Dates for the Month

1 On the Text menu, click Insert Text.

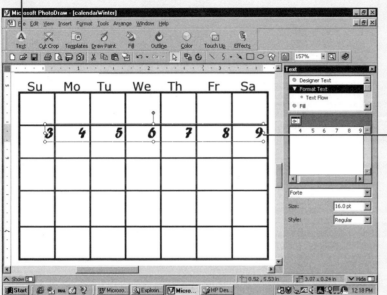

2 Position the text object on the first full week of the month.

3 Select the Forte Font with a size of 16 points. Create and position the dates as shown.

4 When you have created the first week, make duplicates of that week, align the duplicates on the remaining weeks, and adjust the numbering. You may also have to adjust the spacing between the dates.

Choosing a font. Use a font you like and a size that leaves room within the square for notes.

Creating a Personalized Calendar

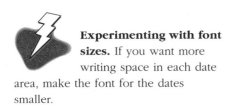

Experimenting with font sizes. If you want more writing space in each date area, make the font for the dates smaller.

Add the Dates for the Month *(continued)*

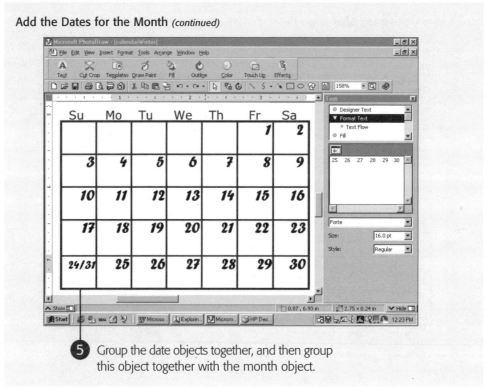

5 Group the date objects together, and then group this object together with the month object.

Creating the Name of the Month and the Year

The name of the month should be easily visible yet not intrusive. We'll create a new text object with the name of the month. Then we'll make it partially transparent and send it toward the back. Since the dates of the month we just created do not take up the entire square, the name of the month will show through just fine.

Create the Name of the Month and the Year

1 Create a new text object with the name of the month, in this case "January."

2 Click Custom Rotate on the toolbar.

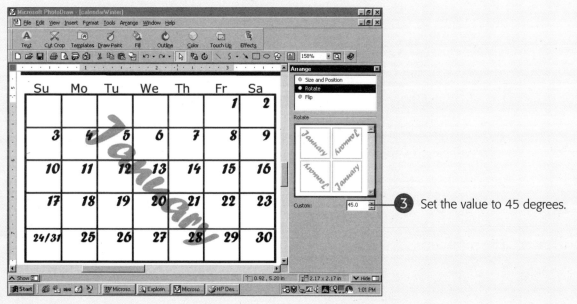

3 Set the value to 45 degrees.

4 On the Effects menu, click Transparency and set Transparency to 60 percent; then press Ctrl+Down Arrow twice to send it back two levels on the Z-order.

Create the Name of the Month and the Year *(continued)*

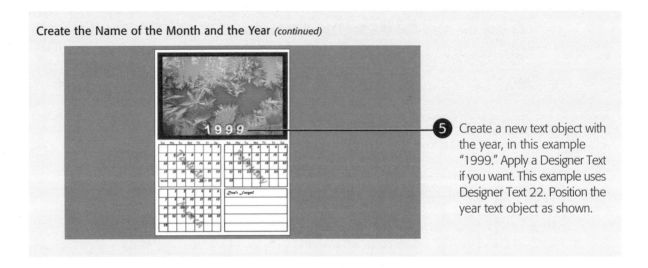

5 Create a new text object with the year, in this example "1999." Apply a Designer Text if you want. This example uses Designer Text 22. Position the year text object as shown.

To truly personalize your calendar, you can go on to highlight special dates using callouts, additional images, or any other items you can think of. Using the tools available in PhotoDraw, you'll create a project that reflects your personality.

Index

workpanes

    default location, 21

    defined, 21

    docking, 47

    hiding/displaying, 43

    illustrated, 16, 22

    repositioning, 47

workspace

    customizing, 47

    illustrated, 8

Z-order

    changing object, 210, 365

    defined, 38

    hot key for increasing (Ctrl+Up),
      277

zooming, 58–60, 133

Will Tait was born in Edinburgh, Scotland, and came to America at an early age. His interest in art led him to study drawing and painting at the Art Students League of New York. In addition to painting, he has worked extensively in printmaking, a discipline perfectly suited as a background for creating art on computers. He has been involved in various educational projects. They include developing an art program for schools in Berkeley, California, printmaking and multimedia programs through the Oregon Coast Council for the Arts, for the Lincoln county schools, and the initial interface design curriculum for the San Francisco State University Multimedia Studies Program. His personal artwork is included in the Achenbach print collection at the California Palace of the Legion of Honor in San Francisco, as well as many private and corporate collections.

The manuscript for this book was prepared using Microsoft Word 97. Pages were composed by Microsoft Press using Adobe PageMaker 6.52 for Windows, with text in Garamond and display type in Formata Bold. Composed pages were delivered to the printer as electronic prepress files.

Cover Graphic Designer

Patrick Lanfear

Cover Illustrator

Tom Draper Design

Interior Graphic Artist

Joel Panchot

Principal Compositor

Elizabeth Hansford

Principal Proofreader/Copy Editor

Norreen Holmes

Indexer

Stephen Bach

MICROSOFT LICENSE AGREEMENT
Book Companion CD

IMPORTANT—READ CAREFULLY: This Microsoft End-User License Agreement ("EULA") is a legal agreement between you (either an individual or an entity) and Microsoft Corporation for the Microsoft product identified above, which includes computer software and may include associated media, printed materials, and "online" or electronic documentation ("SOFTWARE PRODUCT"). Any component included within the SOFTWARE PRODUCT that is accompanied by a separate End-User License Agreement shall be governed by such agreement and not the terms set forth below. By installing, copying, or otherwise using the SOFTWARE PRODUCT, you agree to be bound by the terms of this EULA. If you do not agree to the terms of this EULA, you are not authorized to install, copy, or otherwise use the SOFTWARE PRODUCT; you may, however, return the SOFTWARE PRODUCT, along with all printed materials and other items that form a part of the Microsoft product that includes the SOFTWARE PRODUCT, to the place you obtained them for a full refund.

SOFTWARE PRODUCT LICENSE

The SOFTWARE PRODUCT is protected by United States copyright laws and international copyright treaties, as well as other intellectual property laws and treaties. The SOFTWARE PRODUCT is licensed, not sold.

1. GRANT OF LICENSE. This EULA grants you the following rights:

a. **Software Product.** You may install and use one copy of the SOFTWARE PRODUCT on a single computer. The primary user of the computer on which the SOFTWARE PRODUCT is installed may make a second copy for his or her exclusive use on a portable computer.

b. **Storage/Network Use.** You may also store or install a copy of the SOFTWARE PRODUCT on a storage device, such as a network server, used only to install or run the SOFTWARE PRODUCT on your other computers over an internal network; however, you must acquire and dedicate a license for each separate computer on which the SOFTWARE PRODUCT is installed or run from the storage device. A license for the SOFTWARE PRODUCT may not be shared or used concurrently on different computers.

c. **License Pak.** If you have acquired this EULA in a Microsoft License Pak, you may make the number of additional copies of the computer software portion of the SOFTWARE PRODUCT authorized on the printed copy of this EULA, and you may use each copy in the manner specified above. You are also entitled to make a corresponding number of secondary copies for portable computer use as specified above.

d. **Sample Code.** Solely with respect to portions, if any, of the SOFTWARE PRODUCT that are identified within the SOFTWARE PRODUCT as sample code (the "SAMPLE CODE"):

i. **Use and Modification.** Microsoft grants you the right to use and modify the source code version of the SAMPLE CODE, *provided* you comply with subsection (d)(iii) below. You may not distribute the SAMPLE CODE, or any modified version of the SAMPLE CODE, in source code form.

ii. **Redistributable Files.** Provided you comply with subsection (d)(iii) below, Microsoft grants you a nonexclusive, royalty-free right to reproduce and distribute the object code version of the SAMPLE CODE and of any modified SAMPLE CODE, other than SAMPLE CODE, or any modified version thereof, designated as not redistributable in the Readme file that forms a part of the SOFTWARE PRODUCT (the "Non-Redistributable Sample Code"). All SAMPLE CODE other than the Non-Redistributable Sample Code is collectively referred to as the "REDISTRIBUTABLES."

iii. **Redistribution Requirements.** If you redistribute the REDISTRIBUTABLES, you agree to: (i) distribute the REDISTRIBUTABLES in object code form only in conjunction with and as a part of your software application product; (ii) not use Microsoft's name, logo, or trademarks to market your software application product; (iii) include a valid copyright notice on your software application product; (iv) indemnify, hold harmless, and defend Microsoft from and against any claims or lawsuits, including attorney's fees, that arise or result from the use or distribution of your software application product; and (v) not permit further distribution of the REDISTRIBUTABLES by your end user. Contact Microsoft for the applicable royalties due and other licensing terms for all other uses and/or distribution of the REDISTRIBUTABLES.

2. DESCRIPTION OF OTHER RIGHTS AND LIMITATIONS.

- **Limitations on Reverse Engineering, Decompilation, and Disassembly.** You may not reverse engineer, decompile, or disassemble the SOFTWARE PRODUCT, except and only to the extent that such activity is expressly permitted by applicable law notwithstanding this limitation.

- **Separation of Components.** The SOFTWARE PRODUCT is licensed as a single product. Its component parts may not be separated for use on more than one computer.

- **Rental.** You may not rent, lease, or lend the SOFTWARE PRODUCT.

- **Support Services.** Microsoft may, but is not obligated to, provide you with support services related to the SOFTWARE PRODUCT ("Support Services"). Use of Support Services is governed by the Microsoft policies and programs described in the user manual, in "online" documentation, and/or other Microsoft-provided materials. Any supplemental software code provided to you as part of the Support Services shall be considered part of the SOFTWARE PRODUCT and subject to the terms and conditions of this EULA. With respect to technical information you provide to Microsoft as part of the Support Services, Microsoft may use such information for its business purposes, including for product support and development. Microsoft will not utilize such technical information in a form that personally identifies you.

- **Software Transfer.** You may permanently transfer all of your rights under this EULA, provided you retain no copies, you transfer all of the SOFTWARE PRODUCT (including all component parts, the media and printed materials, any upgrades, this EULA, and, if applicable, the Certificate of Authenticity), **and** the recipient agrees to the terms of this EULA.

- **Termination.** Without prejudice to any other rights, Microsoft may terminate this EULA if you fail to comply with the terms and conditions of this EULA. In such event, you must destroy all copies of the SOFTWARE PRODUCT and all of its component parts.

3. **COPYRIGHT.** All title and copyrights in and to the SOFTWARE PRODUCT (including but not limited to any images, photographs, animations, video, audio, music, text, SAMPLE CODE, REDISTRIBUTABLES, and "applets" incorporated into the SOFTWARE PRODUCT) and any copies of the SOFTWARE PRODUCT are owned by Microsoft or its suppliers. The SOFTWARE PRODUCT is protected by copyright laws and international treaty provisions. Therefore, you must treat the SOFTWARE PRODUCT like any other copyrighted material **except** that you may install the SOFTWARE PRODUCT on a single computer provided you keep the original solely for backup or archival purposes. You may not copy the printed materials accompanying the SOFTWARE PRODUCT.

4. **U.S. GOVERNMENT RESTRICTED RIGHTS.** The SOFTWARE PRODUCT and documentation are provided with RESTRICTED RIGHTS. Use, duplication, or disclosure by the Government is subject to restrictions as set forth in subparagraph (c)(1)(ii) of the Rights in Technical Data and Computer Software clause at DFARS 252.227-7013 or subparagraphs (c)(1) and (2) of the Commercial Computer Software—Restricted Rights at 48 CFR 52.227-19, as applicable. Manufacturer is Microsoft Corporation/One Microsoft Way/Redmond, WA 98052-6399.

5. **EXPORT RESTRICTIONS.** You agree that you will not export or re-export the SOFTWARE PRODUCT, any part thereof, or any process or service that is the direct product of the SOFTWARE PRODUCT (the foregoing collectively referred to as the "Restricted Components"), to any country, person, entity, or end user subject to U.S. export restrictions. You specifically agree not to export or re-export any of the Restricted Components (i) to any country to which the U.S. has embargoed or restricted the export of goods or services, which currently include, but are not necessarily limited to Cuba, Iran, Iraq, Libya, North Korea, Sudan, and Syria, or to any national of any such country, wherever located, who intends to transmit or transport the Restricted Components back to such country; (ii) to any end user who you know or have reason to know will utilize the Restricted Components in the design, development, or production of nuclear, chemical, or biological weapons; or (iii) to any end user who has been prohibited from participating in U.S. export transactions by any federal agency of the U.S. government. You warrant and represent that neither the BXA nor any other U.S. federal agency has suspended, revoked, or denied your export privileges.

DISCLAIMER OF WARRANTY

NO WARRANTIES OR CONDITIONS. MICROSOFT EXPRESSLY DISCLAIMS ANY WARRANTY OR CONDITION FOR THE SOFTWARE PRODUCT. THE SOFTWARE PRODUCT AND ANY RELATED DOCUMENTATION IS PROVIDED "AS IS" WITHOUT WARRANTY OR CONDITION OF ANY KIND, EITHER EXPRESS OR IMPLIED, INCLUDING, WITHOUT LIMITATION, THE IMPLIED WARRANTIES OF MERCHANTABILITY, FITNESS FOR A PARTICULAR PURPOSE, OR NONINFRINGEMENT. THE ENTIRE RISK ARISING OUT OF USE OR PERFORMANCE OF THE SOFTWARE PRODUCT REMAINS WITH YOU.

LIMITATION OF LIABILITY. TO THE MAXIMUM EXTENT PERMITTED BY APPLICABLE LAW, IN NO EVENT SHALL MICROSOFT OR ITS SUPPLIERS BE LIABLE FOR ANY SPECIAL, INCIDENTAL, INDIRECT, OR CONSEQUENTIAL DAMAGES WHATSOEVER (INCLUDING, WITHOUT LIMITATION, DAMAGES FOR LOSS OF BUSINESS PROFITS, BUSINESS INTERRUPTION, LOSS OF BUSINESS INFORMATION, OR ANY OTHER PECUNIARY LOSS) ARISING OUT OF THE USE OF OR INABILITY TO USE THE SOFTWARE PRODUCT OR THE PROVISION OF OR FAILURE TO PROVIDE SUPPORT SERVICES, EVEN IF MICROSOFT HAS BEEN ADVISED OF THE POSSIBILITY OF SUCH DAMAGES. IN ANY CASE, MICROSOFT'S ENTIRE LIABILITY UNDER ANY PROVISION OF THIS EULA SHALL BE LIMITED TO THE GREATER OF THE AMOUNT ACTUALLY PAID BY YOU FOR THE SOFTWARE PRODUCT OR US$5.00; PROVIDED HOWEVER, IF YOU HAVE ENTERED INTO A MICROSOFT SUPPORT SERVICES AGREEMENT, MICROSOFT'S ENTIRE LIABILITY REGARDING SUPPORT SERVICES SHALL BE GOVERNED BY THE TERMS OF THAT AGREEMENT. BECAUSE SOME STATES AND JURISDICTIONS DO NOT ALLOW THE EXCLUSION OR LIMITATION OF LIABILITY, THE ABOVE LIMITATION MAY NOT APPLY TO YOU.

MISCELLANEOUS

This EULA is governed by the laws of the State of Washington USA, except and only to the extent that applicable law mandates governing law of a different jurisdiction.

Should you have any questions concerning this EULA, or if you desire to contact Microsoft for any reason, please contact the Microsoft subsidiary serving your country, or write: Microsoft Sales Information Center/One Microsoft Way/Redmond, WA 98052-6399.

Register Today!

Return this
Microsoft® PhotoDraw™ 2000 by Design
registration card today

Microsoft·Press

mspress.microsoft.com

OWNER REGISTRATION CARD   **1-57231-938-0**

Microsoft® PhotoDraw™ 2000 by Design

_____   _____   _____
FIRST NAME   **MIDDLE INITIAL**   **LAST NAME**

_____
INSTITUTION OR COMPANY NAME

_____
ADDRESS

_____

_____   _____   _____
CITY   **STATE**   **ZIP**

                                                        (   )
_____   _____
E-MAIL ADDRESS   **PHONE NUMBER**

U.S. and Canada addresses only. Fill in information above and mail postage-free.
Please mail only the bottom half of this page.

For information about Microsoft Press®
products, visit our Web site at
mspress.microsoft.com

Microsoft *·Press*